TWICE UPON A TIME

ELIZABETH WANNING HARRIES

Twice upon a Time

*Women Writers and the History of
the Fairy Tale*

170201

PRINCETON UNIVERSITY PRESS

Library of Congress Cataloging-in-Publication Data

Harries, Elizabeth Wanning.
Twice upon a time : women writers and the history of the fairy tale /
Elizabeth Wanning Harries.
p.   cm.
Includes bibliographical references and index.
ISBN 0-691-07444-5 (alk. paper)
1. Fairy tales—History and criticism. 2. Fairy tales—France—History
and criticism. 3. Fairy tales—England—History and criticism.
4. French fiction—Women authors—History and criticism.
5. American fiction—Women authors—History and criticism.
PN3437.H37   2001
398.2′09—dc21   00-051645

This book has been composed in Caledonia
Designed by Jan Lilly
Composed by Eileen Reilly

Printed on acid-free paper. ∞

www.pup.princeton.edu

Printed in the United States of America

10   9   8   7   6   5   4   3   2   1

To the memory of

Coburn Haskell Britton

1936–1997

always the best teller

of tales

Neither do men put new wine into old bottles: else the bottles break, and the wine runneth out, and the bottles perish: but they put new wine in new bottles, and both are preserved.

Matt. 9:17

Reading is just as creative an activity as writing and most intellectual development depends upon new readings of old texts. I am all for putting new wine in old bottles, especially if the pressure of the new wine makes the bottles explode.

Angela Carter, "Notes from the Front Line"

 CONTENTS

ILLUSTRATIONS

✺ ACKNOWLEDGMENTS

ANYONE who writes about revising stories must be acutely conscious that the story she is telling is also just one of many possible versions. But many "helping figures" have made my way to this one easier. David Hayman first mentioned the name Madame d'Aulnoy to me, many years ago; neither of us had any idea at the time that I would eventually write about her. David, Helmut Reinicke, Margaret Higonnet, Uli Knoepflmacher, Vicki Mistacco, and Lewis Seifert encouraged me when I began work on the tales of the late seventeenth century in France. I also learned a great deal from the participants in a Guthrie Workshop on early French and Italian tales at Dartmouth in March 1995—as well as from comments about talks I've given at the MLA, at the Five College Women's Studies Research Center, and at Smith.

My work has been aided and abetted by many colleagues at Smith, in English, Comparative Literature, and Women's Studies. Susan Van Dyne has given me many ideas about Anne Sexton over the years; her comments on the section about Sexton were particularly helpful. Ann Rosalind Jones not only supplied some suggestions for illustrations but was encouraging throughout. Nancy Bradbury gave me good hints about the oral/literary debate over good lunches. Ruth Solie and Luc Gilleman both patiently read the entire manuscript when they were overwhelmed with other work, and made many incisive comments. (Thanks to Ruth, too, for reading an early version of the first chapter and for suggesting that I read Byatt's *The Djinn in the Nightingale's Eye*.) Bruce Sajdak, the best of reference librarians, found things when I despaired, and ordered books I should have ordered. Sharon Seelig and Bill Oram are always rocks in a tempestuous sea. Smith College itself supplied generous sabbaticals, research funding, released time, and a series of resourceful student research assistants: Sarah Smalheer, Katie Peebles, Amanda Darling, Joanna Patterson, and Laura Passin.

I'm also grateful to a number of libraries for preserving and making available early editions of the *conteuses*: the Dartmouth College Rare Book Room, the Beinecke Library at Yale, the Bibliothèque nationale and the Arsénal in Paris, the Mortimer Rare Book Room at Smith, and particularly the Pierpont Morgan Library in New York. The curator there, Dr. Mary Lou Ashby, could not have been more thoughtful or more knowledgeable. We scholars tend to take such holdings and access to them for granted, but (in these days of shrinking resources and library de-accessioning policies) we shouldn't.

Jack Zipes and Maria Tatar read versions of this book for the Press at two different stages; I'm grateful for their incisive comments, stern though some of them were. Mary Murrell is one of the few remaining editors who actually edit; her comments and theirs have made this a much better book. Fred Appel took good care of the book during Mary Murrell's sabbatical; Lauren Lepow, a wise and careful copyeditor, saved me from myself many times over.

An earlier version of part of chapter 1 appeared in Nancy Canepa's volume *Out of the Woods: The Origins of the Literary Fairy Tale in Italy and France* (1997). A much shorter version of chapter 2 appeared in *College Literature* in 1996. The section on women's autobiography in chapter 5 appeared in *Marvels and Tales* in April 2000. Thanks to Wayne State University Press and to *College Literature* for permission to reprint.

My children and grandchildren have provided distraction at just the right moments. Lisa Harries-Schumann also helped with translations from German, particularly the difficulties of Christa Wolf's prose. Martin Harries has always made good suggestions about things I should read. And Jennifer Whiting, though she hasn't read much of this book, can always make me laugh.

TWICE UPON A TIME

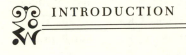

Once, Not Long Ago

> A little formalism turns one away from History,
> but . . . a lot brings one back to it.
>   Roland Barthes, *Mythologies*

WHY DO we still read fairy tales? And why, at the turn of the millennium, are they so popular? The blurbs on the back of the many paperback collections of tales reveal some recurring justifications for printing yet another fat book. The tales are said to be "timeless" or "ageless" or "dateless"; they seem removed from history and change. They "offer insights into the oral traditions of different cultures" or have "the unadorned direct rhythm of the oral form in which they were first recorded" or "retain the feeling of oral literature"; they seem to give us access to a more primitive and more authentic oral culture. "Universal" and "classless," they "offer insight into universal human dilemmas that span differences of age, culture, and geography," and are told by "titled ladies in the salons of the aristocrats, by governesses in the nursery, and by peasant farmers around the hearth." In spite of their varied national origins and the varied ways in which they have been written and published, they seem to be evidence for common human experiences, hopes, and fears that transcend nation and class. At a time when the world is splintering into many ethnic factions, fairy tales seem to provide some binding force.

If we read the history of fairy tales thoughtfully, however, we see that these conventional notions are completely mistaken, part of the nostalgia and traditionalizing that have accompanied our construction of our own modernity. We need to begin by acknowledging that all fairy tales *have* a history, that they are anything but ageless or timeless. Though they may have roots in oral narratives, all the stories we now call fairy tales have been written and rewritten, printed and reprinted over centuries. Some versions of the tales are simpler and more familiar to us than others, and therefore may seem more authentic, but we have no access to any original versions or urtexts. Rather, all we have are versions of versions, narratives spun and respun for hundreds of years. Though the early writers of fairy tales in Italy and France in the seventeenth century often claimed that they were reproducing stories they had been told (by their nurses or grandmothers, from peasant sources), they were usually following written models. The history of fairy tales is not primarily a history of oral transmission but rather a history of print.

Folklorists have recently become acutely aware of the "politics of folklore," articulating "the conceptual problems inherent in our representations of authentic, traditional, folk culture."[1] But, though many people doing research on fairy tales are conscious of what has been happening in folklore, they do not consistently reflect on their own traditionalizing practices. We need to reread the history of fairy tales—and to watch ourselves rereading it. Not that this is easy: the pieties inscribed on the back pages of our fairy-tale collections are hard to shake, even as we are criticizing them. But we should think of the tales we know as belonging to a "distressed genre," as "new antiques," to borrow Susan Stewart's terms.[2] They are often *imitations* of what various literary cultures have posited as the traditional, the authentic, or the nonliterary. They have been "distressed" like a supposedly antique pine chest, given the patina of age, surrounded by signs that suggest simultaneously their great age and their agelessness.

What we now know as fairy tales have always been deeply affected by the practices of writing—and never existed in anything like their present form until long after the invention of print. (People rarely comment on the ironies of the multiplication of printed versions of supposedly oral texts.) In fact, the tales we now call fairy tales were created primarily by highly educated and literate people, sometimes imitating what they claimed were the tales of less-educated or illiterate people. To be quite honest, I sometimes wish I did not believe these things. The nostalgic dream of a simple, coherent oral culture, so different from our complicated and fragmented one, still haunts me. There is something comforting about knowing stories that seem somehow to connect you to a past before writing, before printing, before "Art" with a capital A. But in fact fairy tales rarely do.

As we reread the history of fairy tales, we also need to pay attention to those tales that have been almost forgotten. When we speak of fairy tales, the names that tend to come immediately to mind are Charles Perrault, the Brothers Grimm, Hans Christian Andersen, perhaps John Ruskin, or Oscar

Wilde, or Andrew Lang's late-nineteenth-century rainbow fairy-tale collections. But there is also a long tradition of tales written by women, beginning in France in the 1690s and continuing for over three hundred years. This book highlights this neglected tradition, to show how one-sided and narrow our conception of the fairy tale has become and to link twentieth-century revisions of classic fairy tales with earlier models.[3] The first two chapters focus on the *conteuses* (female tale-tellers) who wrote and published fairy tales in France in the 1690s, to show why they have been overlooked and what their literary strategies actually were. The last two chapters focus on the similar strategies of late-twentieth-century women writers who retell and revise fairy tales: the narrative voices they construct, their framing techniques, their reinterpretations of details from well-known tales. Like the versions of tales by the *conteuses*, recent tales by Angela Carter and Anne Sexton also play on our readerly delight in repetition and in difference. My rereading of the history of fairy tales is an act of inclusion, an attempt to make readers understand the genre as wider and more capacious than they have supposed, more open to a variety of forms and themes.

In the middle of the book, in chapter 3, I trace the invention of the fairy tale in England, from the first translations of Charles Perrault and the *conteuses* through the early nineteenth century. In order to see the ways our dominant Anglo-American ideas about fairy tales are mistaken, we need to understand how they were constructed, or where they came from. Most of the fairy tales we know and repeat were not originally British but rather pan-European. How they came to be thought of as an intrinsic part of our Anglo-American heritage, fully naturalized, is one of the questions that animates this book. In the late seventeenth and early eighteenth centuries, many writers lamented the disappearance of the indigenous fairies. By the middle of the nineteenth, many fairy tales had entered the tradition, mainly from French and German sources. Notions about their necessary shape (short and simple) and their chief audience (children) had become widespread. The movement between these two points, influenced both by Enlightenment rationalism and by romantic nationalism, determined the later shape of our fairy-tale canon.

If we continue to read only a restricted list of fairy tales, limited by common assumptions about their requisite shape and concerns, we will miss some of the most interesting and challenging examples of the genre. If we think all fairy tales must be narrated by an invisible, third-person teller, we will be unable to hear the play of voices in many tales. If we believe that some tales are much more "authentic" than others because they sound ageless, we will be falling into a carefully laid narrative trap. Studying the European literary fairy tale in its historical complexity also gives us a chance to explore some crucial theoretical problems in miniature: canon formation, the simulation of storytellers' voices in print, the practices and politics of literary adaptation and revision. This minor genre, so often the center of arguments about its traditional authenticity and its modernity, can help us untangle some of the persistent problems of literary history. Though these may seem to be exclusively academic concerns, the way we approach these problems ultimately affects our access to a wide range of older texts and to various ways of interpreting them.

But what *are* fairy tales? Our term in English comes directly from the French, the "contes de fées" that became popular in France at the end of the seventeenth century. (As J.R.R. Tolkien pointed out long ago, the first citation for "fairy-tale" in the supplement to the *Oxford English Dictionary* is 1750, though there are many references to "fairies" from the fourteenth century on. There are actually a few scattered uses of the term before 1750— in Sarah Fielding's 1749 novel *The Governess*, for example.) Nothing is more difficult than to try to define the fairy tale in twenty-five words or less, and all dictionaries fail miserably. The *OED* defines it as "a. A Tale about fairies. Also *gen.*, fairy legend, faerie. b. An unreal or incredible story. c. A falsehood." Or another example, simpler but amazingly similar, particularly given the roughly hundred years' distance between them: "1. A story about fairies. 2. A fictitious, fanciful story or explanation" (*The Concise Heritage Dictionary*). But many, even most, of the stories we call fairy tales do not have any fairies in them. (Think of "Little Red Riding Hood" and "Snow White," for example. Wolves that speak, magic mirrors, yes. But no fairies.) And, though it is true that "fairy tale" has become a synonym for an ingenious lie and that fairy tales are of course fictions, I think we have clearer, though still somewhat inchoate, ideas about what makes a tale a fairy tale—ideas that need some examination.

When we speak of fairy tales, we seem to mean several things at once: tales that include elements of folk tradition and magical or supernatural elements, tales that have a certain, predictable structure. Maria Tatar has suggested that the fairy tale "has been associated with both oral and literary traditions but is above all reserved for narratives set in a fictional world where preternatural events and supernatural intervention are taken wholly for granted." She distinguishes the fairy tale from the folk tale because, though it often has folk elements, it rarely has the "earthy realism" of the true folk tale. She places the Grimms' fairy tales midway between folklore and literature in a helpful diagram:[4]

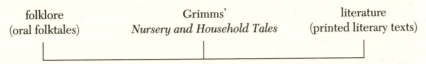

folklore	Grimms'	literature
(oral folktales)	*Nursery and Household Tales*	(printed literary texts)

The common word in German for the Grimms' and other similar collections is *Buchmärchen*, or traditional oral tales with folk elements that have been written down and printed. (One awkward term for these in English is "orature.") They are always opposed to *Volksmärchen* (tales in an oral form), on the one side, and *Kunstmärchen* (invented, literary tales like Goethe's *Märchen*) on the other:

Volksmärchen	*Buchmärchen*	*Kunstmärchen*
(oral tales)	(transcribed oral tales)	(invented or literary tales)

Unlike Tatar, however, I would push the Grimms' tales further to the right-hand side of the continuum, much closer to *Kunstmärchen* than to *Buchmärchen*. Most fairy tales, as we now know them, do have elements of folk tradition. But all of them, and particularly the Grimms', have been extensively shaped and codified by successive literate tale-tellers. To give just one example, the Grimms' tale "Rapunzel," tale number twelve in the *Kinder- und Hausmärchen*,[5] comes from an eighteenth-century German version of the tale, published by Friedrich Schulz in his *Kleine Romane* in 1790; which was an adaptation of Charlotte Caumont de La Force's story "Persinette," first printed in 1697; which probably was taken from Giambattista Basile's collection of fairy tales, *Lo cunto de li cunti* or *Pentamerone* (published after his death in 1634–1636). Elements of this "princess in the tower" story go back at least to medieval romance. What makes "Rapunzel" a fairy tale is not so much its more obvious folk elements (like the eating of the herb, parsley in the French, "Rapünzchen"—rampion, *mâche* or lamb's lettuce—in the German) as the mysterious powers of the old woman (a fairy or "fée" in the French version), the magical isolation of the tower, the separation and final union of the princess and the prince who happens by. Each new written version is in effect a new "reading" of the basic configuration. (For example, as Tatar and others have pointed out, the Grimms—those nervous nineteenth-century Nellies—never mention the princess's pregnancy in later editions of the *Kinder- und Hausmärchen* until her twins mysteriously appear, while Basile and La Force are quite matter-of-fact about it.) Though Max Lüthi praised the Grimms for their storytelling genius as they "translated the seventeenth-century fairy tale back into the style of the folk fairy tale,"[6] they were really shaping it into a style that they themselves had invented as particularly appropriate for their *Märchen*. The writers of fairy tales rarely attempt to uncover or rediscover the folk elements in a tale. Rather, they build on, revise, and change the story as it has come down to them, rereading it in their own ways, pouring new wine into the old bottle that they know from the written tradition.

This old bottle often has a predictable shape. Generations of folklorists, structuralists, and formalist theorists of narrative have worked to show the basic plot elements that most fairy tales share.[7] They identify character roles and basic plot motifs, showing that fairy tales all over the world tend to follow similar patterns. Recently, in a cartoon in the *New Yorker*, Roz Chast brilliantly condensed all these theories into one simple four-frame cartoon called "Story Template" (fig. 1). Like Tzvetan Todorov in his book *The Fantastic*, she emphasizes the movement from stasis to conflict to stasis again; as he says, "All narrative is a movement between two equilibriums which are similar but not identical."[8] In Chast's cartoon the beginning and ending are in fact nearly identical, "once upon a time" and "happily ever after" taking the same shape with the same cast of characters. In fairy tales, of course, at least one new character usually appears in the family circle by the end: a prince, a princess, some character from outside the family who transforms the original configuration. Or, in some cases, a character from the original family has disappeared—as do the wicked mothers/stepmothers in "Hänsel and Gretel" (*KHM* 15) and "The Juniper Tree" (*KHM* 47). But, as Chast's diagram shows, we usually move from one family to another, new-created one, similar in their apparent stability.

Chast's two-frame delineation of the progression of most stories is breathtaking in its accurate simplicity. The blocking figure, a fire-breathing dragon from another undefined world, "suddenly" erupts into the everyday family scene. The helping figure, a superman carefully placed in Central Park with

Fig. 1. Roz Chast, "Story Template."
© The New Yorker Collection 1998
Roz Chast from cartoonbank.com.
All Rights Reserved.

the New York skyline behind him, "luckily" appears, clearly just in the nick of time, to restore the original order. With only four frames, four captions, and five characters as our guides, we easily construct a narrative plot movement, partly because we know the pattern so well.

The template Chast has constructed here is only a rough guide—and would never lead us to imagine the complexity and depth of many fairy tales, particularly those written at the end of the seventeenth century by the French *conteuses* and recently by many women writers like Angela Carter and A. S. Byatt. But I think she has caught, in an economical and amusing way, the paradigms that have informed the reading and rewriting of fairy tales for at least the last three hundred years. These paradigms are still there—in our narrative expectations, in our narrative desires (to use a peculiarly fashionable word in recent narrative theory that depends on the insights of psychoanalysis). When we say, "It's just like a fairy tale," or "It has a fairy-tale ending," we mean that something has turned out mysteriously, even unnaturally, well; that an equilibrium has been reestablished when only catastrophe seemed possible. In fact, a number of fairy tales turn out badly— Perrault's version of "Little Red Riding Hood," Marie-Catherine d'Aulnoy's "The Ram," and many more, particularly some tales by the French *conteuses* that I will discuss in the first two chapters. These are all stories that deliberately violate our sense of the typical fairy-tale pattern. We expect the sequence Chast has outlined: stability, disruption, intervention, and stability regained, "once upon a time" to "happily ever after."

These expectations have been reinforced by our reliance on an essay Walter Benjamin wrote in the 1930s: "The Storyteller" ("Der Erzähler: Betrachtungen zum Werk Nikolai Leskow's," 1936).[9] Writers about fairy tales, as well as theorists of narrative, often refer and defer to this essay. Benjamin praises Leskov as a great example of the kind of storytelling that he sees as doomed: "[T]he art of storytelling is coming to an end. Less and less often do we encounter people with the ability to tell a tale properly" (83). He argues that the rapid changes in modern life, the multiplicity and fragmentation of twentieth-century experience, have made true storytelling almost impossible. And he singles out the fairy tale as the clearest and most powerful example of that true storytelling: "The fairy tale, which is to this day the first tutor of children because it was once the first tutor of mankind, secretly lives on in the story. The first true storyteller is, and will continue to be, the teller of fairy tales" (102).[10]

Here Benjamin also makes the common assumption that the fairy tale is appropriate for children because it was the first "literary" form, that children need and crave the same experiences that people had somewhere in our misty cultural beginnings ("Ontogeny recapitulates phylogeny"). As many scholars have recently shown, fairy tales came to be thought of primarily as literature for children only in the course of the eighteenth century. The equation of fairy tales and childhood is not a sensible one, as J.R.R. Tolkien pointed out long ago (1938).[11] It depends on two related and mistaken romantic notions: that fairy tales are relics of a culture's early beginnings, and that children are beings who trail "clouds of glory" from that ideal, mythic past to which only they have unmediated access. Benjamin associates children with simpler, clearer, more "natural" forms: "There is nothing that commends a story to memory more effectively than that chaste compactness ["keusche Gedrungenheit"] which precludes psychological analysis. And the more natural the process by which the storyteller forgoes psychological shading, the greater becomes the story's claim to a place in the memory of the listener" (91). His postromanticism here seems to blot out his usual ironic powers of analysis. The "chaste compactness" of the archetypal fairy tale, he claims, guarantees that it will be handed on and down.

Benjamin's delineation of the fairy tale is telling. Like many other writers on the fairy tale, and more beautifully than most, he stresses its connections to a community of listeners and the oral tradition. Borrowing from Georg Lukács's *Theory of the Novel* (1920), he insists on the difference between the audience of the storyteller and the reader of a novel: "A man listening to a story is in the company of the storyteller; even a man reading one shares this companionship. The reader of a novel, however, is isolated, more so than any other reader" (100). According to Benjamin, the story creates a particular bond between the listener (or even the reader) and its teller; it is peculiarly intimate, bound up with gesture and voice, even voice as transcribed onto the written page, or what he calls the interaction of "soul, eye, and hand" (108).

And the storyteller, unlike the novelist or the modern writer, is not an "artist" but rather a craftsman or artisan. Benjamin repeatedly returns to phrases and metaphors that place the storyteller in a tradition of manual labor: "Thus traces of the storyteller cling to the story the way the handprints of the potter cling to the vessel" (92). The best storytellers were, on the one hand, seafarers and traveling journeymen; on the other, tillers of the soil

("Ackerbauer") and all those who worked with their hands in one place. Benjamin also mourns the disappearance of the weaving rooms where he thinks stories were told and retold (91). He is anxious to make the true story something that not only is rooted in cultural memory but also bears the traces of its supposed origins as a primitive artifact.

Benjamin's vision of the story and the storyteller is profoundly appealing. It speaks to our sense that the human community is disintegrating and that we have no common wisdom (what Harry Zohn translates as "counsel," German "Rat") to draw on. A reflection of the dark European situation in the mid-1930s, the essay also offers a kind of messianic hope, the hope that we can draw on old customs and stories to create a sense of human community in a disenchanted world.[12] But Benjamin's ideas about the story, and about the fairy tale in particular, are both deeply conventional and deeply misleading. We tend to believe that children have always been the primary audience for fairy tales and that fairy tales are particularly appropriate for them. We tend to believe that the fairy tales we know and love come from ancient oral sources, that their appearance in print is a late and somewhat disturbing development. And we tend to believe that they are an expression of the deep wisdom and knowledge of the "folk," those artisans and spinners and travelers who shaped and crafted them in an unconscious but knowing way.

We also mistakenly expect fairy tales to be short and simple. When Benjamin speaks of the "chaste compactness" of a fairy tale, he is probably referring to the model the Grimms established in their *Märchen*. They are "compact" or concise ("gedrungen") because the Grimms thought they were re-creating the simplicity and directness of folk narrative, without digressions or secondary plots. They are "chaste" ("keusch") because they do not indulge in psychological exploration; the narrator is laconic and nonjudgmental. But this paradigm is not typical of all fairy tales. The early French tales were often convoluted, complex, and full of sly psychological observations—as are many nineteenth- and twentieth-century fairy tales. Our unspoken understanding of the fairy tale is not expansive enough to include them—but, as I will argue in the first chapter, this means writing some of the most interesting tales out of the genre. It is not surprising that Perrault's and the Grimms' tales have been dominant in much fairy-tale research and theory, but I think we need to understand and reassess their influence on our thinking about the forms fairy tales take.

Feminists, of course, have been criticizing the Grimms' patriarchal assumptions and nineteenth-century bourgeois attitudes for nearly three decades. A brief and very selective list of titles shows the general trend: " 'Someday My Prince Will Come"; *Kiss Sleeping Beauty Good-Bye*; *The Cinderella Complex*; "Tale-Spinners: Submerged Voices in Grimms' Fairy Tales"; *Don't Bet on the Prince*.[13] As the second wave of feminist thinking got under way in the 1970s, many critics fixed on fairy tales as condensed expressions of social expectations for women and as dangerous myths that determined their lives and hopes. The "sleep" of Sleeping Beauty or of Snow White in her glass coffin, the uncomplaining self-abnegation of Cinderella, the patience and silence of the sisters who work to save their seven or twelve brothers, the princesses who must be rescued from towers or briar hedges or forests or servitude—all these seem to provide the patterns for feminine passivity and martyrdom. The wicked stepmothers, witches, and fairies have come to represent the dangers older, powerful women seem to pose in our culture. (Many of these patterns have been repeated ad nauseam in the Disney versions of the tales and have been duplicated in the expensive illustrated versions that fill bookstore shelves, as Jack Zipes and others have pointed out.) The "images of women" in the fairy tale have come in for extensive (and needed) critique; Marina Warner's recent *From the Beast to the Blonde* (1995) is a late and particularly incisive example of this—and includes some interesting and necessary work on the woman as storyteller: Mother Goose, Mother Bunch, Scheherazade, and all their mythical avatars.

But we have been less conscious and less critical of the ways the Grimms have determined our conception of the structure of the fairy tale, of the shapes it is supposed to take. The "chaste compactness" of its best-known form, its predictable structure help make its gender inequalities and family structures also seem inevitable. But the literary fairy tale has taken a number of shapes in its history, shapes now often seen as aberrant or subversive. We need to look carefully at the structure of early tales written by women, often very different from the compact tales favored by Perrault and the Grimms. We need to pay attention to the way tales, both old and new, have been framed. We need to look much more closely at the narrative voices various fairy-tale writers have chosen for their tale-telling. The literary fairy tale is much more varied in shape—protean, in fact—than we have assumed, and has been for three hundred years.

Much feminist literary criticism operates on the premise that women writers modify and challenge patterns established by earlier male writers. As Nancy Walker says in her interesting book *The Disobedient Writer*,

> Appropriating a literary genre in order to revise or even reverse its assumptions, ideologies, or paradigms is one of several ways in which a writer may alter an inherited tradition, and such a method is by no means the exclusive property of women. Indeed, literary history—particularly the history of fiction—is frequently constructed by successive writers turning to their own purposes the patterns and materials created by other writers. And yet it is also true that women's relationship to such an inheritance has normally been fundamentally and dramatically different from that of men.[14]

"Re-vising" or revisiting the canon with a cold and critical eye has been part of many women writers' projects.[15] They reread and challenge the canon, and the modes of feeling and writing it embodies, as many feminist critics have shown. Often these critics have posited a difference between the agonistic, Freudian model of canonical revision that male writers subscribed to (as delineated by W. J. Bate and Harold Bloom)[16] and the more muted, palimpsestic, "dis-eased" subversions that women writers invented.[17] All writers write in dialogue with the traditions they have inherited, either openly or covertly; women writers, however, often understand and frame their revision of traditional models in sharply different ways. Our task as readers is to create for ourselves a more inclusive sense of those traditions and of the possible responses to them.

Because the tales written by Perrault and by the Grimms had become the dominant, canonical fairy-tale mode, women writers of fairy tales in the nineteenth and twentieth centuries often wrote against that canon, defining their work as subversive and oppositional. Certainly much of the recent fairy-tale revival has involved the comic or tragic inversion of traditional fairy-tale expectations. Jack Zipes speaks tellingly in the introduction to his *Fairy Tale as Myth / Myth as Fairy Tale* of two different contemporary modes of dealing with fairy tales, what he calls "duplicates" and "revisions." Duplicates simply repeat the structures and norms of traditional tales, reinforcing "the deeply entrenched modes of thinking, conceiving, believing that provide our lives with structure." (An example would be a new translation of one of the Grimms' tales, with elaborate new illustrations, that does not question or significantly change the "original" it is copying.) Revisions, on the other hand, try "to alter the reader's views of traditional patterns, images, and codes."[18] (An example would be Angela Carter's story "The Bloody Chamber," which is based on earlier "Bluebeard" narratives but sees its patterns and meaning in a sharply different way.)[19]

Most retellings of traditional or classic fairy tales are duplicates; any "new" collection of well-known fairy tales will bear this out. They do not change or question their existing forms or cultural assumptions. Some retellings are revisions; most of the tales, novels, and poems I will be looking at in this book belong in this category. But we need to develop a new word for procedures in retellings that go beyond simple revision. Christina Bacchilega has recently called these techniques "postmodern," a term she uses to include the "conflictual dialogue with a pervasive tradition" that many contemporary fairy tales engage in. Postmodern narrative transformations, she argues, "do not exploit the fairy tale's magic simply to make the spell work, but rather to unmake some of its workings." Postmodern suspicion of the authentic subject, of fixed gender positions, and of the primacy of the spoken word informs the tales written in the last twenty-five years or so. She emphasizes the role of mirrors, frames, and carefully constructed first-person narrative voices in the recent revisions of traditional tales: "Postmodern fictions, then, hold mirrors to the magic mirror of the fairy tale, playing with its framed images out of a desire to multiply its refractions and to expose its artifices."[20]

The term "postmodern," however, is a period term, a term that refers only to (roughly) the last quarter century. (It is also a term that has been the subject of much argument and theoretical difficulty, though Bacchilega reduces it to a common denominator that most critics would accept.) But the "postmodern" narrative techniques Bacchilega so brilliantly explores are strikingly similar to the narrative preoccupations of Giambattista Basile and of the late-seventeenth-century *conteuses*. Their tales, too, are often carefully framed, usually within a telling dialogue or contrasting novella. Their tales, too, often feature distorting mirrors and curious *mises-en-abyme*, or reflections of themselves, that expose their own artificiality and fictionality. The narrative voices the *conteuses* construct, while usually in the third person, never try to be "universal" or reproductions of what Benjamin calls "the speech of the many nameless storytellers" (84). Rather, the *conteuses* often emphasize their own position as knowing, educated, worldly-wise, female subjects, with a wry and sometimes sardonic view of the narrative constellations they are reusing and revising.

In other words, our pervasive and one-sided understanding of the fairy-tale tradition as conforming to the shapes and patterns that writers like Benjamin have described leads us to see the revisionary techniques of recent writers as "postmodern," new, unprecedented. Because we have ignored or forgotten other moments in the history of fairy tales, we fail to see the continuities that run through it. Certainly recent writers go much further in their play with and critique of the forms of the fairy tale, but such play and critique have been part of the genre of the literary tale almost from the beginning. Nancy Canepa has recently and convincingly argued for the "modernity" of Basile's tales, "the figural and ideological interpolations, the references to diverse social realities and narrative traditions, that crowd the *cunti* and disturb their illusory 'happy-ever after' linearity."[21] Lewis Seifert, Patricia Hannon, and others have shown us the complexity of the *conteuses'* creations. Many fairy tales are not the compact monologues we tend to expect, but rather examples of what Bakhtin called "heteroglossia," the point of intersection of conflicting and competing voices and levels of speech.[22] Throughout the history of the written, literary fairy tale, from its very beginnings in Italy and France, insistent internal voices and narrative strategies have called the shapes and patterns we now see as "traditional" into question.

Are there in fact *two* genres of fairy tales—one the compact model Perrault and the Grimms favored; one the longer, more complex, and more self-referential model?[23] I would rather say that our current understanding of what the fairy tale must be like is too narrow. Both models have existed since the genre began. But rather than call them the "traditional" and the "postmodern" or "performative" models, as Bacchilega does, I want to stress the long tradition behind both models by calling them simply "compact" and "complex." This does not mean that all complex tales are long; some of Angela Carter's most compelling (and chilling) revisions, like "The Snow Child" and "The Werewolf," are very short indeed, as are some of Basile's and the *conteuses'*. But they are complex in their reimaginings of well-known and more conventional fairy-tale patterns and motifs. They insist that their audiences constantly keep "compact" or "traditional" or "classic" versions in mind as they read or listen, reflecting on the differences between them.[24] Their doubleness, their insistence on representing "the other side of the story" (to borrow Molly Hite's title), makes their complexity necessary:

The notion that stories inevitably both obscure and encode other stories has been axiomatic to our understanding of narrative since at least the eighteenth century; when construed as repressed or suppressed stories *of the Other*, these other stories become the enabling conditions for the writing and reading of . . . narrative.[25]

"Compact" fairy tales are usually presented as foundational or original, literally as stories that tell us of origins, as stories that do not seem to depend on other stories but come to us as unmediated expressions of the folk and its desires. Their carefully constructed simplicity works as an implicit guarantee of their traditional and authentic status. "Complex" tales, on the other hand, work to reveal the stories behind other stories, the unvoiced possibilities that tell a different tale. They are determinedly and openly "intertextual" and "stereophonic," Roland Barthes's terms for the ways all writing is intertwined with other writing.[26]

Neither model of the tale is new. In France, the literary fairy tale was a genre initially established by a group of women (and a few men, including Perrault, who frequented their circles and salons). Lewis Seifert has estimated that more than two-thirds of the tales that appeared during the first wave of fairy-tale production in France (between 1690 and 1715) were written by women.[27] For more than a century the tales of d'Aulnoy, Lhéritier, La Force, Bernard, and other women dominated the field of fairy tales and were the touchstones of the genre. They were often long, intricate, digressive, playful, self-referential, and self-conscious—far from the blunt terseness that Benjamin and many others associate with the form. (Their friend and competitor Charles Perrault was creating tales much closer to this model at the same time.) The *conteuses* played with earlier romance patterns and sometimes called them into question, but they were conscious that they were participating in the creation of a new genre.

What happens when a genre begins in two very different modes, the compact and the complex? What explains the gradual eclipse of these writers, their tales, and the kind of storytelling that they invented? Why did the simple Perrault model of the fairy tale win out? Why have we ignored, until very recently, the ways the *conteuses* challenged patterns of plot and feeling articulated in earlier written tales (by Straparola and Basile in Italy, in particular) and attempted to establish new ones? Why do we now tend to define the fairy tale in a way that excludes the tales the *conteuses* wrote? In the chapters that follow, I will show how the two models have coexisted and competed at least since the late seventeenth century, or for slightly more than three hundred years.

No book on fairy tales can be comprehensive. I regret that I have been able to do so little with the relationship between folklore and fairy tales;[28] with the collections of tales produced by Straparola and Basile in Italy in the sixteenth and early seventeenth centuries; with the many tales produced during the nineteenth century, in England,[29] in France, or in Germany, particularly tales written by women at about the same time as the Grimms were producing their tales;[30] with tales from outside Europe. But I have concentrated on the development of our current understanding of the fairy tale and on the ways rereading the complex tales of the *conteuses* and of our contemporaries can help us refine that understanding. As Salman Rushdie has said, "every story one chooses to tell is a kind of censorship. It prevents the telling of other tales."[31]

The history of the written fairy tale is a history of pouring old wine into new bottles, forcing new wine into old bottles, and often "distressing" new bottles to make them look old. In my exploration of that history, I'll be practicing a feminist formalism,[32] trying to see how gender and this peculiar genre have interacted, or why it matters who is making or recycling the bottles and fermenting the wine. Marina Warner has spoken of fairy tales as "a language of the imagination, with a vocabulary of images and a syntax of plots."[33] I will be exploring the ways that language has been inflected, the various idiolects or *paroles* that fairy-tale writers have chosen to use, the ways they have "negotiated"[34] their paths to new forms, transposed images, and replotted plots. In this book I reread the shifting history of that language and the different, gendered ways it has been spoken over the last three hundred years.

CHAPTER ONE

Fairy Tales about Fairy Tales: Notes on Canon Formation

> To what extent do we continue to read, and teach, and write about the already read because it *has already been written about*?
>
> Nancy K. Miller, *Subject to Change*

WHY DO we read the books we read? How do we choose the fairy tales we read or retell? Why do we teach the books we teach? How do we decide which books or tales to print and reprint? How does the process of selection and winnowing work? What criteria should determine the selections? These and other, related questions have been hotly debated in the academy and in the media for the last twenty years or so. The so-called culture wars have been the locus for an ongoing discussion (to use a term more neutral than the debates have actually been) of literary tradition and the judgment of literary value, the continuing transmission of "Western tradition" and other traditions, and the representation of various groups of writers in the syllabi and reading lists of the academy.

Most of the arguments in these "wars" focus on questions of inclusion and exclusion: what writers are included in which anthologies and syllabi, and why? If we include writers who have normally not been part of the acknowledged "canon" (the list of writers "traditionally" taught in literature courses), which writers will we leave out? (Anthologies often just get thicker and thicker, but syllabi are always limited in scope.) Which writers and traditions should our students be required to know, or at least have a nodding acquaintance with? Often the participants in the "culture wars" perceive these questions primarily as political: the exclusion of women writers, or African American writers, or postcolonial writers seems to mirror their marginal political status. If we require fewer of the "dead white males" (to use the term that often comes up in these debates), we seem to be contributing to the shift in political power that the participants in the debate either celebrate or fear. As Joan DeJean has said, "controversy over issues such as which authors should be taught in schools becomes of significant importance because it stands for a larger upheaval, as a result of which culture, and even society, come to be defined in significant ways."[1]

John Guillory has argued, in his book *Cultural Capital: The Problem of Literary Canon Formation* (1993), that the terms of the argument I have sketched here are misconceived on both sides. Guillory criticizes the bases of the current "canon debate"—the way both sides tend to assume that the existing canon reflects an unchanging and monolithic Western culture. Any canon, he argues, is only a selection, and that selection changes—sometimes quite rapidly—over time. The canon should not be the result of identity politics; "representation" in the canon is not the same thing as political representation. Furthermore, the "values" that both sides perceive as inherent in the texts we have chosen to teach reside not only there but also in the reading community that has selected them. Both sides have misunderstood what is at stake in the debate about the canon. Canon questions, according to Guillory, are academic questions only.

Yet Guillory, though he claims to talk about "literary canon formation," does not seem to have any way of describing or accounting for change. When a text becomes canonical, it is constantly reread, discussed, and written about. Other texts from the same era fade into the background, or the shadowy recesses of the stacks, or archives, or rare book rooms. Yet he relegates the work of finding and studying forgotten texts to what he calls "research programs," scholarly projects that take place at the highest levels of the university system. Finding forgotten or neglected texts has been an important part of the agenda of feminist criticism, of course; since the mid-1970s feminists have often engaged in what Elaine Showalter called "gynocritics" or the recovery and study of texts written by women.[2] But Guillory seems content to contain the work of recovery in academic institutions, particularly in graduate schools. He makes no provision for the ways the work of recovery might influence the construction of undergraduate syllabi or reading lists or anthologies—or, for that matter, the publication and transmission of rediscovered texts to a wider public.

Guillory also claims that in the past we did not study writing by women because they produced relatively little before the eighteenth century, and because after that they wrote in genres considered "minor," like the novel.[3] (In some ways his book is not just an explanation but also a justification of the current canon.) One of the crucial factors in the study of literary history is what he calls "access to literacy."[4] And it is certainly true that before the mid–seventeenth century, women in Europe produced far less writing than men did because literacy among women was at first restricted to a few aristo- crats, and because later many women were taught to read, but not to write.[5] This cannot explain, however, what has happened to many texts written and published by women since then. In France, for example, women were the primary producers of novels and, later, fairy tales, from about 1650 on. Yet by the mid–nineteenth century their texts were all but unknown. Not only were these women literate, but they had "access to the means of literary production," another important determinant of standing in literary history as Guillory sees it;[6] they knew how to get their work circulated, published, and discussed. Yet the texts they produced were often quite systematically denigrated and, by the nineteenth century, deliberately forgotten.[7]

One of the things "research programs" have shown, in fact, is precisely the repetitive processes of exclusion that obscure the construction of catego- ries we tend to take for granted, like "*the* fairy tale." And canons do have considerable influence outside the precincts of the university—a fact that the dissemination of the fairy tale makes particularly apparent. We read and reread and write about Perrault's and the Grimms' tales because they are the ones that have been available to us. Our understanding of what a fairy tale should be is limited to the characteristics of the examples of the genre we have known. In order to understand literary history in general, and the history of fairy tales in particular, however, we must continue to explore the ways gender has influenced not only access to literacy and to the means of production but also what we read. As Nancy K. Miller suggests in my epi- graph for this chapter, the texts we know are the texts people have chosen to write about—and what we choose to write about is in part a function of the ways gender has determined literary reception. Our view of earlier literary landscapes should be wider.[8]

To study the history of the written fairy tale is essentially to do this work in miniature. Many, indeed most, of the early writers of fairy tales in the 1690s in France were women. (They produced more than two-thirds of the roughly seventy tales written and published during the 1690s.) Yet the only name from this group most readers still know is Charles Perrault, and the only tales that are still endlessly reproduced are Perrault's. To understand why this is so is to begin to understand how gender operates in canon formation.

My methodological moves may seem predictable. As Susan Gubar has commented, "With recovery, often the woman writer being excavated is claimed to be central because of the highly charged (again, feminist or misogynist) sexual ideologies of her productions, or the standards of evaluation by which she had been judged are said to be skewed by generic and gendered criteria inappropriate to her accomplishment."[9] I will be claiming, as Gubar foresees, that the work of these women seems strange and unfamiliar because of the literary strategies they use and the ways these strategies have been judged. These judgments, however, did not occur in a vacuum. They are linked to the complex cultural history of the literary fairy tale itself, particularly its relationship to romantic ideas about popular culture and the "folk." Since the Brothers Grimm were the architects of many of our received ideas about tales, their explicit comments on this history seem a good place to start.

I I

In the introduction to the first edition of their *Kinder- und Hausmärchen* (1812), Jacob and Wilhelm Grimm refer briefly to some of the fairy-tale collections that had come before theirs, particularly the tales known as Perrault's (first published in 1697):

> Frankreich hat gewiß noch jetzt mehr [Märchen], als was Charles Perrault mittheilte, der allein sie noch als Kindermärchen behandelte (nicht seine schlechteren Nachahmer, die Aulnoi, Murat); er giebt nur neun, freilich die bekanntesten, die auch zu den schönsten gehören.

> (France must surely have more [fairy tales] than those given us by Charles Perrault, who alone still treated them as children's tales (not so his inferior imitators, Aulnoy, Murat); he gives us only nine, certainly the best known and also among the most beautiful.)[10]

The Grimms go on to praise Perrault for his "naive and simple manner" and for his refusal to embellish the tales. His fairy tales, they say, have nearly the flavor and purity of the true folktale. The Grimms' opinions rest on a number of romantic notions about fairy tales that we still tend to share: that they are (or should be) primarily for children; that the best of them are accurate reproductions or transcriptions of oral tales; that oral tales are a kind of natural but marvelous growth from the folk itself, an expression of a primitive but therefore authentic national spirit; that oral storytelling is on the wane, and its traces must be preserved in print. They believe, in short, that their collecting is an attempt to recover something valuable and primitive that is being lost. Their work is based on a nostalgic and futile quest to recover a past that never quite existed.[11] They say explicitly that the authentic fairy tale cannot be invented.[12]

The Grimms' preface is a very good example of the romantic interest in folk culture in the decades just before and after 1800. As Susan Stewart says, "in order to imagine folklore, the literary community of the eighteenth century had to invent a folk, singing and dancing 'below the level' of 'conscious literary art.' "[13] The Grimms, in other words, participated in the invention of a tradition of a particular kind of oral storytelling among the folk. Though storytelling has undoubtedly existed for thousands of years, the Grimms had to imagine it in a certain way in order to ground their own collecting efforts. They had to posit a rupture or separation between literate and oral culture, between modern, self-conscious writing and older, supposedly natural, spontaneous storytelling or ballad singing. Their nostalgia for a vanishing or vanished culture—assumed to be simpler and more poetic than their own—still permeates most fairy-tale collecting and research. We expect the written tale to be what Stewart calls a "distressed genre," a genre that is given all the patina of age and of oral transmission. Our studies of written tales have been, at least until recently, primarily attempts to find and catalog their oral sources. And the Grimms' anxieties—about the relationship of "high" art and popular culture and about the interplay of the written and the oral—are still our own.

My quotation from the Grimms also has an important subtext, buried within parentheses: "(not so his inferior imitators, Aulnoy, Murat)." Marie-Catherine le Jumel de Barneville, baronne d'Aulnoy, and Henriette-Julie de Castelnau, comtesse de Murat, were among the aristocratic women who began the vogue of writing fairy tales down in France at the end of the seventeenth century. In 1690 Marie-Catherine d'Aulnoy published a fairy tale, "L'île de la félicité," in her novel *Histoire d'Hypolite, comte de Duglas*. This tale—a strange amalgam of Greek myth and folk belief—is now consid-

ered to be the first literary fairy tale written in France, the earliest in a wave
of tales published throughout the 1690s and much of the earlier eighteenth
century, many of them by women. The Grimms seem unable to praise Perrault without belittling these women, calling them his "imitators," though in
fact they began writing tales earlier.[14] The growth of interest in a supposedly
simpler "folk culture" at the end of the eighteenth century, an interest that
the Grimms both followed and promoted, made it impossible for them and
for many later commentators to appreciate the tales d'Aulnoy, Murat, and
many other women in France wrote.

These tales, in all their glitter and artificiality, actually work against the
emerging association of fairy tales with the primitive, with the folk, and with
the oral tradition as they were beginning to be understood, with illiterate
and anonymous female tellers of tales, and with children. The women's tales,
rather than existing in the supposed "timeless space" of folk culture, are
consciously invented as a complex and ironic comment on the historical moment in which they were produced. The style, length, and timeliness of their
narratives do not fit the ideology of the fairy tale as it has been constructed
in the last three centuries. They have been effectively written out of the
history of fairy tales, an erasure that began even before the Grimms.

In 1699, for example, the abbé de Villiers wrote a dialogue between a
Parisian and a Provincial about the vogue for fairy tales, *Entretiens sur les
contes des fées et sur quelques autres ouvrages du temps, pour servir comme
préservatif contre le mauvais goût* (Dialogues on fairy tales and some other
works of our time, to act as an antidote against bad taste). Throughout the
text Villiers struggles to establish the boundaries of good taste—or what he
thinks of as correct and established literary standards. The volume is dedicated to the members of the Académie française, the supposed "juges na-
turels de tous les livres" (*natural* judges of all books [my emphasis]).[15] And
Villiers goes on to praise Perrault ("un celebre Academicien" [a well-known
member of the Academy]), one of the fraternity of learned male authors, for
imitating the style and simplicity of "nurses" so cleverly in his tales: "il faut
être habile pour imiter bien la simplicité de leur ignorance"[16] (one must be
clever to imitate their ignorant simplicity well). Villiers insists, in fact, on
the simulation of the primitive and the oral as hallmarks of the good fairy
tale, while dismissing the women's tales for their length, lack of unity, and
precious language. Throughout he criticizes women writers' ignorance and
lack of learning, the learning that paradoxically makes it possible for Perrault

to imitate the voice of the "ignorant" storyteller so well. The Parisian, often apparently a mouthpiece for Villiers himself, articulates the nascent set of beliefs that govern the evaluation of fairy-tale production: written fairy tales should replicate or recapture the style and tone of "authentic" folk narrative; they should appeal to children, though written with at least one ear cocked for the reactions of adult readers; they should have "morals" that contribute to what Maria Tatar calls the "pedagogy of fear" in the education of children.[17]

At the same time, the Parisian continually insinuates that women writers are more interested in sales than in quality. He tells a story, for example, about a woman who, pretending to be a well-known princess, sends a coach-and-six to bring a printer to the princess's house in order to drive up the price he is willing to pay for her novel. This fable—interesting both in its treatment of class and in its feigned disdain for the profit motive—is typical of Villiers's anxiety about women's writing and money, about the literary marketplace as a site where, he claims, lazy and ignorant women readers read the productions of lazy and ignorant women writers.[18] As the Parisian says:

> la plûpart des femmes n'aiment la lecture, que parce qu'elles aiment l'oisi-veté & la bagatelle; ce n'est pas seulement dans la Province, c'est aussi à Paris et à la Cour qu'on trouve parmi elles ce goût pour les Livres frivoles. Tout ce qui demande un peu d'application les fatigue et les ennuïe; elles s'amusent d'un Livre avec le même esprit dont elles s'occupent d'une mouche ou d'un ruban, êtes-vous étonné après cela que les Contes & les Historiettes aïent du débit.[19]

> (most women enjoy reading only because they enjoy laziness and the trivial; not only in the provinces, but also in Paris and at the court one finds among women this taste for frivolous books. Everything that requires a little effort tires and bores them; they amuse themselves with a book in the same way they play with a fly or a ribbon. So does it astonish you that tales and little stories are popular?)

For Villiers, this invasion of the marketplace by women—as writers and as consumers—interrupts what he sees as the "natural" economy of literature and the unchanging value of its monuments, giving undeserved credit and sales ("débit") to fairy tales and other short fiction. He also complains that women and provincials are unselective in their reading habits and therefore create literary fads: "Et qui ne se persuade pas que les Livres sont une marchandise qui change de mode comme les garnitures & les habits?"[20] (And who is not convinced that books are now a modish merchandise like accessories and gowns?) Books have become commodities like fashionable clothing, both governed by the fickle and superficial taste of women. Fairy tales written by women are then doubly suspect: because they do not aspire to the rigorous simplicity of Perrault's tales, and because they are part of a new literary economy that threatens the stability of the old.[21] Like Boileau in his diatribes against the novels written by women earlier in the century, particularly in his tenth Satire (1694), Villiers carefully constructs literary standards that exclude women's tales.[22]

In spite of Villiers's and others' complaints, the tales by women like d'Aulnoy, Murat, and Lhéritier continued to be reprinted throughout the eighteenth century. They formed the major part of the monumental, forty-one-volume *Cabinet des fées* published from 1785 to 1789. During and after the French Revolution, however, these tales were reprinted less and less often and were rarely, if ever, included in school anthologies or classroom texts. Perrault became *the* French fairy-tale writer.

The growth of romantic nationalism contributed at the same time to a dramatic narrowing of the fairy-tale canon. Johann Gottfried Herder's essay "Von Ähnlichkeit der mittlern englischen und deutschen Dichtkunst" (On the similarity of medieval English and German poetry) (1777) emphasizes the crucial role of folklore in establishing a national identity:

> Und doch bleibts immer und ewig, daß der Teil von Literatur, der sich aufs Volk beziehet, volkmäßig sein muß, oder es ist klassiche Luftblase. Doch bleibts immer und ewig, daß wenn wir kein Volk haben, wir kein Publikum, keine Nation, keine Sprache und Dichtkunst haben, die unser sei, die in uns lebe und wirke.[23]

> (And yet it is always true that the literature that is about the folk must be popular, or it is just a classical air-bubble. Yet it is always true that if we have no "folk," we have no public, no nation, no language nor literature that is truly ours, that lives in and has an effect on us.)

Herder's essay is really an appeal to German scholars to recover old folk material in German, as Percy had (and Macpherson and Chatterton pretended they had) in English. But this process of recovery—a process that the Grimms, as well as their friends Clemens Brentano and Achim von

Arnim, were deeply involved in—was guided, as we have seen, by a fairly narrow and exclusive notion of what folk culture and particularly fairy tales (or *Märchen*) ought to look like. Tales by d'Aulnoy and Murat—often cited or parodied in German literature toward the end of the eighteenth century[24]—were no longer considered authentic or moral enough to be reproduced or even to be mentioned, except in parentheses.

In 1826, a volume by C. A. Walckenaer, *Lettres sur les contes des fées* (Letters about fairy tales), echoes many of Villiers's themes and anxieties as well as Herder's notions about the superiority of Northern culture. The volume is structured as a series of letters from an older male adviser to a young mother who is trying to decide on appropriate material to read to her daughter. Are fairy tales really for children? If so, which ones should she choose? What can her daughter learn from fairy tales? (Significantly we are given none of the mother's letters but only her friend's magisterial replies.) Walckenaer returns again and again to the origins of the "contes de fées" in Northern mythology and links the "fées" to the Latin *fata* as well as sibyls and Celtic fairies.[25] Though he is concerned with tracing the links of fairy tales to traditional or mythological "wisewomen," he, like Villiers, explicitly condemns the versions of the tales written by women. He argues that Marie-Jeanne Lhéritier's story "L'adroite princesse"(The clever princess) should never have been added to editions of Perrault's *Contes* because "les aventures qui y sont racontées sont de nature à ne devoir pas être mises sous les yeux de l'enfance, et encore moins de l'âge qui suit. Perrault n'aurait pas commis cette faute"[26] (the adventures that are told there are of a nature that should never be seen by children, and even less by those who are a little older. Perrault would never have made that mistake). Like the Grimms, he claims that Perrault published his tales first and that the women imitated him. ("Le succès des contes de Perrault produisit une foule d'imitations" [35] [The success of Perrault's tales produced masses of imitations].) And he explicitly criticizes the elaborate style of the women's tales:

> Mais aucun de ces recueils n'eut un succès aussi grand et surtout aussi durable que celui des contes de Perrault; et il est facile d'en trouver la raison: aucune de ces nouvelles productions ne ressemblait aux modèles auxquels Perrault avait eu le bon esprit de se conformer. Ces nouveaux contes n'étaient plus les *Histoires du temps passé, et de la Mère l'Oye*, répétées sans cesse par les bonnes et les nourrices, à qui leur propre instinct et leur défaut même d'éducation avaient enseigné les tournures de

phrases les plus simples, les plus claires, les plus naïves, et les mieux
appropriées à la faible intelligence de leurs élèves. (36)

(But none of these collections had a success that was as great or as long-
lived as that of Perrault's tales; and it is easy to see the reason why: none
of these new productions resembled the models that Perrault had the wit
to follow. These new tales were no longer the *Stories of Bygone Days and
of Mother Goose*, repeated endlessly by serving-women and nurses, whose
good instincts and even lack of education had taught the turns of phrase
that were the simplest, the clearest, the most naive, and the best suited to
the feeble intelligence of their pupils.)

Walckenaer then goes on to quote one of Villiers's criticisms of the women's
tales: "Ils les ont faits si longs, et d'un style si peu naïf, que les enfants
mêmes en seraient ennuyés" (39) [27] (They made them so long, and the style
so sophisticated, that even children would have been bored). And he repeats
Villiers's argument that the *conteuses* of the 1690s simply wanted to make a
name for themselves, to arrive at literary celebrity by an easy route (132).

Like Villiers and the Grimms, then, Walckenaer continues to criticize the
learned ladies who wrote fairy tales, and to praise the lower-class woman
storyteller and her simple tales. The myth of this storyteller has been pervasive in most writing about fairy tales from 1699 to the present, even in work
that is otherwise quite skeptical about the supposed "tradition." The frontispiece of Perrault's original collection has imprinted certain notions about the
telling of tales on generations of readers. It gives us, in miniature, a version
of what the traditional storytelling situation has traditionally been thought
to be (see fig. 2). The frontispiece shows a fireside scene: three fashionably
dressed children seated by a fireplace, listening to a simply dressed older
woman, perhaps a nurse, shown with a spindle.[28] The fire and the candle
suggest that the storytelling is taking place in the evening, as in the traditional *viellée* or evening storytelling session; the lock on the door and the
cat curled up by the fireplace underscore the intimacy and the comforting
domesticity of the scene. The older title of the collection, the title that Perrault had used for an earlier manuscript edition of the *Contes* in 1695, appears as a placard affixed to the door in the background, just above the spindle that is traditionally associated with women's storytelling: *Contes de ma
Mere Loye* (Stories of Mother Goose). The writing on the placard is more
irregular and clumsy than the somewhat more elegant type used on the title
page, just as the title on the placard contrasts with the more elaborate and

Fig. 2. Frontispiece by Clouzier, Charles Perrault, *Histoires ou contes du temps passé* (1697). Courtesy of the Houghton Library, Harvard University.

distanced formal title: *Histoires ou Contes du temps passé, avec des Moralitez* (Stories of times past, with morals).

Perrault signals his ambivalence about the new genre of written fairy tale in several small but telling ways. First, he does not sign his name to the edition of the *Contes* published in 1697 but rather ascribes them to his son Pierre Darmancourt, then nineteen. No one knows, of course, whether his son had a hand in the composition of the tales, but it is significant that the tales were widely thought to be by Perrault himself at the time. In an obituary notice for Perrault in the *Mercure* in 1703, the writer has no doubt that "La belle au bois dormant" (Sleeping Beauty) was one of his works:

> L'heureuse fiction où l'Aurore et le petit Jour sont si ingénieusement introduits, et qui parut il y a neuf à dix années, a fait naître tous les contes de fées qui ont paru depuis ce temps-là, plusieurs personnes d'esprit n'ayant pas cru ces sortes d'ouvrages indignes à leur reputation.[29]

> (The happy fiction in which Aurora and the little Day are so cleverly introduced, and which appeared nine or ten years ago, gave birth to all the fairy tales that have appeared since then, many talented people believing that this kind of work would not sully their reputations.)

In this passage, the writer not only attributes the prose tales to Perrault but also reinforces the fiction (begun by Villiers and others who damned the *conteuses*) that he was the first to write tales. It is Perrault, the writer claims, who "changeait en or tout ce qu'il touchait"[30] (changed everything he touched into gold); his brilliance has transformed the little folk "bagatelles" into something rich and strange. Perrault may not have been confident in 1696 (when "La belle au bois dormant" first appeared in the *Mercure*) or in 1697 (when the *Contes* were first published) that the tales were worthy of him. Or perhaps, as Marc Soriano suggests, he wanted to enhance his son's reputation at court.[31] The evasiveness of the signature, however, is part of the elaborate set of strategies that Perrault established—in the frontispiece, in the typography, in the dedication—to frame his tales and direct his readers' responses.

Certainly Perrault was conscious of the importance of having standing in court circles. The dedication to "Mademoiselle," the niece of Louis XIV, is part of his anxious balancing between high and popular cultures. Even more significant is the manuscript version of the *Contes*, dated 1695 and apparently given to the same "Mademoiselle."[32] If the volume is indeed authentic, we see Perrault participating in courtly manuscript culture in 1695, then publishing his *Contes* in a rough and rather unsophisticated format in 1697. (Most of his other books, as Gilbert Rouger points out,[33] were much more carefully and elaborately printed, often by Coignard, an official printer to the king, as were his tales in verse in 1695.) The manuscript is bound in red morocco with the arms of "Mademoiselle" gilt-stamped on both covers and is carefully copied in a calligraphic hand. The first printed editions, however, look rather like the cheap chapbooks and almanacs *colporteurs* carried from door to door and from village to village, with coarse wood engravings and irregular fonts. Perrault disseminates his tales in two very different ways, for two very different audiences. He is poised between the manuscript culture of court patronage and the newer modes of printing for a mass reading public.[34]

Perrault, then, carefully staged his entry into the new field of fairy tales. He played up and played on his connections to the court at Versailles, as an Academician and as a servant of the king, by creating an elaborate dedication copy as well as dedicating the printed version to a member of the royal family. At the same time, however, he seems to have attempted to appeal to the growing market for cheaply printed books. Insisting on and reemphasizing his membership in the coteries of the court and the court-sanctioned Académie, he also was canny enough to see the ways he could profit from circulating his material to a wider audience. It seems unlikely that he realized that three hundred years later he would be remembered chiefly for his fairy tales, and it is difficult to imagine that he would have been happy about it. But we have to see him as a savvy entrepreneurial writer, taking advantage of various codes of literary production to reach different audiences. Though critics then and now have been eager to see him as dignified and disinterested, magisterially above the claims of the marketplace, everything we know suggests otherwise. He was at least as interested in marketing his work as Villiers claimed the *conteuses* were. Far from simply copying or imitating the tales he may have heard (but probably read), he consciously framed them in a way that seemed to guarantee their stylistic naïveté and their connection to an oral folk tradition.

III

In contrast, the women who wrote tales in the 1690s presented themselves—both in their frontispieces (see chapter 2) and in their stories themselves—as sophisticated writers rather as than simple peasant storytellers. They never identified themselves with "nurses" or peasant women or "Mother Goose"; in fact, they tended to refer to themselves, in the salons and in their frontispieces, as sibyls or fairies. There was some element of class consciousness

here, of course, but something much more important was also at work. If
they identified themselves primarily as *tellers* of tales, they would find it
more difficult to see themselves as *writers* of tales. Like Perrault, they were
conscious of the implications of the "paratexts" that surrounded their work
and the print mediums they used: frontispieces, title pages, choices of fonts
and illustrations.[35] Like Perrault, they were writers mindful of their places in
a highly developed cultural sphere.[36] But, unlike Perrault, they were writing
explicitly for adults, not children, as their frontispieces suggest. And their
stories, unlike Perrault's, tend to be long, complex, often full of digressive
episodes and decorative detail.

Their *contes*, in fact, are often self-referential, "fairy tales about fairy tales"
(one of the meanings of the ambiguous title of this chapter) or *mises-en-
abyme*. Far from the simple, direct narratives that Perrault and the Grimms
preferred, the *conteuses'* tales tend to make self-conscious commentaries on
themselves and on the genre they are part of. In d'Aulnoy's "La chatte
blanche," for example, a prince lost in the woods finds a castle covered with
scenes from her own earlier tales and from Perrault's. In another of d'Aulnoy's tales, "Le pigeon et la colombe," the good fairy "lisait dans les astres
avec la même facilité qu'on lit à présent les contes nouveaux qui s'impriment
tous les jours" (2:283)[37] (read the stars with the same ease that one now reads
the many new tales that are being printed every day). In her 1698 story
"Anguillette," Murat gives her hero an ancestor who comes from one of
d'Aulnoy's tales: "Le Prince qui alors regnoit descendoit en droite ligne de
la celebre Princesse Carpillon, & de son charmant Epoux dont une Fée
moderne plus sçavante & plus polie que celles d'antiquité, nous a si galam-
ment conté les merveilles"[38] (The Prince who reigned then was a direct descendant of the famous Princess Carpillon and her charming husband whose
story has been told by a modern fairy, more learned and more courtly than
those of antiquity). In 1702, at the end of her tale "La tiranie des fées détruite," Louise d'Auneil brings many earlier fairy-tale heroines together—d'Aulnoy's "Biche blanche" and "Chatte blanche" among them—to celebrate both
a wedding and the subjugation of the evil and powerful fairies:

> Toutes ces aymables personnes, quoy que de pays different, se trouverent
> parler la même langue, pour reconnoître une si charmante Souveraine.[39]

> (All these delightful people, although from different countries, found them-
> selves speaking the same language, to recognize such a charming queen.)

The *conteuses'* heroines do indeed all speak the same language, are part of the same literary culture and way of writing. Their glittering tales often become mirrors of themselves and each other, as well as of the court of Louis XIV. They are anything but naive.

We might compare, for example, two versions of a similar scene, the first from Perrault's "Cendrillon" or "Cinderella":

> Le lendemain les deux soeurs furent au Bal, et Cendrillon aussi, mais encore plus parée que la première fois. Le Fils du Roi fut toujours auprès d'elle, et ne cessa de lui conter des douceurs; la jeune Demoiselle ne s'ennuyait point, et oublia ce que sa Marraine lui avait recommandé; de sorte qu'elle entendit sonner le premier coup de minuit, lorsqu'elle ne croyait pas qu'il fût encore onze heures: elle se leva et s'enfuit aussi légèrement qu'aurait fait une biche. Le Prince la suivit, mais il ne put l'attraper; elle laissa tomber une de ces pantoufles de verre, que le Prince ramassa bien soigneusement. Cendrillon arriva chez elle bien essoufflée, sans carosse, sans laquais, et avec ses méchants habits. (162)

> (The next evening the two sisters went to the ball, and so did Cinderella, dressed even more splendidly than before. The king's son never left her side and kept saying sweet things to her. The young lady enjoyed herself so much that she forgot her godmother's advice and was dumbfounded when the clock began to strike twelve, for she did not think it was even eleven. She rose, and fled lightly as a fawn. The prince followed her but could not catch her. However, she dropped one of the glass slippers, which the prince carefully picked up. Without coach or footmen, Cinderella reached home out of breath and in shabby clothes.)[40]

The second version is from d'Aulnoy's "Finette Cendron":

> Un soir que Finette avait plus dansé qu'à l'ordinaire, & qu'elle avait tardé assez tard à se retirer, voulant réparer le temps perdu & arriver chez elle un peu avant ses soeurs, en marchant de toute sa force, elle laissa tomber une de ses mules, qui était de velours rouge, toute brodée des perles. Elle fit son possible pour la retrouver dans le chemin, mais le temps était si noir qu'elle prit une peine inutile; elle rentra au logis, un pied chaussé & l'autre nu.

> Le lendemain le prince Chéri, fils aîné du roi, allant à la chasse, trouve la mule de Finette. Il la fait ramasser, la regarde, en admire la petitesse

et la gentillesse, la tourne, retourne, la baise, la chérit & l'emporte avec
lui. Depuis ce jour-là, il ne mangeait plus; il devenait maigre & changé,
jaune comme un coing, triste, abattu. Le roi et la reine, qui l'aimaient
éperdument, envoyaient de tous côtés pour avoir du bon gibier & des
confitures. C'était pour lui moins que rien: il regardait tout cela sans ré-
pondre à la reine, quand elle lui parlait. L'on envoya quérir des médecins
partout, même jusqu'à Paris & à Montpellier. Quand ils furent arrivés, on
leur fit voir le prince, &, après l'avoir considéré trois jours & trois nuits
sans le perdre de vue, ils conclurent qu'il était amoureux, & qu'il mourrait
si l'on n'y apportait remède. (*Contes*, 1:380–81)

(One evening when Finette had danced more than usual and had delayed
her departure to a later hour, she was so anxious to get home before her
sisters that she walked too hurriedly and lost one of her slippers, made of
red velvet and embroidered with pearls. She tried to find it on the road,
but the night was so dark that she searched in vain. Thus she entered the
house with one foot shod and one foot not.

   The next day, Prince Chéri, the king's eldest son, went out hunting and
found Finette's slipper. He picked it up and examined it, admiring its
diminutive size and elegance. After turning it over and over, he kissed it
and carried it home with him. From that day on he refused to eat, and
his looks underwent a great change: he became yellow as a quince, thin,
melancholy, and depressed. The king and queen, who were devoted to
him, had the choicest game and best jam brought in from everywhere, but
they meant nothing to him. He gazed blankly at everything and did not
respond when his mother spoke to him. They summoned the best physi-
cians from all around even as far as Paris and Montpellier. After observing
him continually for three days and three nights, they concluded that he
was in love and that he would die if they did not find the only remedy that
would cure him.)

Most writers about fairy tales, from the 1690s until the present, would
point out the greater economy, speed, and simplicity of the Perrault version
of this series of events. (The glass slipper, perhaps an invention of Perrault's,
has become a crucial part of the versions of "Cinderella" we now usually tell;
Perrault's version has become ours.) Another way to look at the differences,
however, might be to comment on the comic psychological interest of d'Aulnoy's portrayal of the prince, on her telling use of contemporary detail (from

the embroidered, fetishistic slipper to the doctors from Paris and Montpellier), and on her ingenious, mocking elaboration of a well-known motif. Only if we believe—with Villiers, the Grimms, and Walckenaer—that the language of the fairy tale must be simple, stripped-down, and pseudo-naive would we necessarily prefer Perrault's version. We might also look at another pair, based on similar motifs: the two tales called "Riquet à la houppe," one by Perrault (first published in his *Contes* in 1697, not included in the manuscript edition of 1695), one by Catherine Bernard (first published in 1696 in her novel *Inés de Cordoüe*).[41] Though there has been a fair amount of speculation about priority, no one has been able to prove which one came first— and that, in any case, is not central to my argument.[42] In fact, we should probably think of them as tales told the same afternoon in a salon, rival versions based on a common donnée—just as, in the salons, one composed poems based on the same collection of rhyming words ("bouts-rimés") or made up different interpretations for the same dreams. The two tales seem to be answers to the same question: what happens when absolute beauty is combined with stupidity, and ugliness with high intelligence? In most fairy tales the princes and princesses are both beautiful and smart—but what if they weren't? What if the beautiful princess were abysmally stupid and the clever prince hideously deformed? What if they encountered each other? How would their meeting differ from the classic "love at first sight" that dominates most tales?

Perrault and Bernard make some of the same choices. They both present the prince as the deformed, intelligent one, the princess as the beautiful one with no brains. They both give the prince an underground kingdom and a retinue of gnomes. Both play on a central exchange: the prince gives the princess the gift of intelligence, with the power the fairies had given him at birth to make up for his deformities; the princess in return must promise to marry him. Both set the crucial meetings between them exactly a year apart, the year that the prince has given the princess to enjoy and exercise her new intelligence before their marriage. And, in both stories, the marriage takes place.

Within this common framework, however, the differences are striking. Perrault begins with his usual formula: "Il y avait une fois" (once upon a time), establishing the fairy-tale milieu in the first few words. He starts with the birth of the prince, the horror of his mother at this "si vilain marmot" (ugly little monkey), and the compensatory gift of the fairy. Then he goes on to the birth, seven or eight years later, of twin girls in a neighboring kingdom:

one beautiful but stupid, one clever but ugly. (The clever but ugly princess does not appear in Bernard's version, and gradually fades from Perrault's, having served primarily as a foil for her sister.)

Bernard, on the other hand, begins her tale with a sentence that might lead to a very different kind of story: "Un grand seigneur de Grenade, possédant des richesses dignes de sa naissance, avoit un chagrin domestique qui empoisonnait tous les biens dont le comblait la fortune" (A great nobleman of Grenada, possessing riches worthy of his birth, had a domestic sorrow that poisoned all the gifts that fortune had bestowed on him). The setting she creates is not immediately identifiable as a fairy-tale landscape; the mention of Grenada makes it seem that she might be beginning one of the many "nouvelles" set in Spain, popular at the time, rather than a fairy tale. She begins with the birth of one princess, named Mama (oddly enough), and the "chagrin domestique" that her stupidity and lack of grace cause. Then Bernard moves swiftly, in a paragraph and a half, to the meeting with Riquet, the prince/monster, who, in her version, is given no previous history at all. Perrault's opening, with its symmetrical families and fairy gifts, is immediately in the realm of fantasy; Bernard's, with its quasi-realistic focus on the princess and her family, initially inhabits a different kind of narrative space.

This difference seems to narrow as the stories continue, since both recount the meeting of the prince and princess in rather similar ways. But in Perrault's version Riquet acknowledges that his power to give the princess some wit comes from the fairies, while in Bernard's version he gives her a verse to recite, rather than stressing the magic of his gift. This verse, apparently simple and banal in the extreme, nevertheless has a subtle incantatory power:

> Toi qui peut tout animer,
> Amour, si pour n'être bête,
> Il ne faut que savoir aimer,
> Me voilà prête.

> (272)

(Cupid, you who can bring everything to life, if it is only necessary to know how to love in order not to be stupid, see that I am ready.)

The princess is not simply made intelligent, as in Perrault's version; she must contribute to her own transformation by repeating these words: "A mesure que Mama prononçait ces vers, sa taille se dégageait, son air devenait plus vif, sa démarche plus libre; elle les répéta" (272) (As Mama uttered these verses, her poise improved, her posture became more lively, her movements freer; she repeated them). And everything that happens *after* her transformation in the two stories is almost completely different. In both versions, the transformed princess finds an admirer who is rich, handsome, and intelligent. In Perrault's version, however, the princess seems to forget him as soon as she reencounters Riquet. Perrault's princess agrees to marry Riquet without hesitation when he tells her that she has the gift to make him handsome, just as he had the gift to make her intelligent.

> La Princesse n'eut pas plus tôt prononcer ces paroles, que Riquet à la houppe parut à ces yeux l'homme du monde le plus beau, le mieux fait et le plus aimable qu'elle eût jamais vu. Quelques-uns assurent que ce ne furent point les charmes de la Fée que opérèrent, mais que l'amour seul fit cette Métamorphose. . . . Dès le lendemain les noces furent faites, ainsi que Riquet à la houppe l'avait prévu, et selon les ordres qu'il en avait donnés longtemps auparavent. (180)

> (No sooner had the Princess finished uttering these words, when Riquet à la houppe appeared to her eyes as the most beautiful, well-formed, and charming man that she had ever seen. Some say that it was not the fairy's charms at work here, but rather simply Love that caused this Metamorphosis. . . . The wedding took place the next day, just as Riquet à la houppe had planned it, and following the orders that he had given long before.)

Perrault mockingly suggests that Riquet is not transformed at all but rather has become handsome only in the eyes of the deluded Princess; his new beauty is only an illusion. But he ends his tale here: Riquet and the Princess, having given each other their symmetrical gifts, presumably live happily ever after, just as Riquet has planned. The story begins and ends with Riquet: his birth, his plans, and his power.

In Bernard's version, the other suitor—here given a name, Arada—is always present in the princess's thoughts, and in fact her fear of his disdain if she should become stupid again is one of the reasons she agrees to marry Riquet. But even after her marriage—and it is significant that Bernard continues to write her story "beyond the ending"[43] that we tend to expect—she continues to think of him and finally arranges for him to join her in Riquet's subterranean kingdom. Riquet is not transformed; he remains the clever but hideous gnome he has been since the beginning. Though the princess is temporarily able to outwit him, now being clever herself, and visits her lover Arada at night, Riquet discovers her treachery and takes his revenge by turning Arada into a gnome identical to himself. Mama, no longer able to distinguish between them, lives on unhappily in the subterranean kingdom:

> Elle se vit deux maris au lieu d'un, et ne sut jamais à qui adresser ses plaintes, de peur de prendre l'objet de sa haine pour l'objet de son amour; mais peut-être qu'elle n'y perdit guère: les amants à la longue deviennent des maris. (278)

> (She lived with two husbands instead of one, and never knew who to complain to, for fear of taking the object of her hatred for the object of her love. But perhaps she hardly lost anything at all: in the long run lovers always become husbands.)

In place of Perrault's conventional wedding and happy ending, Bernard gives us this disillusioned "moral."[44] Marriage is not a static and blissful state, and lovers do not remain the faultless creatures they have seemed. Perrault's tale is one of mutual transformation; in Bernard's there is no such magical reciprocity.

Jack Zipes once claimed that both tales are designed to discipline women into compliant daughters and wives, showing that women's unruly desires must be tamed by constant surveillance.[45] It seems to me, however, that Bernard's tale is about the dangers for women in fairy-tale marriage patterns, the patterns that Perrault both reproduces and mystifies. Perrault's tale is indeed "male-centered," to use Zipes's term,[46] beginning and ending with the history of Riquet à la houppe. But Bernard's—as her very different introduction and conclusion show—is focused on the plight of a woman whose desires do *not* transform the ugly prince into a dream-boat, and whose situation is never completely under her own control. (Her illusion of autonomy in the year following her transformation is cruelly shattered after Riquet's reappearance and the forced marriage.) Though perhaps not suitable for the eyes of children, as Walckenaer complained, Bernard's tale is a comic and clear-eyed subversion of romance or what we now think of as "fairy-tale" patterns. Riquet as husband becomes a tyrant who can even clone himself to enforce his wife's absolute isolation in his underground kingdom. Rather than living "happily ever after," the princess lives on in adulterous bigamy, with two indistinguishable and repulsive husbands and no one she can safely confide in. The tale, in fact, may be a fairly transparent allegory of the position of women in the marriage economy of France under Louis XIV.[47]

Perhaps we should not be surprised that Bernard's tale has not been widely reproduced or anthologized since the eighteenth century. Though her tale is approximately the same length as Perrault's, unlike many of the *conteuses'* very long tales, and though its language is often as terse and compressed as his, Bernard's pessimism and her critique of contemporary patriarchal marriage patterns would certainly not have endeared it to the Grimms or their successors. As fairy tales gradually became naturalized as guarantors of good behavior, bourgeois family stability, and submissive female purity, tales like Bernard's became less and less acceptable.[48]

IV

The most prolific and the most gifted of the *conteuses* was Marie-Madeleine d'Aulnoy, who inaugurated the vogue of fairy-tale writing in France in her story "L'île de la félicité" (1690). In her tales she often played freely with folkloric motifs—combining a version of the abandoned-children motif (Perrault's "Petit Poucet," the Grimms' "Hänsel and Gretel") with the Cinderella story in her "Finette Cendron," for example. She also often included motifs and figures from Greek mythology: various personified mythological winds, particularly Zephyr, meet the medieval figure of Death with his scythe in "L'île de la félicité"; later she makes many references to "Amour" (Cupid) and to the story of Cupid and Psyche, most overtly in "Le serpentin vert" (The great green worm) when the heroine is cautioned to *read* the story before she demands to see her monstrous husband in the daylight.[49] D'Aulnoy repeatedly and imaginatively deals with metamorphoses, transforming her characters into plants or animals, and sometimes leaving them in that state, as in "L'oranger et l'abeille" (The orange tree and the bee) or, tragically, in "Le mouton" (The ram). Like many of her contemporaries—Lhéritier, Murat, the abbé de Choisy—she often deals with heroines who dress as men, to travel in safety or to redeem their families' honor; her inventive treatment of this persistent motif in "Belle-Belle ou le chevalier Fortuné" (Beauty, or the fortunate knight) often questions seventeenth-century assumptions about invariable gender characteristics.

D'Aulnoy's tale "La chatte blanche" (The white cat), published in her *Contes nouveaux ou Les fées à la mode* (1698), begins like an aristocratic version of Perrault's "Chat botté" (Puss in boots). Perrault's hero, the third of three sons of a miller, is forced to go out into the world to seek his fortune after his father dies, leaving his mill to the oldest son and his donkey to the next, while the youngest inherits only a cat. D'Aulnoy's hero, the youngest of three princes, is forced to go out into the world to obey his father, the king; like his brothers, he must submit to a series of three trials: to find the most beautiful little dog in the world, then to find a long and beautiful piece of cloth that will pass through the eye of a needle, then to find the most beautiful bride. But this initial folkloric competition among brothers becomes submerged in the central story of the White Cat, a beautiful and mysterious anthropomorphic being who lives in a beautiful and mysterious castle. Though the tale begins as a story about the prince's quest, it quickly turns into the story of the highly educated and intelligent female cat. The delights of her castle and of her conversation, in fact, repeatedly cause the prince to forget his duty; it is always the cat herself who reminds him that the proverbial year is coming to a close, and supplies him with the things his father has requested.

As Lewis Seifert has pointed out, " 'La Chatte blanche' is first and foremost about the power of female storytelling."[50] In the tale, d'Aulnoy follows the outlines of traditional "Animal-Bride" stories (AT 402, "The Mouse as Bride");[51] the motif of the three brothers, their competition, and the animal-bride who gives the tiny gifts occur over and over in tales like Calvino's "The Prince Who Married a Frog."[52] But in her version the story of the prince recedes as she emphasizes the cat's realm and powers. The cat is a writer herself, though her works are unknown:

> Souvent même la belle chatte composait des vers & des chansonettes, d'un style si passionné qu'il semblait qu'elle avait le coeur tendre . . . ; mais son secrétaire, qui était un vieux chat, écrivait si mal, qu'encore que ses ouvrages aient été conservés, il est impossible de les lire. (*Contes*, 2:172)

> (Often the beautiful Cat would even compose verses and little songs in a style so passionate that one might have thought her in love . . . ; but her secretary, an old cat, wrote so illegibly that, even though these works have been preserved, it is impossible to read them.)

D'Aulnoy here may be referring to the difficulty readers have in deciphering texts by women; though the cat's poems have not disappeared, like so much other writing by women, they cannot be "read" because they have been handed down so imperfectly by a male scribe. Elsewhere in the story, d'Aulnoy points to another failure of reading: her cat orchestra is playing what sounds to the prince like caterwauling and screeching. She assures him, though, that "nous avons ici des poètes qui ont infiniment de l'esprit, & si vous restez un peu parmi nous, vous aurez lieu d'en être convaincu" (2:169) (we have poets here with infinite powers of wit, and if you stay a while among us, you will certainly be convinced). She implies that the cats' language will seem like mere noise until the prince has become used to it and learned to interpret it. D'Aulnoy signals her readers not to be too quick to condemn her writing as barbaric or monstrous; she seems to suggest as well that one must always read women's texts in their context, patiently, not rushing to judgment.

The cat's castle also mirrors her power and luminous intelligence. It is covered with "carboucles" or carbuncles, mythological gems that were said to emit radiant light. Its tower walls are a picture gallery of scenes representing "l'histoire de toutes les fées depuis la création du monde jusqu'alors" (2:166) (the history of all the fairies, from the creation of the world to the present), including several from d'Aulnoy's own tales and Perrault's "Peau d'âne" and "Belle au bois dormant," as we have seen. (The prince is amazed and pleased to see a picture of Prince Lutin, supposedly his cousin, a character from another of d'Aulnoy's tales, and later a miniature on the White Cat's table that looks exactly like himself.) Her salon is decorated with portraits of famous literary cats, from Rabelais's Rodillardus to Puss-in-boots.[53] Both she and the prince have a literary lineage as well as a royal one, inscribed in the decoration of the castle itself. It is the site of royal entertainments—ballets, fireworks, a hunt, even a naval battle the prince can observe from a terrace— but it is also a house of fictions, elaborately constructed like the royal *divertissements* that mirror the entertainments at Versailles.

The most elaborate fiction within the tale is the White Cat's own story, a version of Rapunzel that she finally tells, after she has become a woman again, in answer to the prince's many questions. Like Rapunzel, she was promised to the fairies by her pregnant mother in exchange for some enticing fruit;[54] like Rapunzel, she is hidden away from the world in a tower by the fairies/witches but falls in love with a passing cavalier. This princess, however, turns out to have a will of her own: she refuses to do the spinning the fairies expect, rejecting the distaff "d'un petit air mutin" (2:197) (with a mutinous little gesture), and she refuses to marry the hideous dwarf they have selected for her. The fairies in turn refuse to let her die with her cavalier but rather turn her into a white cat. Her disobedience brings about her first metamorphosis; her second depends on the prince: only he can release her from her feline form by cutting off her head and tail and throwing them into the fire. He must be ready to dismember her at her command; transformation, d'Aulnoy seems to be saying, does not come without risk and even violence.

The White Cat's story is embedded in the story of the prince, just as her gifts to the prince's father are all embedded in something tiny: an acorn, a seed within a grain of wheat within a cherry stone within a hazelnut within a walnut, a rock crystal.[55] (In fact, her story is doubly embedded, a story within a story within a wider frame-tale, "Le gentilhomme bourgeois," as we will see in chapter 2.) The tale-within-a-tale is mirrored in the fantastic forms of the tiny encapsulated objects. The delicate piece of linen that the prince finally draws out from its hiding place within the seed is so miraculous that

> tous les oiseaux, les animaux & les poissons y étaient peints avec les arbres, les fruits & les plantes de la terre, les rochez. les raretés & les coquillages de la mer, le soleil, la lune, les étoiles, les astres & les planètes des cieux. Il y avaient encore le portrait des rois & des autres souverains qui régnaient pour lors dans le monde; celui de leurs femmes, de leurs maîtresses, de leurs enfants & de tous leurs sujets, sans que le plus petit polisson y fût oublié. (2:181)

> (all the birds, animals, and fish were depicted on it, along with the plants of the earth; the rocks, the curiosities and shellfish of the sea; the sun, the moon, the stars, the heavenly bodies and planets of the heavens; as well as the portraits of the kings and other sovereigns who reigned on earth at the time; those of their wives, their mistresses, their children, and all their subjects, down to the last street urchin.)

The wonderful, delicate piece of cloth is infinitesimally small and yet can encompass the whole world and the heavens, just as an apparently trivial fairy tale can. (In Calvino's "The Prince Who Married The Frog," the cloth is long and fine, but it does not reflect the universe: "Out [of the walnut] came cloth as fine as gossamer that continued to unroll until the throne room was covered with it")[56] D'Aulnoy again turns the details of her tale into an allegory of writing, justifying her own ways of telling a story. The structural complexities of the tale and its elaborate descriptions are not mere excess or self-indulgent play, but rather subtle guides for reading it.[57] The "carboucles" and the many other gems that stud the castle suggest and reflect the power of female storytelling. Even the strange, disembodied white hands that serve the prince in the castle, "qui lui semblaient fort belles, blanches, petites, gressettes & bien proportionnées" (2:167) (that seemed to him very beautiful, white, small, plump, and well proportioned), are clearly feminine; though they may seem to be playing women's traditional domestic role, they too reflect the cat's ability to create a mysterious order in the domain she controls.

The White Cat's power is not unlimited, of course. Her early life is circumscribed by her mother's immoderate desire and by the power of the fairies; she never can act with perfect freedom. But, even after her marriage, she dominates the kingdoms she retains for herself and the prince, as well as our attention. As Seifert has remarked, the last sentence of the tale focuses exclusively on the princess:[58] "La belle Chatte blanche s'y est immortalisée autant par ses bontés & ses liberalités que par sa rare mérite & sa beauté" (2:207) (The lovely cat was long remembered, as much for her kindness and generosity as for her rare merit and beauty). D'Aulnoy has transformed a tale about a wandering prince into a tale about a powerful princess, whose storytelling, both written and oral, is part of her power.

Why is this tale so much less familiar than Perrault's "Cinderella" or "Sleeping Beauty"? Though it is probably d'Aulnoy's best-known tale, often reprinted in France and included by Andrew Lang in *The Blue Fairy Book* (1889), there have been few recent popular editions, for adults or for children. In the English-speaking world, Lang's abridged version may have contributed to its quasi-disappearance. Though the adaptation by Minnie Wright he chooses to reproduce retains d'Aulnoy's story outline and some of her details, it omits what is most characteristic and most telling. For example, instead of the list of fairy tales pictured on the walls of the White Cat's castle, we hear only that "[t]he walls were of the finest porcelain in all the most delicate colours, and the Prince saw that all the stories he had ever read were pictured upon them."[59] Rather than d'Aulnoy's specific homage to contemporary tales, by other *conteuses* and by herself, we get a vague reference to stories in general. The adapter leaves out all references to the cat as a writer, to the other talented cats in her kingdom whose work the prince cannot yet understand, and to the miniature world portrayed on the fine cloth. Perhaps most tellingly, the last sentence dwindles into a conventional fairy-tale ending: "The festivities lasted several months, and then each king and queen departed to their own kingdom and lived happily ever after."[60] Though Lang includes the story, in other words, he omits most of what is distinctive and original about it. His stripped-down version makes "The White Cat" seem like a faded imitation of traditional fairy-tale style and motifs, instead of an active transformation of the genre as d'Aulnoy knew it.

Perhaps, too, readers have been unable to warm to d'Aulnoy's elaborate, baroque descriptions and romance situations. If you come to a fairy tale expecting the simple tales popularized by Perrault and the Grimms, "The White Cat" may well seem overstuffed and overcomplex. (As one of my research assistants—a sophomore—said about the stories by the *conteuses*: "Too many diamonds and emeralds.") Like the prince, we must get accustomed to the distinctive sounds the *conteuses* make in order to hear anything other than elaborate and sometimes annoying noise. It takes time and open-minded reading to appreciate their significant contributions to the genre—and to begin to recognize the paths they have broken for later writers. Their sophisticated play with narrative structure and telling detail, their sardonic critiques of the seventeenth-century French marriage economy, their explorations of the psychology and limitations of women's political and artistic power—all these elements make their tales an important contribution to the history of the fairy tale.

V

Our current canon of fairy tales—those tales produced and reproduced in endless collections and illustrated editions of single tales—includes very few written by women. ("Beauty and the Beast" is an exception I will discuss in chapter 3.) But this is not the result of differing access to literacy or to the mechanisms of the literary marketplace, as Guillory might claim. The *conteuses*—all of them either aristocrats or well-connected middle-class women—were highly literate and sophisticated writers in a culture that found their writing both delightful and deeply disturbing. Though they had "access to the means of literary production,"[61] to use Guillory's phrase, their work was almost immediately criticized and marginalized by threatened writers like Villiers. Like the female writers of romances in the seventeenth century, or Hawthorne's "damned mob of scribbling women" in the mid–nineteenth century in the United States, they were in fact gradually excluded from the canon of fairy tales—a process that we need to examine and understand.

As we read and analyze these noncanonical texts, we will also have to reconsider the evaluative terms that have been part of the aura surrounding the canonical ones. Canons tend to be self-validating; that is, the qualities they possess become the qualities that we look for in our reading and praise all over again when we find them.[62] The Grimms wanted fairy tales to be simple, "naive," economical, a reflection of their ideas about the folk, and appropriate for the social education of children; the ones they chose became canonical; and now, when we read fairy tales, we want them to be like the ones the Grimms promoted. Reexamining the early French fairy tales written by women and attempting to understand the formation of the minor canon of fairy tales has implications for all canon investigations and all literary history. To think about a canon often means to take a hard look at the terms we use to evaluate our texts—and that's never easy. It means as well trying to analyze and make explicit the assumptions that governed the formation of the canon in the first place. Assumptions about a good or "authentic" fairy tale created the canon of the genre, a canon that has come to include Perrault but exclude most of his female contemporaries. We've unconsciously accepted notions that were beginning to form as Perrault was writing in the 1690s and that were made explicit by the Brothers Grimm in the early nineteenth century. Ignoring the sophisticated "fairy tales about fairy tales" the *conteuses* wrote, we've continued to believe other "fairy tales about fairy tales."

CHAPTER TWO

Voices in Print: Oralities in the Fairy Tale

> In appropriating folklore genres, the literary tra-
> dition is able to create an idealization of itself
> through a separation of speech and writing. Such
> a separation . . . always posits speech as a form of
> nature.
>
> Susan Stewart, *Crimes of Writing*

> [W]e must give up the fiction that collects all
> these sounds under the sign of a "Voice," of a
> "Culture" of its own—or of the great Other's.
> Rather, orality insinuates itself . . . into the
> network—an endless tapestry—of a scriptural
> economy.
>
> Michel de Certeau, *The Practice
> of Everyday Life*

FAIRY TALES and orality seem intimately connected. We think of written tales as transcribing stories handed down orally for hundreds of years, as simply "putting into print" the traces of that long-standing tradition. Most writers of fairy tales have done their best to reinforce that impression. Charles Perrault's alternative title, *Tales of Mother Goose*, suggests a traditional, spoken origin. The Brothers Grimm work hard to create a simple and naive narrative voice. Hans Christian Andersen's stories often begin with formulas like "Now then, here's where we begin" that imitate oral storytelling. I am not denying that many fairy tales have been (and continue to be) part of an on-going oral, popular culture, but I do want to show that our sense of access to that culture through reading written fairy tales is an illusion—an illusion carefully and deliberately created by many fairy-tale collectors, editors, and writers.

We can become conscious of that illusion by looking further at another strand in the tangled history of written fairy tales—the tales written by women in the 1690s in France. Unlike Perrault, their contemporary, these women only occasionally appealed to the oral, popular tradition and never attempted to imitate an illiterate or uneducated voice. Rather, they simulated a different kind of orality—the conversation that framed the tales they knew by Straparola and Basile, and that animated the salons of the later seventeenth century in France. Most of the long, elaborate tales they wrote are set within a conversational frame, a frame that often reproduces the milieu and the carefully formulated repartee that was part of salon culture.

The frontispiece of the 1697 edition of Perrault's *Contes* that I discussed in the first chapter defines the traditional version of the oral storytelling situation. If we look at it again, from a slightly different angle, we can see the kind of orality Perrault means to suggest (see fig. 2 again). The central female figure, dressed in the simple costume and sabots of a domestic servant or nurse, is simultaneously spinning and telling a story, spinning wool or flax and "spinning a yarn."[1] The thumb and forefinger of her left hand, carefully delineated, are guiding the filament; the next two are raised in the traditional gesture that asks for a listening audience's attention. The frontispiece sets her in the tradition of the spinning woman with distaff, a tradition that also links her to the oral transmission of stories. The simple peasant woman in Perrault's frontispiece may be simply that, but the distaff and her raised fingers suggest her unsettling verbal power, a power that Perrault both mimes and controls. Her distaff and her dress mark the storyteller's gender, social position, and place in the literary economy: she is an emblem of the mythical oral tradition that Perrault claimed to draw on and at the same time carefully distanced himself from.

The distaff is always a mark of gender; it often anchors the woman in the domestic sphere but sometimes is used to stress her unruly distance from it. Witches and harridans often carry one. In two engravings of about 1500, Albrecht Dürer's savage depiction of a witch riding backward on a goat (fig. 3) and Israhel van Meckenem's *The Angry Wife* (fig. 4), the spindle is thrust through the distaff, suggesting that the domestic implement is no longer used for spinning but rather has become a subversive banner or a weapon. The distaff often stirs up undercurrents of misogyny and fear of women's voices and gossip. One particularly telling woodcut from a French seventeenth-century pamphlet, an example of the old "silent woman" topos, shows a headless woman holding a distaff, with the motto "Si Tu La Cherche La Voicy" (If you are looking for her [the silent woman], here she is) (fig. 5).[2]

Fig. 3. Albrecht Dürer, *The Witch Riding Backwards
on a Goat* (engraving, 1511). Courtesy of the
Metropolitan Museum of Art, New York, Fletcher
Fund, 1919. (19.73.75)

The presence of the distaff suggests that the woman has effectively been
silenced and relegated to her domestic functions; she is no longer a speaker
or a teller of tales, but rather a mute sexualized object. As Marina Warner
says, "Women dominated the domestic webs of information and power";
this domination always made male observers uneasy.[3] In Perrault's choice of
frontispiece, however, all these negative connotations are subdued. The central figure continues to spin while she is telling her stories; she is both nurse
and tale-teller, trustworthy domestic and *raconteuse*.

Fig. 4. Israhel van Meckenem, *The Angry Wife* (engraving, ca. 1500). Rosenwald Collection. Photograph © 2000 Board of Trustees, National Gallery of Art.

Women are often supposed to be tellers of tales: those anonymous, lower-class nurses and grandmothers who taught and entertained children by telling them stories. The murky legend of "Mother Goose" is an instance of this belief; Sévigné's well-known letter of October 30, 1656, refers to it casually as if this were part of the common lore about fairy tales:

Et si, Mademoiselle, . . . , ce n'est pas un conte de ma mère l'oie,
  Mais de la cane de Montfort
  Qui, ma foi, lui resemble fort.

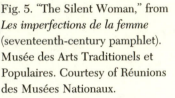

Fig. 5. "The Silent Woman," from *Les imperfections de la femme* (seventeenth-century pamphlet). Musée des Arts Traditionels et Populaires. Courtesy of Réunions des Musées Nationaux.

(And if, Mademoiselle, . . . , this is not a tale of Mother Goose, but of the drake of Montfort, there are strong resemblances between them.)

For Sévigné, the Mother Goose tale is the generic title for a whole group of popular stories. The *Dictionnaire de l'Académie* (1694) gives many folk synonyms for *conte*:

> *Le vulgaire appelle* conte au vieux loup, conte de vieille, conte de ma Mère l'Oye, conte de la cicogne, conte à la cicicogne, conte de peau d'asne, conte à dormir debout, conte jaune, bleu, violet, conte borgne, *Des fables ridicules telles que sont celles dont les vielles gens entretiennent et amusent les enfants*.[4]

> (*The common people call* old wolf's tale, old wives' tale, Mother Goose tale, tale of the stork, tale told by a stork, donkey skin tale, tale to fall asleep by standing up, yellow, blue, violet tale, one-eyed tale, *all those ridiculous tales told by old women to entertain and amuse children*.)

Many, if not all, of these definitions are linked to the traditions of gossip and tale-telling by women—not only the old wives' and Mother Goose tales, but also the tales of and by the stork, as Warner has pointed out. Angela Carter has described the situation in her usual trenchant prose: "Old wives' tales— that is, worthless stories, untruths, trivial gossip, a derisive label that allots the art of storytelling to women at the exact same time as it takes all value from it."[5] Perrault's frontispiece perpetuates the prevailing myth about the appropriate role for women in the transmission of fairy tales: as aging, patient, nurturing conduits of oral culture or spinners of tales.

This belief has not completely faded. Vladimir Propp in his essay "The Nature of Folklore" imagines the prehistory of literature using exclusively feminine metaphors: "Folklore is the womb of literature; literature is born of folklore. Folklore is the prehistory of literature. . . . Literature, which is born of folklore, soon abandons the mother that reared it. Literature is the product of another form of consciousness."[6] He locates folklore at the beginning of time, in a feminine realm. Or, as Trinh Minh-ha says, in her *Woman, Native, Other* (1989), "The world's earliest archives or libraries were the memories of women. Patiently transmitted from mouth to ear, body to body, hand to hand. . . . Every woman partakes in the chain of guardianship and of transmission."[7] Trinh still imagines oral culture as literally handed down by women, in a particularly physical, intimate way ("from mouth to ear, body to body, hand to hand"). Women are still said to be the guardians of tradition, passing on to their children and grandchildren the stories of their culture. But, as folklorists like Linda Dégh have shown, women are and were not the only, or even the primary, storytellers in most oral cultures.[8] The myth of the anonymous female teller of tales, particularly strong in the legends of Mother Goose and Mother Bunch, is just that: a myth—but a myth that has several important functions and corollaries. If women are the tellers of tales, storytelling remains a motherly or grandmotherly function, tied (to use the language of French feminist criticism) to the body and nature, as we see in the quotation from Trinh. Stories are supposed to flow from women like milk and blood. And if women are thought of as *tellers* of tales, it follows that they are not imagined as the collectors or writers of tales. As fairy tales were transmuted from oral tales into "book tales" (*Buchmärchen*, or tales that have been written down) into written, invented tales (*Kunstmärchen*), women were subtly relegated to the most "primitive" stage. Perrault's frontispiece may have been an attempt to etch his female writing competitors out of existence.

As Catherine Velay-Vallantin has shown us, the frontispiece also suggests the fictive reading situation that Perrault and his printer wanted to prescribe, a simulation of oral tale-telling, or what she calls "factitious orality."[9] In his prose tales, Perrault mimes the voice of the peasant storyteller, always elegantly walking the line between the practices of writing and supposed "oral" transmission "within a culturally more aristocratic mode of reading."[10] He presents the voice as "authentic," as a transcription of traditional storytelling. As we have seen, contemporary commentators like the abbé de Villiers particularly admired his ability to feign this voice, to be clever enough to sound naive. But we must remember that this voice is a deliberate simulation, existing in an uneasy tension with the more sophisticated language of the worldly verse morals at the end of each tale and with the sophisticated verse tales he wrote earlier. Perrault abandons the intricate, courtly style he used for those verse tales in his *Contes*, choosing instead a simpler narrative voice.

The frontispieces of volumes of tales women wrote in the 1690s often seem to be designed to contest the ideological force of Perrault's. In the frontispiece of early editions (1698 and 1711) of d'Aulnoy's *Contes nouveaux* (fig. 6), a woman dressed in the flowing robes and turban usually associated with a sibyl is writing the title of one of d'Aulnoy's tales, "Gracieuse et Percinet," in a large folio or book. Again she has children as her audience, but these children are dressed in rather the same way and probably are of the same class as the storyteller. The storyteller is represented *not* with the domestic and gendered spindle, but rather with a large book that demonstrates her literacy. There is a fireplace, but the fire is out. Instead of the simple candlestick, there are sconces surrounded with elaborate scrollwork. Instead of the locked door, there is a window opening out on a summer country scene. Instead of the domestic cat, there is an exotic monkey—again perhaps a reference to another of d'Aulnoy's tales, "Babiole," published earlier that same year. This mirror effect—the reflection of some of the tales in the introductory picture—heightens the conscious artificiality of the scene and of the tales that follow.[11]

The frontispieces of a 1725 Amsterdam edition of d'Aulnoy's *Contes nouveaux ou les Fées à la mode* also work against the image of the woman as lower-class storyteller. The frontispiece of volume 1 shows a fashionably dressed woman seated on an elevated dais, gesticulating as she speaks to an audience, similarly dressed, that seems to be primarily adult (fig. 7). Far from an enclosed, domestic, fireside scene, this is a large room with classical

Fig. 6. Frontispiece, Marie-Catherine d'Aulnoy, *Suite des contes nouveaux* (Paris: Compagnie des libraires, 1711). Courtesy, the Bancroft Library, University of California, Berkeley.

columns and an open window that looks out on a faintly classical landscape with obelisks and a tower. The decorative rocaille around the title at the top of the page underscores the aristocratic milieu of this storyteller.

The frontispiece of volume 2 again represents a woman writing (fig. 8), a woman with a helmet on her head—probably Pallas Athena, since she is accompanied by an owl—writing on a large tablet with a quill and apparently speaking at the same time. Behind her a spear replaces the distaff. In the foreground there is an audience of fashionably dressed adults, sitting at lei-

Fig. 7. Frontispiece, Marie-Catherine d'Aulnoy,
Nouveaux contes de fées, vol. 2 (Amsterdam:
Etienne Roger, 1725). Courtesy of the Pierpont
Morgan Library, New York. PML 84636.

sure on the ground. The scene in the background might represent, in miniature, the plot of one of d'Aulnoy's tales, with its fleeing figures and pursuing
horseman.

The frontispieces used for the *conteuses'* tales, then, usually represent
them as sibyls, or as aristocratic storytellers, or as Greek goddesses, not as
spinning peasant women.[12] In another paradoxical illustration of the interweaving of the oral and the written, they often are represented as "writing

Fig. 8. Frontispiece, Marie-Catherine d'Aulnoy,
Nouveaux contes de fées, vol. 2 (Amsterdam:
Etienne Roger, 1725). Courtesy of the Pierpont
Morgan Library, New York. PML 84637.

to an audience," inscribing words on a tablet or folio in front of a listening group. Because women have been perennially associated with the *telling* of tales—in nurseries, in spinning and weaving circles, in quilting bees, by the fireside—it has been difficult for them to think of themselves, and to be thought of, as fairy-tale *writers*. As Joan DeJean points out in *Tender Geographies*, France was the only country where "the written transcription of fairy tales was not totally controlled by men,"[13] at least until the nineteenth century. It was not primarily the traditional passivity of most female protagonists of fairy tales that made it difficult for women to take the active step of writing them down and inventing them, but rather the pervasive notion that women were the designated oral transmitters of those tales.

But the women who wrote tales in the 1690s chose frontispieces and created narrative structures that contested this limiting prescription. The tales the women wrote—again in contrast to Perrault's—are full of references to a feminine, aristocratic, listening audience: "Perhaps you are going to think, Madame . . ."; "Isn't it true, Countess, that . . ."; "I'm sure you have heard, Madame. . . ." The typographical forms in which their tales were printed rarely reflect any interest in suggesting popular origins for the tales; rather, they tend to be identical with those forms in which the many novels and "nouvelles" of the late 1600s in France were printed. Perrault's tales in his 1697 volume always have a crude, illustrative engraving on the first page; the tales in the women's collections often have only the same decorative, stylized headpieces that they use for their other writing. The tales embedded in the women's novels are sometimes not set off from the rest of the text at all, as in d'Aulnoy's "L'île de la félicité" (in her 1690 novel *Histoire d'Hipolyte, comte du Duglas*); sometimes they are separated by a chaste and simple border of florets. The *conteuses'* words do not often appear "in costume" to delight children or to simulate popular orality;[14] their fairy tales are in part reflections of an ongoing (though perhaps fading) salon practice.

Sometimes, in fact, they present their tales in deliberate opposition to Perrault's model. Murat, in the introduction to her *Histoires sublimes et allegoriques* (1699), explicitly dedicates her tales to "Les Fées Modernes" (modern fairies), the writers who are anything but the old-fashioned, naive, female storytellers of times past:

> Les anciennes Fées vos devancieres ne passent plus que pour des badines auprés de vous. Leurs occupations étoient basses & pueriles, ne s'amusant qu'aux Servantes & aux Nourrices. Tout leur soin consistoit á bien ballayer la maison, mettre le pot au feu, faire la lessive, remuer & endormir les enfans, traire les vaches, battre le beurre, & mille autres pauvretez de cette nature; . . . Leur divertissement étoit de dancer au clair de la Lune, de se transformer en Vieilles, en Chats, en Singes, & en Moynes-bourus, pour faire peur aux enfans, & aux esprits foibles. C'est pourquoy tout ce qui nous reste aujourd'hui de leurs Faits & Gestes ne sont que des Contes de ma Mere l'Oye. Elles étoient presque toûjours vielles, laides, mal-vétuës, & mal logées.[15]

(The old fairies, your predecessors, were just gossips compared to you. Their occupations were low and childish, amusing only for servants and nurses. All they did was to sweep the house well, put the pot on the fire, do the washing, rock the children and put them to sleep, take care of the cows, churn the butter, and a thousand other little things of that kind . . . their diversions were to dance by the light of the moon, or to transform themselves into old women, cats, monkeys, or bogeymen, to frighten children and feeble minds. That is why all that remains today of their deeds and actions are only tales of Mother Goose. They were almost always old, ugly, badly dressed and badly housed.)

Murat here deliberately mocks the kind of tale that Perrault produced, his "Contes de ma mere l'Oye" that had been published only two years earlier.[16] She suggests that these tales are only "old wives' tales," crude and outmoded, certainly not suitable for an adult and sophisticated audience. She contrasts his model storytellers, the nurse/gossips busy doing mundane and menial female tasks, with the elegant and educated *conteuses*:

Mais pour vous MESDAMES, vous avez bien pris une autre route: Vous ne vous occupez que de grandes choses, dont les moindres sont de donner de l'esprit à ceux & celles qui n'en ont point, de la beauté aux laides, de l'éloquence aux ignorans, des richesses aux pauvres, & de l'éclat aux choses les plus obscures. Vous estes toutes belles, jeunes, bien-faites, galament & richement vétuës & logées, & vous n'habitez que dans la Cour des Rois, ou dans des Palais enchantez.[17]

(But you, my ladies, you have chosen another way: you occupy yourselves only with great things, the least of which are to give wit to the men and women who have none, beauty to the ugly, eloquence to the ignorant, riches to the poor, and luster to the most hidden things. You are all beautiful, young, well formed, nobly and richly dressed and housed, and you live only in the courts of kings, or in enchanted palaces.)

Murat insists on the distinction between the traditional lower-class female storyteller and the late-seventeenth-century *conteuses*, a group she both praises and implicitly includes herself in. Her literary contemporaries are often aristocratic, certainly well born, well dressed, and well housed; their writing reflects the elegance of their milieu. As modern "fées," they have a magical power of discourse that transforms their lowly materials into stories fit for a discerning audience. They form and frame their narratives echoing the voices heard in the salons.

I I

To trace the tales written in the 1690s by women, then, is to trace a kind of writing based on a very different conception of the "oral" from Perrault's dominant model. The *conteuses* do write stories based on traditional material, though their sources are usually written (Straparola in particular); they also occasionally echo traditional formulas that seem to define women as the oral conduits of popular culture. For example, Perrault, in his verse tale "Peau de l'âne" (1694), and his niece Marie-Jeanne Lhéritier, in her tale "Les enchantemens de l'éloquence" (1696), include almost identical verses:

> Ils ne sont pas aisez à croire;
> Mais tant que dans le monde on verra des enfants,
>> Des meres & des mere-grands,
>> On en gardera la memoire.

(These stories are not easy to believe, but as long as there are children, mothers, and grandmothers in the world, they will be remembered.)[18]

These lines, and other similar ones, occur once in a while in the women's tales, linking the written stories to an ongoing tradition of storytelling and marking that tradition as transmitted by women to children. But much more often, and sometimes simultaneously, the *conteuses* place their tales in the complex and playful ambience of salon conversation. The "oral" for them is not primarily naive and primitive, but rather a highly charged, high-cultural event.

We still tend to identify the oral with peasant, illiterate, or "folk" culture. Like the Grimms, we tend to think of the oral as coming before the written, or as part of the origins of culture. As John Guillory has pointed out, "the generic category of the popular continues to bear the stigma of nonwriting, of mere orality, within writing itself, since popular works are consumed, from the point of view of High Culture, as the textual simulacra of ephemeral speech."[19] Or, to translate, popular writing is usually treated as simply a transcription or a written echo of the speech of the "folk," a less sophisticated, less intellectual activity. (Perrault's imitation of the voice of a member of the folk could be seen as an early instance of this practice.) But, as folklorists like Alan Dundes have shown, there are many different kinds of "folks" and illiteracy is not a requirement.[20] The "oral" can appear in many different social contexts and does not necessarily precede writing. In many cultures, oral narrative and written texts continually influence and change each other.[21]

Walter J. Ong has pointed to a different kind of orality: the residues of ancient rhetorical practices that continued to be taught in schools for boys throughout the seventeenth century.[22] In his book *Orality and Literacy*, Ong makes an interesting guess about women's leading role in the invention of the novel:

> A great gap in our understanding of the influence of women on literary genre and style could be bridged or closed through attention to the orality-literacy-print shift. . . . [E]arly women novelists and other women writers generally worked from outside the oral tradition because of the simple fact that girls were not commonly subjected to the orally based rhetorical training that boys got in school. . . . Certainly, non-rhetorical styles congenial to women writers helped make the novel what it is: more like a conversation than a platform performance.[23]

It seems to me, however, that Ong's guess about the relationship of early women writers to orality is off the mark, at least in France. Or rather, his primary conception of secondary orality (orality that persists after the introduction of writing) is in fact a very narrow, academic, and elite one—and not very "oral" at all. The women who wrote fairy tales, though they were "outside" the oral tradition he is considering, were interested in simulating another kind of oral transmission, a practice that Ong never mentions. He suggests, at the end of the passage above, that women's writing tended to be based on "conversation" rather than on platform rhetoric—but he never acknowledges that conversation, including the ritualized conversation of the salons, is after all an oral practice too. In spite of his laudable attempt to think about women in relation to orality and writing, he in fact defines the oral tradition in a way that excludes them.

We need to develop more nuanced categories of the oral—categories that will permit us to see the ways oral practices that do not derive from supposed "folk narrative" or from the ancient techniques of rhetoric taught in schools continue to leave their traces in written texts. The nostalgia for the oral that permeates most written narrative can take on very different forms. The orality that has left its marks in many fairy tales is rarely the disputational "harangue" of Ong's school-based oratorical rhetoric, and not always the pseudo–folk situation that is sketched in Perrault's frontispiece. Rather, the women of the 1690s attempted to reproduce the conversational ambience of the salons that had formed them as writers. As Joan DeJean has shown in *Tender Geographies*, "the conversational style . . . is originally a female concept, invented in the salons and reinscribed in prose fiction when, following Scudéry's example, women found a new power base in the republic of letters."[24] While her claim seems too broad, ignoring the conversational basis of earlier texts like Plato's dialogues, or the *Decameron*, or the collections of tales by Straparola and Basile, DeJean rightly emphasizes the importance of conversation in women's writing of the later seventeenth century in France.

Like the earlier novels by Scudéry or Villedieu, the *conteuses'* tales grew in part out of the competitive, scintillating dialogues that were an integral part of the salons. First the tales were probably a diversion, one of the many collaborative "divertissements" that formed part of salon culture, like riddles, metamorphoses, portraits, and "maximes d'amour"; then they were written down. But both practices seem to have continued simultaneously throughout the 1690s; as Roger Chartier has said, "the opposition of oral and written fails to account for the situation that existed from the sixteenth to the eighteenth century when media and multiple practices still overlapped."[25] This was true in popular culture, where evening tale-telling probably coexisted with the publication of fairy tales in chapbooks and *colporteur* literature. And it was equally true in the aristocratic practices of the salons. Tale-telling and tale-writing went on simultaneously, as many of the frontispieces suggest.

Like all oral cultures, the culture of the salons is difficult to recover, because it was fluid, ephemeral, constantly changing. We know much more about it than about many other oral cultures, however, since the participants were literate; they wrote about what went on at the salons in their letters, memoirs, even novels. The evidence we have of the ways stories were told and received is spotty and unreliable—found mostly in letters like Sévigné's and novels like Segrais's *Les nouvelles françaises ou les divertissements de la princesse Aurélie* (1656), about the group around the Grande Mademoiselle during her exile at Saint-Fargeau, or La Force's *Jeux d'esprit* (1701), about the "divertissements" that the princesse de Conti promoted during her exile at Eu in the early seventeenth century. Madame de Sévigné, in another well-known letter—this one dated August 6, 1677—suggests all the artificiality and the incongruities of a fairy-tale-telling scene at court, as well as its links with the opera, in order to establish the oral situation in which it took place:

> Mme de Coulanges, qui m'est venue faire ici une fort honnête visite qui durera jusqu'à demain, voulut bien nous faire part des contes avec quoi l'on amuse les dames de Versailles: cela s'appelle les *mitonner*. Elle nous *mitonna* donc, et nous parla d'une île verte, où l'on élevait une princesse plus belle que le jour; c'étaient les fées qui soufflaient sur elle à tout moment.[26]

> (Mme de Coulanges, who has come here to pay me a gracious visit that will last until tomorrow, wanted to acquaint us with the stories that are currently amusing the ladies of Versailles: that is called cajoling [literally, simmering] them. She cajoled us then, and told us about a green island, where a princess more beautiful than the day was being brought up; it was the fairies who breathed on her at every moment.)

Sévigné, with her usual clear-eyed irony, is not much amused by the fantastic fairy tale, with its pastoral "green island," or its length: it lasts "une bonne heure" (a good hour). She makes use of the new word *mitonner* in order to mock the tone and flavor of the storytelling.[27] But in 1677, neither Mme de Coulanges, her court source, or Mme de Sévigné herself thinks of fairy tales primarily as written material; they see the tales, rather, as part of a concrete social milieu—a milieu that is far from the homely, domestic milieu sketched in Perrault's frontispiece.

Recently several writers have attempted to look at the conversation of the salons in its relationship to French intellectual and artistic life in the seventeenth and eighteenth centuries.[28] While acknowledging its elusiveness, they have brought out some of its crucial features: the allusive word-play, the emphasis on repartee and collaborative exchange, the emphasis on improvisation, the absence of weighty "sujet." Erica Harth believes that the salons became "a discursive dead end for women"[29]—and, if one is primarily interested in women's becoming recognized as philosophers, this is probably true. But I see the discourse or, to use a less weighty term, "talk" of the salons as a literary proving ground—not only for the novel, as DeJean has shown, but also for fairy tales. Just as salon talk influenced the suggestive brush strokes of Watteau's canvases, it also provided the airy framework for the castles and enchanted islands that were staples of the fairy tales women wrote.

And here I mean "framework" in a rather literal way. Though Perrault often used the dialogue form in his more "serious" works—the *Parallèle des anciens et des modernes* (1692), for example—he abandoned it when he wrote his *Contes*, preferring to create the naive, solitary voice of "Ma Mère Loye." His women contemporaries, however, saw in the give-and-take of salon dialogue a useful way to introduce and frame the stories they were writing. Though they may not have collaborated on individual stories (I have found no evidence that they did), they situated themselves and their stories in this sparkling, collaborative interchange. Both Raymonde Robert and Lewis Seifert argue that the framing device functioned primarily to give a nostalgic illusion of "social cohesion" or class solidarity.[30] I want to argue here, however, that the frames had a different, and important, narrative function.

Reading tales like Lhéritier's "The Adroit Princess" (1696) in their original form, in fact, we discover that most later editions and translations have wrenched her tales out of their conversational frame. "The Adroit Princess" is dedicated to the comtesse de Murat and begins as if Lhéritier were carrying on a dialogue with her:

> Vous faites les plus jolies Nouvelles du monde en Vers; mais en Vers aussi doux que naturels: je voudrois bien, charmante Comtesse, vous en dire une à mon tour; cependant je ne sai si vous pourrez vous en divertir: je suis aujourd'huy de l'humeur du Bourgeois-Gentilhomme; je ne voudrois ni Vers, ni Prose pour vous la conter: point de grands mots, point de brillans, point de rimes; un tour naif m'accomode mieux; en un mot, un recit sans façon et comme on parle.[31]

> (You create the most beautiful "nouvelles" in the world in verse, but in verse as sweet as natural: I would like, charming Countess, to tell you one in my turn; however, I'm not sure it will amuse you: today I feel like [Molière's] Bourgeois Gentilhomme; I don't want to use verse or prose to tell it to you: no grand words, no startling effects, no rhymes; a naive tone suits me better; in a word, a story ["récit," which retains the aura of the oral] told without any ceremony and as one speaks.)

There are lots of interesting things here, particularly Lhéritier's claim that she has used a language that is simple and "naive," a language that is not formal but rather is written "as one speaks." Simplicity, a key word for both Perrault and these women writers when they talk about the language of their tales, is never a pure transcription, but rather a constructed and carefully pruned version of actual speech.[32] In his similar dedication of one of his verse tales, "Les souhaits ridicules," to "mademoiselle de la C***," Perrault emphasizes her ability to tell stories "dont l'expression est toujours si naïve" (in which the language is always so naïve) and her understanding of the importance of style:

> Qui savez que c'est la manière
> Dont quelque chose est inventé,
> Qui beaucoup plus que la matière
> De tout Récit fait la beauté   (*Contes*, 81)

(who understands that it is the *manner* of invention, much more than the *matter*, that is the beauty of any story)

Like Perrault, Lhéritier is creating a special, stripped-down language for her tales. Unlike Perrault, however, she does not claim to be reproducing the voice of a peasant storyteller. Rather, she is interested in recapturing the elegant simplicity of the language current in the salons, always characterized as "naive" even at its most artificial and constructed. In his recent "Origins of the Fairy Tale," Jack Zipes describes the rhetoric of the *conteuses* this way: "[T]hey placed great emphasis on certain rules of oration such as naturalness and formlessness. The teller of the tale was to make it 'seem' as though the tale were made up on the spot and did not follow prescribed rules."[33] This assumed "naïveté" and simplicity is a crucial feature of the language promoted in the salons.[34] As Murat said of d'Aulnoy's writing, in an unpublished manuscript, "elle écrivoit comme je fais par fantaisie, au milieu et au bruit de mille gens qui venoient chez elle, et elle ne donnoit d'application à ses ouvrages qu'autant que cela la divertissoit" (she wrote the way I do, as her whims took her, in the middle of the noise of the many people who came to her house, and she concentrated on her works only as much as it amused her).[35] Murat here suppresses the labor of writing; what is important is the natural *sprezzatura* of the born aristocrat, writing without constraint and without effort.

We also do not hear this informal, apparently improvisational language as a monologue, the uninterrupted voice of a single storyteller. In the passage above, Lhéritier speaks of telling a story *in her turn*; that is, she conceives of storytelling as an exchange.[36] She imagines a situation rather like the situation in Boccaccio's *Decameron*, or in Marguerite de Navarre's *Heptaméron*, or in Basile's *Pentamerone*, in which the characters in the frame-tale tell stories. This seems to have been the way fairy tales played a role in the salons: members of the group took turns, often adding to and elaborating on the tales others had just told. Lhéritier echoes this reciprocal, sometimes competitive, sometimes collaborative storytelling (a version of what Joan De-Jean calls "salon writing") in her written tales.[37]

In the earliest novels that included fairy tales—d'Aulnoy's *Histoire d'Hipolyte, comte de Duglas* (1690), for example—the tale is always told by a character in the novel, sometimes in very contrived situations. The hero of d'Aulnoy's novel tells the tale of the "Île de la félicité" to an abbess to distract her while her portrait is being painted. He is in disguise as the painter's assistant; his beloved Julie is quasi-imprisoned in the abbey. The tale—a long story that mingles classical references and motifs that the hero remembers from the "contes des fées" he has heard on his travels—seems in part to be a retarding moment, designed to build up the suspense that leads to the lovers' reunion. But it also establishes the convention followed by many of the later writers of fairy tales (though significantly *not* Perrault): the creation of a conversational frame for the tales.

At the height of fairy-tale production, five years later, the tales become a more motivated and "natural" part of the action. In Catherine Bernard's novel *Inés de Cordoüe* (1696), two rival ladies at the Spanish court of the late sixteenth century tell contrasting tales, each trying to outdo the other. Since the queen of Spain, Elizabeth, is French—a point that the novel underlines—she has preserved the custom of holding "conversations" for four or five hours a day; she is always thinking up new amusements for the group that gathers in her "cabinet."[38] Bernard carefully establishes Elizabeth's salon as the place where the court could escape the legendary severity of Philip II, a retreat to French "galanterie" and arts.[39]

In this milieu, the heroine Inés tells the story of "Le Prince Rosier," a story that features appearances of fairies in miniature chariots of ivory, and princes transformed into rosebushes, but that is essentially about the impossibility of unchanging true love. Her rival Leonor responds by telling the story of "Riquet à la houppe," a story that Perrault also retold. As we saw in the first chapter, this is also, unlike Perrault's, a tale in which no one lives "happily ever after." Like "Le Prince Rosier," her version of the tale runs counter to the form we expect fairy tales to take. Both women tell stories that are marked by the marvelous: in "Le Prince Rosier" a guardian fairy and miraculous transformations; in "Riquet à la houppe" fairies and a subterranean realm occupied by gnomes. But though the decor is fantastic, the emotional climate is in fact quite grimly realistic: in both "le mariage, selon la coustume, finit tous les agrémens de leur vie" ("Riquet," 43) (marriage, as is the custom, ended all the pleasures of their lives).

These stories suggest some of the distinctiveness of the tales the women wrote, their tendency to work against the "happily ever after" we now expect as an ending. But, in the context Bernard provides for them, they also show us the way the tales grew out of salon culture, its diversions and rivalries. Inés's tale, for example, is praised by the queen and many other members of the court; her rival Leonor, however,

> fit à Inés plusieurs questions sur ce conte avec autant de malice que d'aigreur. Inés y répondit avec une douceur qui acheva de la faire paroistre une personne parfaite.
>
> Le lendemain Leonor se prepara à conter une Fable, & n'oublia rien pour l'emporter s'il se pouvoit sur Inés. (45)

(asked Inés several questions about the story with as much malice as animosity. Inés answered with a sweetness that had the effect of making her seem to be a perfect person. The next day Leonor got ready to tell a Fable, and did everything she could to make it superior to Inés's.)

To tell a fairy tale well is a way to shine in the salon; Leonor is unable to attract the attention of the marquis de Lerme, who clearly prefers Inés's story, "Prince Rosier." The entire plot of the novel—incredible though it often seems—is driven by Leonor's jealousy of Inés and her desire for revenge; the tale-telling sessions in the queen's salon mark the beginning of the conflict between the perfect Inés and her most imperfect competitor.

When they begin writing fairy tales down, then, d'Aulnoy and Bernard and Lhéritier set them in an oral situation, but an oral situation that is far from the supposed ur-situation that Perrault evokes in his frontispiece. D'Aulnoy continues to frame her tales; in her *Nouveaux contes des fées* (1697, the third and fourth volume of her first collection of stories), for example, she sets them in a double frame: first within the conversational milieu at Saint-Cloud, then within a Spanish "nouvelle": *Dom Gabriel Ponce de Léon* in the third volume, *Dom Ferdinand de Tolède* in the fourth. As the Madame D*** of the preface (a transparent stand-in for d'Aulnoy herself) says,

> Voici un cahier tout prêt à vous lire; &, pour le rendre plus agréable, j'y ai joint une nouvelle Espagnolle, qui est très-vraie & que je sais d'original. (*Contes*, 1:296).

> (Here is a notebook ready to read to you; and to make it more charming, I have connected it with a Spanish novella, which is very true and also I think original.)

The fictionalized "author" of the tales, after being visited by a nymph in the park at Saint-Cloud, offers to *read* her tales aloud to her listeners; again reading and the oral are explicitly invoked together. This motif persists throughout the volumes, as various characters in the Spanish novellas read fairy tales to each other and comment on them. D'Aulnoy, as Patricia Hannon has suggested,[40] blurs the boundaries between novel and *conte de fée*, insisting on the similarities between them. She exploits the conventions of the novel, its digressions and interpolated tales, in the *contes* themselves; the tales crystallize many strategies of the seventeenth-century romance in miniature. At the same time, however, the novellas frame the tales as verbal artifacts, as simulations of an aristocratic dialogue.

D'Aulnoy published another four-volume collection of tales a year later, *Contes nouveaux ou les fées à la mode* (1698). Again she includes a frame-tale in the last two volumes. This one, however, gives us not a series of miniromances within a romance but rather a series of tales that are constantly in friction with, and sometimes interrupted by, a frame-tale that mocks them and questions their validity: "Le gentilhomme bourgeois." The principal figure of this frame-tale—one can hardly call him a hero—begins life as the son of a draper on the rue St. Denis but decides to pass himself off in Normandy as the nobleman M. de La Dandinardière. He's clearly a descendant of Molière's Georges Dandin, but also of Don Quixote; his experience is always at odds with the fairy tales he begins to dream of, listen to, and even write. At the beginning, the daughters of a neighbor offer to send him a "conte" (tale) to read; he says he does not want any more "comptes" (accounts) (*Contes*, 2:161), attempting to erase his mercantile origins. (The pun on "conte" and "compte" suggests d'Aulnoy's persistent play with the tropes of the literary and the fashion marketplaces.) He must be persuaded by one of the daughters that tales are fashionable: "[C]es sortes de Contes sont à la mode, tout le monde en fait, & comme je me pique d'imiter les personnes d'esprit, encore que je sois dans le fond d'une Province, je ne laisse pas de vouloir envoyer mon petit ouvrage à Paris" (*Contes*, 2:161–62) (This kind of tale is à la mode, everyone writes them, and since I pride myself on imitating talented people, even though I'm in the depths of a province, I still plan to send my little work to Paris).

Throughout the frame-tale, d'Aulnoy identifies the writers and the readers of fairy tales as badly educated, provincial or bourgeois, and credulous to an extreme. The tales they are said to write and read out loud, however, do not seem markedly different from the tales in her earlier collection—and, in fact, are among her best known: "La chatte blanche," "Belle-belle ou le chevalier Fortuné," "Le pigeon et la colombe" among them. How are we to understand her strategy? Raymonde Robert claims that the comic and disruptive frame does not and should not affect our reading of the tales, that d'Aulnoy's aim here is not parody.[41] But d'Aulnoy consistently stresses the discrepancies between the frame-tale and the tales themselves, at one point even interrupting "La princesse Belle-Étoile et le prince Chéri" in the middle for a long discussion (*Contes*, 2:373–74).[42] (This interruption is omitted without comment in most versions of the tale I have seen.) The reader must move from the remote elegance of the world of the tale to a farcical conversation in which all the characters of the frame-tale pretend to learning they do not have. (For example, M de la Dandinardière uses a Latin tag he does not really understand and is accused by the provincial baroness of having used dirty language. There is a feminist speech, as Patricia Hannon points out, but the ridiculous self-importance of the speaker effectively nullifies any impact it might have.) D'Aulnoy constantly points up the ignorance and the pretensions of the characters, mocking them and their love for her own *contes*.

Perhaps the most telling moment—the moment when this reader, at least, knows without doubt that d'Aulnoy is fooling—is when the narrator describes the manuscript of a tale that is about to be read as "fort grifonné, car c'étoit une Dame qui l'avoit écrit" (*Contes*, 2:342) (badly scribbled, since it was a woman who wrote it). Here d'Aulnoy insists on the reader's knowledge that this book is written by a woman—and slyly asserts her own literary authority while pretending to undermine it. Like Cervantes, d'Aulnoy plays with the distance between a misguided narrator and her authorial self, as well as with conflicting narrative styles. The crude narrative frame, full of comic dialogue and farcical pratfalls, highlights the ethereal dream-settings of her later fairy-tale romances—and at the same time calls their otherworldliness into question.

Her tactics here also undermine claims that her tales are nostalgic utopias, born of a desire to re-create lost aristocratic spaces or to create new ones. In these *Contes nouveaux*, her last collection of fairy tales, she insists on the comic disparities between the worlds the characters of the tales and of the frame inhabit. The romance drama of the unrecognized princess in a story like "La chatte blanche" is juxtaposed with the comic class drama of the merchant's son trying to rise in a sharply stratified world. Dandinardière's reaction to "La chatte blanche," read to him by the local prior, is typical in its naïveté:

> [J]'étois si charmé de Chatte blanche, qu'il me sembloit estre à la noce, ou ramassant à l'entrée qu'elle fit, les fers d'Emeraudes & les clouds de Diamans de ses chevaux. Vous aimez donc ces sortes de fictions? reprit le Prieur: Ce ne sont pas des fictions, ajouta le Dandinardière, tout cela est arrivé autrefois, et arriveroit bien encore sans que ce n'est plus la mode. (208)

> (I was so charmed by "The White Cat" that I seemed to be at the wedding, or at her entrance, collecting the emerald horseshoes and the diamond nails of her horses. So you like this kind of fiction, replied the Prior. These are not fictions, added Dandinardière, all this happened long ago, and would still happen now except that it's no longer fashionable.)

Dandinardière seems completely unable to recognize a fiction when he sees it—and dreams of living in a time when he could make his fortune by collecting the jewels that are always a feature in the *conteuses'* tales. D'Aulnoy mocks his ridiculous belief that he actually could be present at the marvelous events the tales depend on, his clumsy faith in their literal truth. He and most of the other readers in the frame-tale see neither the joyfully fictive embroidery of the tales nor their subversive social commentary. The White Cat's jewels intrigue him; her political wisdom and power as ruler of her realm and as writer do not.[43]

Why have readers ignored the frames of these tales? Why have most editors (including those who produce versions of the early collections called "complete") omitted them? Why have critics in general failed to discuss the strange comic frame of d'Aulnoy's last printed tales? Partly this is the result of publishing practices, the habit of presenting fairy tales as isolated and unmediated fantasies that exist in a "world apart." (Many of these tales were published alone in chapbooks throughout the eighteenth century. Though the *Nouveau cabinet des fées*, a collection of most of the tales written after 1690, published from 1785 to 1789, included the frame-tales, most publishers continued the practice of printing them as isolated texts.) The *conteuses* often frame individual tales in typical fairy-tale style, beginning with "Once upon a time" and ending with a marriage, but they do not intend these generic gestures to become impermeable barriers between the tales and their world. Setting the tales in a wider frame, the milieu of the Parisian salons—or even in the clumsy and comic imitation salons of the provincial nobility that we see in the "Le gentilhomme bourgeois"—the *conteuses* situate them in a re-creation of a vibrant oral economy. They are not simply symbolic structures, though of course they must be read as symbolic; they are also tokens of an ongoing exchange, an exchange that is part of their meaning and their value.

The conception of the oral that pervades the tales written by women, then, is not the "factitious orality" that Perrault created, the simulation of the supposed stripped-down language of the "folk." And their tales were even less designed for children than Perrault's. Rather, their written fairy tales grew in part out of an aristocratic oral culture, a culture that, though often in opposition to the official culture of the court, always distinguished itself from the culture of the "menu peuple" as well. In the dedication of his prose *Contes* to Louis XIV's niece, Perrault argues that he has included tales that show what goes on "dans les moindres familles" (in the least important families) to give her and other potential rulers some idea of what the life of their subjects is like. Lhéritier, on the other hand, explicitly distinguishes her tales from popular ones; she says that tales told and retold by the folk must have picked up impurities, much as pure water picks up garbage as it flows through a dirty canal: "if the people are simple, they are also crude (*grossière*)."[44]

Lhéritier also claims that stories she tells come from the Provençal troubadours, and that she has attempted to imitate the purity of their morals and style—unlike the writers of the many bad novels being published in her day.[45] Other *conteuses* appeal to other written traditions. For example, Murat in her "Avertissement" to the reader of her *Histoires sublimes et allégoriques* (1699) acknowledges that her source for three of the four tales in her volume is Straparola:

> [J]'ai pris les idées de quelques-uns de ces Contes dans un Auteur ancien intitulé, *les Facecieuses nuits du* Seigneur Straparole, imprimé pour la seiziéme fois en 1615. Les Contes apparemment étoient bien en vogue dans le siecle passé, puis que l'on a fait tant d'impressions de ce livre. Les Dames qui ont écrit jusques icy en ce genre, ont puisé dans la même source au moins pour la plus grande partie.
>
> (I've taken the ideas for these stories from an old author, *The Entertaining Nights* of M. Straparola, printed for the sixth time in 1615. Fairy tales must have been popular in the past century, because there were so many reprintings of this book. The women who have written in the genre so far have also drawn on the same source, at least for the most part.)

This passage is fascinating for several reasons. Murat makes no bones about taking the outlines of most of her tales from another, written source. ("Le sauvage," "Le roy porc," and "Le turbot" all come directly from the first volume of Straparola's tales, though her versions are much longer and more complex.) She also suggests her interest in the history of written tales, and in the publishing history of Straparola's collection. (Six editions of the French translation of Straparola between 1573 and 1612 does seem like a lot.) She places herself—and her fellow *conteuses*—squarely in the tradition of *written* tales,[46] just as Lhéritier does by appealing to the *troubadours* and medieval romance. But they framed their tales the way they did in part to make it clear that they had little to do with the simple, uneducated teller of tales Perrault gives us. They saw their tales not as a continuation of an illiterate female tradition but as a new and powerful intervention in the world of letters.

III

Though the *conteuses* often refer to and simulate oral practices, then, they do not attempt to re-create a mythical or ur-storytelling situation. Theirs is not primarily a nostalgic art. Rather, they attempt to resist or undo the cultural notions that were coming into being as they wrote: the equation of the oral with the unformed and primitive, the equation of the written with the sophisticated. As Michel de Certeau once said, modern Western culture defines the oral as "that which does not contribute to progress; reciprocally, the 'scriptural' is that which separates itself from the magical world of voices and tradition."[47] In their simulation of interwoven voices, in the elaborate conversational frames of their tales, the *conteuses* show that the oral can be progressive, and that the written can and often must bear the traces of tradition and myth. They implicitly challenge the contemporary assumption that the language of history, of science, of learning in general must necessarily be an abstract written language, divorced from the language of the everyday—and that women's language is necessarily trivial and childish.

The *conteuses* also do not pretend that the language of their tales had anything to do with the language of the "folk." Unlike Perrault, they do not suggest that the voices they simulate are primitive, unlettered, grounded in a long peasant oral tradition. Rather, they evoke the voices they heard every day, in the palaces, in the salons. As Marc Fumaroli has pointed out, they were interested in "l'art de la conversation et de l'entretien entre honnêtes gens, où l'art de narrer joue un si grand rôle" (the art of conversation and of dialogue between gentlefolk, where the art of narrating plays such a great role).[48] Their tales are based primarily on written models—Straparola, Basile, medieval romances, accounts of Greek mythology, probably the chapbooks that circulated in all levels of society during the seventeenth century.[49] But their "scriptural economy," as de Certeau calls it, is a celebration and interweaving of narrative voices.

Written simulations of the oral are nothing new, of course. The old tradition of frame-tales is only one example of this persistent strategy of writing. (Think of Boccaccio's nobles outside Florence, or Chaucer's pilgrims, or Basile's wicked old women.) But our persistent romantic identification of the oral with the unlettered has made it difficult for us to appreciate the many possibilities of voice in writing that the *conteuses* exploit. D'Aulnoy, for example, gives us many different voices, from the aristocratic sibyl of Saint-Cloud to the bumbling nouveau-riche Dandinardière. The voice she never mimics, however, is the voice of the old peasant woman telling her tales.[50]

This leads to a final series of paradoxes: Perrault in his prose *Contes* manipulates conventions of the book, both typography and illustration, in order to create the illusion of "folk orality"—in the frontispiece, on the title page, and in the crude illustrative headpieces of the tales. Lhéritier, Bernard, Murat, d'Aulnoy, and the other women writers of the 1690s, on the other hand, usually rely on the apparent transparency or neutrality of current print practices to carry on what seems to have been a living oral tradition. Instead of surrounding their tales with all the typographical signals of folk origins, they frame them in a conversational setting, a setting that marks their tales as part of an aristocratic and highly literate milieu.

Perrault, like the king in the *Thousand and One Nights*, pays apparent homage to the skills and cultural power of the female storyteller. He pretends to reproduce her voice, in a peculiar kind of narrative cross-dressing. But he appropriates that voice and that female figure for his own purposes—and, at the same time, represents her as unable to write.[51] The storyteller is female, but the story-writer is male. Perrault creates the illusion that he is reproducing storytelling as it had always existed in oral popular culture; his simulation of its practices became the dominant style and ideology of the fairy tale, as we see in the Grimms' prefaces and most writing on the fairy tale up to our time. But the women who also participated in the invention of the written fairy tale in France created a very different illusion—the illusion that the story is told within the conversational space of the salons.

All these writers try to give the impression that the stories are being told aloud. They all simulate oralities, but the oralities they simulate are radically different and their methods of producing the illusion of orality even more so. Perrault simulates the oral by imitating (or inventing) the language and world of the folk and the image and voice of the lower-class woman tale-teller. D'Aulnoy, Lhéritier, Murat, and Bernard, however, reject the models of orality and of femininity that Perrault both accepts and promotes. By framing their tales with traces of salon conversation, they represent their tales as part of an aristocratic oral culture. By writing their tales down, they contest the notion that women can only tell the tales that men transcribe and transmit in print. By explicitly setting their work within the traditions of fairy-tale *writing*, they establish themselves as not only literate but learned. And, in a final paradox, by including traces of the oral culture of the salons, they create a new model of femininity: the woman who not only talks—by the fireside to children or in the salon—but also writes.

CHAPTER THREE

The Invention of the Fairy Tale in Britain

> There is no "natural" form here, but a set of documents shaped by the expectations that led to their artifactualization in the first place.
>
> Susan Stewart, *Crimes of Writing*

OUR CULTURE sharply divides telling stories aloud from writing stories down. We tend to think of story*telling* as an older form, linked to peasant or lower-class culture, somehow archaic, perhaps more authentic. Story *writing*, on the other hand, is a high-cultural activity, sophisticated, somehow modern. As Karl Kroeber has said in *Retelling/Rereading*, we often "categorize story-telling as 'primitive,' as an activity peculiar to 'undeveloped' people either lost within or marginal to 'advanced' Western culture."[1] Although we now almost always encounter fairy tales in printed form, we still persist in imagining them as a primarily *oral* genre that puts us in contact with a vanished or submerged, less advanced culture.

The tales we now call "fairy tales," however, came to be known in England and America almost exclusively through printed translations. Unlike fairy tales in Germany or France or Italy, most classic fairy tales in England were not "collected" or "recovered" by later editors or folklorists. Rather, they were really "invented," much like Scottish tartans and royal rituals, in the early nineteenth century.[2] These imported tales were often seen as a substitute for the earlier British fairy lore that had been lost, the native tradition that had inexplicably faded from view. In his influential book *Before Novels*, J. Paul Hunter claims that fairy tales disappeared in England during the seventeenth century—and that their disappearance was responsible in part for the rapid growth of the novel in the eighteenth.[3] As he sees it, English culture had become deeply suspicious of oral communities and their methods of transmitting stories. Puritanism, a new consciousness of class, new distinctions between fact and fancy all joined to drive out, or at least to

suppress, a thriving oral tradition. English reading audiences in the eighteenth century, he argues, were nostalgic for popular forms that once had
been available to all. Like Edwin Muir in his "Complaint of the Dying Peasantry," he mourns the eclipse of an oral culture by print culture:

> Our old songs are lost,
> Our sons are newspapermen
> At the singer's cost.
> There were no papers when
>
> Sir Patrick Spens put out to sea
> In all the country cottages
> With music and ceremony
> For five centuries.[4]

Hunter criticizes the romantic, "child-is-father-of-the-man" nostalgia that
he finds in much current fairy-tale research. But his own nostalgia for a
comprehensive oral community plays an important part in his diagnosis of
the "losses" in eighteenth-century culture. We could say that the eighteenth
century was deeply involved in attempts to "recover" supposedly lost cultural goods; ballads, epics, fables, and proverbs, as well as fairy tales, were
both sought and written as evidence of faded traditions. But, as we saw in
chapter 2, these traditions were largely invented rather than rediscovered;
the Rowley poems of Thomas Chatterton, the poems supposedly by the
Celtic bard Ossian, and the rest of the epidemic of fakes and forgeries were
simply the most obvious part of the eighteenth century's attempt to create
a meaningful past for itself—and to create an oral, nonliterate culture to
distinguish itself from.[5] The kind of oral community Hunter describes and
longs for probably never existed. His evidence for its reality consists primarily of laments for the passing of an older, more cohesive and natural world,
from the late seventeenth century on.

One lament he does not cite, but that seems perfectly to coincide with his
views, comes from John Aubrey's *Miscellanies* (1696):

> Before Printing, Old-wives tales were ingeniose: and since Printing came
> in fashion, till a little before the civil-Warres, the ordinary sort of People
> were not taught to read: now-a-dayes Bookes are common, and most of
> the poor people understand letters: and the many good Bookes, and vari-
> ety of Turnes of Affaires, have put all the old Fables out of dores, and the

The Monarchy of FAIRIES once was great,
As good old Wives, and Nurfes do relate:
Then was the goldenAge, from whence did fpring
A Race of Fairies, dancing round a Ring,
Who in the Night-time did inform Mankind,
Of what the following Tales will bring to mind.

Fig. 9. Frontispiece, Marie-Catherine d'Aulnoy,
The History of the Tales of the Fairies (London:
John Harris, 1716). Courtesy of the Pierpont
Morgan Library, New York. PML 86068.

divine art of Printing, and Gunpowder have frighted away Robin-good-
fellow and the Fayries.[6]

Aubrey believes that the spread of literacy and of printed books has driven
earlier "fables" and "Old-wives tales" out of British lives, even the lives of
"the ordinary sort of People." A pervasive book culture has replaced a thriving oral culture.[7]

The frontispiece of an early translation of d'Aulnoy twenty years later
(1716) shows exactly the same sort of nostalgia for a vanished "Golden Age":

The King and Queen of Hearts, seated in a royal pavilion, preside over a group of fairies dancing in a ring (fig. 9). As the caption says, "The Monarchy of FAIRIES once was great, / as good old Wives, and Nurses do relate." Like Aubrey, the caption writer both regrets the passing of an age when the fairies were always present, and attributes the tales about them to a fading oral tradition dominated by wives and nurses. These laments, and thousands like them, were common in England around the turn of the eighteenth century and may have led to the new enthusiasm for imported fairy tales.

The feeling of living "in the wake of a lost oral community" is part of a pastoral nostalgia for what might once have been. As William Empson showed us long ago (1935), pastoral often passes for lost social solidarity.[8] Jochen Schulte-Sasse has suggested that "the mental structures of eighteenth-century thinking . . . share a cognitive figure that juxtaposes alienation, isolation, and the division of labor in modernity with an absent and longed-for state of communal solidarity or moral sensibility."[9] Hunter's argument, echoing this eighteenth-century way of thinking, depends on a simple and misleading opposition: once there was a cohesive culture that could cement its sense of community by face-to-face telling of stories and singing of songs; in the eighteenth century, when that cohesive culture was gone, the novel was forced to rely on forms of print to create an analogous—though far more abstract and tenuous—relationship between author and reader.[10] Hunter, like John Aubrey, suggests that printed words that cannot "speak" (what Edwin Muir calls "dumb letters" later in the same poem) will always be an inadequate substitute for oral tradition.

But Hunter accepts eighteenth-century attitudes and diagnoses far too easily. As Margaret Spufford and others insist, from the late sixteenth century on, "illiteracy was everywhere face to face with literacy, and the oral with the printed word."[11] The pure rural peasant community, telling stories free from the contamination of print, is really a late-eighteenth-century invention.[12] The Grimms' nostalgic evocation of an older culture in 1812 repeats earlier laments:

> Es war vielleicht gerade Zeit, diese Märchen festzuhalten, da diejenigen, die sie bewahren sollen, immer seltner werden . . . denn die Sitte darin nimmt selber immer mehr ab, wie alle heimlichen Plätze in Wohnungen und Gärten einer leeren Prächtigkeit weichen.

(It is probably just the right time to collect these tales, since those who have been preserving them are becoming ever harder to find.... The custom of telling tales is ever on the wane, just as all the cozy corners in homes and in gardens are giving way to an empty splendor.)[13]

The Grimms believed they were preserving a dying custom, gathering up the fading remnants of a robust tale-telling tradition that had gone on in the "cozy corners" of folk communities. The metaphors they used for their collecting—metaphors drawn from farming and harvest, metaphors of organic growth and wholeness, metaphors of awaking the tales from a long sleep[14]—suggest that they retrieved their *Märchen* as a natural and essential part of German culture. Italo Calvino, echoing the Grimms in his introduction to his 1956 collection of Italian tales, speaks of his "deep-rooted conviction that some essential, mysterious element lying in the ocean depths must be salvaged to ensure the survival of the race."[15]

This nationalistic salvage operation is part of the myth of the fairy tale in most European countries. Yet, as scholars like Heinz Rölleke have shown, most of the tales the Grimms collected or transcribed had roots in earlier European *written* literature. They were certainly not exclusively German in origin, and they were certainly extensively mediated by literate cultures. Moses Gaster recognized the difficulties in our attempts to trace the "origin" of fairy tales more than a hundred years ago. In a now almost forgotten article, he argues that we shouldn't assume that general explanations will work for all branches of folklore, or that the lore of the folk is timeless and homogeneous: "Just as *our* knowledge is a knowledge formed by many *strata*, one upon the other, so also the knowledge of the *illiterate* is not a homogeneous element, but one which has been acquired during centuries, and it only appears to us to form one indivisible unity." He goes on to ask the crucial question: "*Can we* watch the rise and growth of a fairy or popular tale in modern times, and pursue it from the time when it was *no* popular tale through all the vicissitudes and changes it underwent, till it became a genuine popular tale, gathered afterwards from the lips of the illiterate?"[16] This project, showing how a tale entered the popular imagination from printed sources, has been carried out by scholars like Catherine Velay-Vallantin in France, Rudolf Schenda in Germany, and the Opies in Britain. Other scholars have traced the movement of specific tales from, for example, medieval romance to written collection of tales to *conte de fées* to chapbook to oral tale-telling, but persist in believing that such tales must have a preexisting oral substratum that informs them throughout their history.

As Rudolf Schenda asked in 1986, "Is the *Märchen* actually a genre clearly defined by ancient traditions, or has it taken shape only recently under quite specific historical conditions?"[17] Like Albert Wesselski in the 1930s, he questions the notion that the "fairy tale" has existed for centuries; rather, he suggests, the genre as we now understand it "crystallized" only in the early nineteenth century.[18] Though we as postromantics would like to see it as an ancient oral expression of the spirit of various peoples, all the evidence points instead to a complex literary and written process of winnowing, simplifying, and selection. In his book *Von Mund zu Ohr*, Schenda makes another iconoclastic comment: "Es ist vor allem die Ausbreitung der Lesefähigkeit und der Lese-Akte, welche das Erzählen in den unteren Volksschichten fördert"[19] (It is above all the spread of literacy and the act of reading that promotes storytelling in the lower strata of society). It seems that we may have the direction of transmission wrong: rather than moving from the folk to the elite, the fairy tale may at least as often have moved in the other direction, from writing to oral tale-telling.

And this leads to more questions: Did fairy tales really disappear in the seventeenth century in England? What makes us think they ever were current? It seems increasingly clear to me that we have no way of knowing what tales were told in early nonliterate communities. Though the persistence of some stories in the long chapbook tradition may suggest oral roots, we know that many were drawn from medieval romances and were therefore part of a long-lived oral/literate culture.[20] Of the twenty-four well-known tales Iona and Peter Opie collected as *The Classic Fairy Tales* in 1974, only three are clearly of English origin—and only one of those, "Tom Thumb," can be shown to have existed before the eighteenth century. One other English tale, "Jack the Giant Killer," appeared in eighteenth-century chapbooks, but most of the tales we now know as "fairy tales" were imported from France in the 1700s or Germany in the early 1800s.[21] The English fairy-tale "tradition" as we now know it was never lost but rather created, borrowed from other cultures, pieced together as part of a mixed European quilt—as the tales were in Italy (by Straparola and Basile), then in France (by the *conteuses* and Perrault), then in Germany (by Musäus, Schümmel, the Grimms).

In other words, we will never know what tales were told by the fireside or in the spinning rooms of early English communities. But they are likely to have been very different from the stories we call "fairy tales" today. If the chapbooks are any indication—and I think they are—the stories that were told were a wild mixture of Bible stories, ballads, stories from Arthurian legend, local legends, and bawdy tales. We have been trained to believe that fairy tales reflect and preserve the true, essential, authentic nature of the "folk," that they are both timeless and nationally distinct. For example, in his well-known essay "Peasants Tell Tales: The Meaning of Mother Goose" (1984), the cultural historian Robert Darnton argues that "the great collections of folktales made in the late nineteenth and early twentieth centuries . . . provide a rare opportunity to make contact with the illiterate masses who have disappeared into the past without leaving a trace." But his argument depends on two basic assumptions that may not be safe to make: that tales collected in the late nineteenth century really give us access to the stories told in early modern European peasant communities, and that these stories actually took the forms we're familiar with today.[22] We must remember that fairy tales are not just "the product of a cross-cultural oral tradition," as Steven Swann Jones reminds us,[23] but that they have also come down to us through the complex interaction of the written and the oral, silent reading and reading aloud, as well as oral recitation or improvisation. (Here it would be useful to recall the frontispieces of the tales by Frenchwomen published in the early eighteenth century, in which the *conteuse* is represented not as reciting orally but as reading from a book to a listening audience (see figs. 6 and 8 again).

Rather than mourning the eclipse of the "oral tradition," then, we need to look critically at the ways our conceptions of the oral tradition and of the fairy tale have been formed.[24] Our sense of that history has developed in much the way that the supposed history of country music developed in the 1950s and 1960s, with all its fantasy of a pure Southern sound uncontaminated by show business, commercial recording, and other song traditions. As Geoffrey O'Brien has said, "all the scholarship in the world could not keep nonspecialist listeners from finding in the songs the ingredients for a narrative as thoroughly imaginary as *Ivanhoe* or *Ernani*. For a generation that lacked much sense of common tradition, the songs became the equivalent of Percy's *Reliques of Ancient English Poetry* or [the Grimms'] fairy tales."[25] A recent book, by Richard A. Peterson, is called *Creating Country*

Music: Fabricating Authenticity. The fairy tale was "created" in an analogous way, and its authenticity is just as fabricated. What we have in both cases is a dream of an original, pure, oral communication, without written or recorded sources, reflecting an almost completely imaginary past that is thought to be lost.

I I

Our task, then, is to understand how the fairy tale was constructed in eighteenth-century and early-nineteenth-century England. If it was not "recovered" from older oral sources, where did it come from, and how was it understood? The history of the fairy tale in England is largely a history of translation. As Maria Tatar has said, "our fairy-tale canon is drawn, for the most part, from collections produced by Charles Perrault and the brothers Grimm, and those collections are marked by strong rewritings (in the case of Perrault) and by repeated editorial interventions (in the case of the Grimms)."[26] In other words, neither collection is a pure transcription of French or German oral tradition. Perrault's tales were translated into English by Robert Samber in 1729; they circulated in both "polite" and chapbook forms throughout the eighteenth century. The Grimms' tales were translated by Edgar Taylor in 1823–1826, only a few years after they first appeared in Germany, and immediately became staples of the nursery library. Other translations, like the translations into English of Galland's French translation of the *Arabian Nights* (1704–1717) and of d'Aulnoy's tales (starting in 1699), also gradually seeped into the English fairy-tale canon during the eighteenth century—as did translations of Hans Christian Andersen and other Scandinavian tales in the mid–nineteenth century.

In the eighteenth century in England, both translations and "new" tales appeared primarily in two different forms: in the didactic early literature for well-brought-up middle-class children and in the flourishing chapbooks that those well-brought-up children were not supposed to read. Fairy tales existed simultaneously as the didactic and as the fantastic in two different literary fields.[27] In one field they were closely associated with the improving moral, the beast fable, and the proverb—all designed to educate and discipline the child. Often framed by explicitly didactic dialogues and other material, they were printed in the octavos and duodecimos thought appropriate for educational material and designed to be bought by adults for children.

In the other field they were crudely printed chapbooks of twenty-four pages or so, part of the repertory of romance, existing side by side with stories of legendary heroes, "small godly books," and "small merry books" in the peddler's pack.[28] One kind belonged to the world of the middle-class nursery, one primarily to the world of the newly literate classes, though many children in educated, middle-class homes seem to have gobbled them up as well. (Perhaps they were an equivalent of the forbidden comic books I longed for as a child. John Bunyan, Samuel Johnson, James Boswell, and Edmund Burke all specifically regret and recant their fascination with this "subliterature" as boys).[29] Geoffrey Summerfield puts this well: "It is, then, a nice irony that while 'official' adult-sanctioned children's literature was striving tediously and even stridently to promote the orthodox mercantile values, children continued with great determination to devour the vulgar nonsense of the romances under the very noses of the didactic adults."[30] Fairy tales had not vanished, if they had ever existed earlier; rather, they had taken two very different paths into print: the path of the moral tale and the path of the "penny history."

Good examples of the fairy tale as moral exemplum are the tales embedded in Sarah Fielding's novel *The Governess*, first printed in 1749 and now known as the first "school story" for girls. Fielding includes two fairy tales that take up about a quarter of her text—yet she seems ambivalent about their inclusion. As the "governess," whose "speaking name" is Mrs. Teachum, says, "Giants, Magic, Fairies, and all Sorts of supernatural Assistances in a Story, are only introduced to amuse and divert" (34).[31] With this dampening remark Mrs. Teachum tries to put a lid on the fizzing inanities of a tale that one of her pupils has just read to the others. Mrs. Teachum's comments on the tales and on their "high-sounding Language" tend to reduce them to transparent allegories of vice and virtue, and to present as dangerous the ways they differ stylistically from the calm, sensible dialogues of the rest of the novel: "great Care [must be] taken to prevent your being carried away, by these high-flown Things, from that Simplicity of Taste and Manners [and implicitly language] which it is my chief Study to inculcate" (35). But at the same time she suggests that to refuse to read or listen to fairy tales because they might be "childish" is to pretend to false wisdom, like the child who priggishly refused to go to a "Raree-show" (63); at her school the fairy tale as dramatic spectacle becomes a sanctioned, if somewhat suspect, genre.

We first see Mrs. Teachum's pupils as selfish Hobbesian little beasts quarreling over the inevitable Apple of Discord. Far from being Rousseauian innocents, they trail no clouds of glory but rather are chiefly devoted to their own appetites. Only Jenny Peace, the oldest and most "civilized" of the girls, has learned the lessons of generosity, self-forgetfulness, and obedience to authority that the novel is anxious to teach. She, in fact, acts as a "monitor," in an anticipation of Bell's and Lancaster's educational theories of the early nineteenth century, supervising and teaching the younger girls.[32] They must be disciplined into these virtues through self-examination, confession (in a series of brief autobiographies), moral example, and what Orwell would have called "groupthink." Despite some attempts to turn Sarah Fielding into a protofeminist, in this novel she clearly accepts many of the pieties of the nascent bourgeois gender ideology.[33] She presents Mrs. Teachum's dead husband as her superior and teacher: "Mr. *Teachum* was a very sensible Man, and took great Delight in improving his Wife; as she also placed her chief Pleasure in receiving his Instructions" (1). And Mrs. Teachum carefully circumscribes the education the girls in her school receive, "instructing those committed to her Care in Reading, Writing, Working [needlework], and in all proper Forms of Behavior" (1). (Note what's omitted here: mathematics, history, geography, physical science, even music, to name just a few.)

Fairy tales enter the informal curriculum of the school as part of the training in proper "Behavior," rather than in reading or writing. Jenny Peace reads two of them aloud to the younger girls in scattered intervals between school hours and other scheduled obligations; they are both interrupted at least once (a point I want to come back to). The first one, "The Story of the Cruel Giant Barbarico, the Good Giant Benefico, and the pretty little Dwarf Mignon," follows many romance plot conventions: the lovers Fidus and Amata are separated by the huge and wicked giant Barbarico, who is finally bound up by Mignon (a dwarf who is his unwilling page) and then decapitated by Benefico, the smaller, good giant. Many of the details of the tale are purely conventional as well. The giant first spies the lovers in a leafy bower, "a little natural Arbour formed by the Branches of a spreading Tree within the Meadow's flowery Lawn" (22). Amata plays the part of the helpless female, "the fair Disconsolate" who floats "half-expiring" in a stream and rarely has anything to say. The story of terror, imprisonment, and destruction ends with the discovery that the dwarf is Amata's long-lost brother, the marriage of the lovers, and "Tranquillity and Joy thro' all the happy Country round" (34).

Sarah Fielding may well have known d'Aulnoy's tales, probably in the translations that came out in England from 1699 to 1728 and were reprinted until the early nineteenth century.[34] As Victor Watson points out, in an essay on the recently discovered 1744 collection Jane Johnson put together for her children, most well-read women of the day in England were familiar with French tales of the 1690s.[35] But, far more than d'Aulnoy's tales, this tale is based on stark moral contrasts. The good giant is brave and resourceful, while the bad giant is cowardly and given to tantrums: "And whenever he happened to be disappointed in any of his malicious Purposes, he would stretch his immense Bulk on the Top of some high Mountain, and groan, and beat the Earth, and bellow with such a hollow Voice, that the whole Country heard and trembled at the Sound" (21). Barbarico's behavior is as outrageous as his name suggests and as his body is deformed—unlike Benefico, the good giant, and Mignon, the gentle dwarf, who are both explicitly described as "well-formed" or "exactly proportioned." And his punishment, decapitation followed by the exhibition of his "yet grinning Head" (31) on a pole on the top of a mountain, makes him literally a monster (from *monstrum*, something shown forth, and *moneo*, to warn), exhibited for everyone to see as "a joyful Spectacle" (31). Like the "freaks," blacks, and Native Americans exhibited in taverns in eighteenth-century England, Barbarico is represented as the cultural other—but his otherness is also part of Fielding's ongoing attempt to split the good definitively from the bad and to define childish behavior like his as out of the bounds of civilized society.[36] He derives his malign power from his size, but that power is also explicitly oral; as he threatens Mignon, "I am a Giant, and I can eat thee: / Thou art a Dwarf, and canst not eat me" (26). The presence of the good, self-contained, responsible, smaller giant (unusual in fairy tales, as fig. 10 suggests) accentuates Barbarico's "unnatural" violence—categorized as unnatural because, though really natural like all the ruder childish impulses, it should have been regulated and repressed.

Fielding carefully enlists the destruction of the giant and all he represents in the civilizing project that animates the whole book. Mrs. Teachum's commentary on the story—later repeated almost word for word by Jenny Peace to the younger girls—emphasizes the "very excellent Moral" (34) that Jenny's mother had found in it earlier. But she hedges her approval with all kinds

"You and your brother portray a great many wicked giants in these tales of yours, Herr Grimm. Do you think you could balance them by depicting a couple of good ones?"

Fig. 10. Cartoon by Ed Fisher. © The New Yorker Collection 1991 Ed Fisher from cartoonbank.com. All Rights Reserved.

of qualifications. She warns against seeing the magical elements of the story as essential and against the "various sounding Epithets" (34) that Barbarico is given to: "But neither this high-sounding Language, nor the supernatural Contrivances in this Story, do I so thoroughly approve, as to recommend them much to your Reading" (35). Instead, she recommends stories that have "that Simplicity of Taste and Manners which it is my chief Study to inculcate" (34), stories perhaps like the simple autobiographical narratives that each of her pupils tells.

In spite of Mrs. Teachum's grudging response, Jenny Peace reads another tale later in the book, "The Princess Hebe: A Fairy Tale." This time she requests approval in advance and assures Mrs. Teachum that this second tale is "not in such a pompous Stile, nor so full of wonderful Images, as the Giant-Story" (62). In fact, this tale is much less bloody and somewhat more realistic; unlike the first, it emphasizes female characters, obedience, and self-knowledge. The Princess Hebe is the heir to her father's throne but is driven out by her jealous aunt and uncle after his death. She and her mother come under the protection of the fairy Sybella and live quietly in her simple house in a secluded "Placid Grove" for many years, completely separated from society.[37] When the fairy Sybella leaves to do a good deed, however, Hebe meets the fairy's wicked and violent sister Brunetta disguised as a shepherdess, warbling a song about virtue. Though she withstands the shepherdess's blandishments, she is finally tempted to leave the security of the grove; her betrayer is another maiden, seemingly in distress, who then snatches the sacred miniature of her dead father and leads her to the evil Brunetta's "gaudy" castle. After three days of delight, she recognizes the castle for what it is—"Nothing was heard but Quarrels, Jars, and galling Speeches: Instead of sweet Music, the Apartments were filled with Screams and Howling" (87)—and finally escapes (without any magical intervention) to Placid Grove. Eventually, of course, she is made Queen of her father's kingdom:

> [T]he Princess *Hebe* was seated, with universal Content, on her Father's Throne; where she and her People were reciprocally happy, by her great Wisdom and Prudence: And the Queen-Mother spent the Remainder of her Days in Peace and Joy, to see her beloved Daughter prove such a Blessing to such Numbers of human Creatures; whilst she herself enjoy'd that only true Content and Happiness this world can produce; namely, *A peaceful Conscience, and a quiet Mind.* (90–91)

This tale is remarkable chiefly for what it does not include. Though it echoes patterns from d'Aulnoy's tales—the dispossessed princess, the good and powerful fairy in conflict with her evil opposite, the secluded grove or island—it is almost exclusively a story about women. (Even the usurping uncle is a nonentity, egged on by his jealous wife; when she dies, he returns the throne to his niece.) There is no heterosexual romance plot, as there is, if muted and secondary, in the tale about giants. The fairies' virago mother manipulates and eclipses their wiser father; Hebe's father is represented only by a portrait miniature. The story focuses on the test of Hebe's wisdom and virtue by the wicked fairy and her eventual affirmation of the maxim that "True Obedience . . . consists in Submission" (74)—to her mother, to the good fairy. In a sense we could say that Fielding has reproduced the girls'-school situation in the tale: Mrs. Teachum's pupils are to learn to submit their dangerous and unruly wills to her and to her surrogate, the monitor Jenny Peace. There is no grotesque giant to be decapitated and exorcised; both stories take place in an essentially all-female world, and both stress the overriding importance of female obedience.

Mrs. Teachum, of course, is rather more enthusiastic about this tale than the first one. She draws endless (and obvious) morals from it: "The Princess, you see, could have no Happiness till she returned again to her Obedience, and had confessed her Fault. And tho' in this Story all this is brought about by Fairies, yet the Moral of it is, that whenever we give way to our Passions, and act contrary to our Duty, we must be miserable" (93). Like many of the other stories and parables stitched into this strange text—"The Story of Caelia and Chloe"; or Jenny Peace's summary of the play *The Funeral, or, Grief à la Mode*; or the story of "The Assembly of the Birds," with a long excerpt from a particularly depressing collection of moral poems called *Fables for the Female Sex* by Edward Moore and Henry Brooke (1744)—this fairy tale has insistent moral designs on its audiences, both internal (the schoolgirls) and external.

Unlike the other stories, however, the fairy tales are often interrupted. This may be a response to the early translations of d'Aulnoy's tales, which included their frame novellas. It may be simply because they're longer than most of the other interpolated tales. But sometimes the interruptions themselves seem significant, more than just a break for lunch, tea, or dancing lessons. Toward the end of the story of Princess Hebe, for example, the girls are distracted by the "Sound of Trumpets and Kettle-Drums" (87): they

> suddenly started from their Seats, running directly to the Terras; and, looking over the Garden Wall, they saw a Troop of Soldiers riding by, with these Instruments of Music playing before them.
>
> They were highly delighted with gallant and splendid Appearance of these Soldiers, and watched them till they were out of Sight. (87)

Some of the girls want to wait until the second troop of soldiers goes by; the majority, however, want to go back to the story of Hebe, and "the few were ashamed to avow their Inclinations" (88). The contrast between the feminized fairy tale and the interruption seems startling and deliberate: Mrs. Teachum's pupils, safely separated by the garden wall from the masculine world of blaring trumpets and war, are still attracted to it. While, perhaps surprisingly, "The Story of Caelia and Chloe" is the only narrative in the novel that deals explicitly with courtship and marriage, in this interruption Fielding adumbrates the world that is excluded from the tale "The Princess Hebe" and from the school. Both exist in a closed feminine circle.[38] And both celebrate feminine docility, self-control, and dovelike submission.

Stories suitable to be read in girls' schools or about girls' schools were thought at the time to be particularly moral. Eliza Haywood, in her *Female Spectator* (which appeared just before *The Governess*, from 1744 to 1746), prints a complaint that she has provided "Lucubrations . . . [which are but] fit . . . to be read in Boarding-Schools, and recommended as Maxims for the well regulating private Life."[39] Haywood wanted to have an effect on a wider and even political field, the world of the coffee-house; Fielding carefully confines her field in this novel to the domestic and quasi-familial. In her hands the fairy tale becomes a civilizing instrument, designed to produce women who conformed to a restrictive set of gender norms (and perhaps to produce those norms as well).

Jeanne-Marie Le Prince de Beaumont, a Frenchwoman who was for a time actually a governess in England, also saw the fairy tale as suitable for the moral education of young women. Her version of "Beauty and the Beast," first published in her *Magazin des enfants* in 1756 in London, revises and transforms the first version of the story published in 1740 by Mme de Ville-neuve as part of her novel *La jeune Amériquaine, et les contes marins*.[40] Per-haps imitating Fielding in *The Governess*, Beaumont surrounds her tales with moral dialogues between a governess, Mrs. Affable, and her charges, six "young ladies of quality" with names like Lady Sensible, Lady Witty, and Lady Tempest. As the title page of the English version tells us, "The Useful is blended throughout with the Agreeable, the Whole being interspersed with proper Reflections and Moral Tales."[41] Beaumont designed her maga-zines primarily as educational instruments, but (unlike some of her contem-poraries) she understood the value of fiction, and particularly fairy tales, as part of her educational project. Her reaction to the French fairy tales of the 1690s is both interesting and symptomatic:

On me dira, nous avons douze volumes de Contes de Fées, nos enfans peuvent les lire. A cela je réponds: outre que ces contes ont souvent des difficultés dans le stile, ils sont toujours pernicieux pour les enfans, aux-quels il ne sont propres qu'à inspirer des idées dangereuses & fausses. . . . [J]'ai relu avec attention ces contes; je n'ai pas lu un seul que je pusse racommoder selon mes vuës; & j'avoüe que j'ai trouvé les contes de la *mère l'Oye*, quelques puériles qu'ils soient, plus utiles aux enfans, que ceux qu'on a écrits dans un stile plus relevé.[42]

(Someone might say, we have twelve volumes of fairy tales; our children could read those. But to that I respond: not only do these tales often have difficulties of style, but they are always pernicious for children, in whom they inspire only dangerous and false ideas. I have reread these tales carefully; I have not read one I could revise according to my views; & I acknowledge that I have found the tales of Mother Goose, however childish they are, more useful for children than those written in a more elevated style.)

Beaumont is not being completely honest here: in fact, as we have seen, she borrowed tales, not only from Perrault but also from Villeneuve (whose version of "Beauty and the Beast" is certainly long, ornate, and complex) and other, less-known writers. And, though she echoes the praise of Perrault's simple style that had been current at least since the abbé de Villiers in 1699, she seems perfectly happy to embellish and drag out her own tales, particularly the "Conte du Prince Tity" (originally by Saint-Hyacinthe), which dominates three whole dialogues in volume 3 of the *Magazin*. She also often borrows names from the *conteuses'* work—the Princes Charmant, Fortuné, and Chéri; Princess Gracieuse, and the Fairy Candide, for example—though it is often a shock to discover how mundane and moral the tales they're featured in have become. In order to create tales "selon mes vuës," she consistently minimizes the marvelous and translates the supernatural into the faintly tedious.[43]

This is perhaps most evident in her version of "Riquet à la houppe" in dialogue 24, volume 4. As we saw in chapter 1, both Perrault and Bernard emphasize Riquet's connection with an underground kingdom and his retinue of gnomes, but these magical features disappear completely in Beaumont's version. Like Bernard, she refuses to transform Riquet (here called "Spirituel" or witty) into a beautiful young man at the end, or even to suggest (as Perrault does) that he at least has become beautiful in the heroine's eyes. But Beaumont's moral project is different: Princess Astre, who *has* become both witty and wise, says that "Spirituel me plaît tel qu'il est; je ne m'embarrasse guère qu'il soit beau; il est aimable, cela me suffit"[44] (Spirituel pleases me just as he is; I don't care if he's handsome; he is amiable, and that is enough for me). To underline this point, Beaumont has Mrs. Affable follow the tale itself with a long critique of the failings of handsome men, so feminized in their attention to their "ajustement," and then the story of Narcissus, whose vanity is his undoing. The multiple ironies of the tale, in both Perrault's and Bernard's versions, disappear in Beaumont's.

The best-known fairy tale in the *Magazin* is, of course, her "Beauty and the Beast," a much-condensed retelling of Villeneuve's version that has become the standard all over Europe.[45] On the third day, after "chiding" all her pupils for eating too quickly and one pupil for swearing "upon [her] conscience," Mrs. Affable finally launches into her promised tale, the second in the *Magazin*. Again, Beaumont strips away many of the supernatural features of the earlier tale, including magic mirrors that permit Beauty to see what is going on everywhere in the city she left (an early adumbration of television or spy satellites?) and the frequent appearance of fairies. She also gets rid of the complex drama of class origins and missing babies that provides some of the tension (and length) of Villeneuve's tale. (In Villeneuve the merchant's daughter turns out to be a displaced princess; Beaumont is apparently not interested in such class recuperation.) Most important, however, is her careful refocusing of the fairy's curse: the prince is forced not only to live in beastly form but also to hide his sharp wits: "[A] wicked fairy had condemned me to remain under that shape till a beautiful virgin should consent to marry me: the fairy likewise enjoined me to conceal my understanding; there was only you in the world generous enough to be won by the goodness of my temper."[46] Because Beauty is able to see his *goodness* underneath his shaggy exterior and inarticulate remarks, she "receive[s] the reward of [her] judicious choice." Though in this case the prince is transformed, the emphasis is on the importance of virtue in both prince and merchant daughter. And, in a parallel development, the wicked sisters are transformed into sentient statues, because of their "malicious and envious mind[s]." In the discussion that follows, Mrs. Affable continues to stress the importance of Beauty's self-abnegating obedience, both to her father and to the Beast, and the unimportance of looks.[47] As Marina Warner has suggested in *From the Beast to the Blonde*, the Beast is not only transformed but "transfigured," changed into a type of almost holy goodness.[48]

Both Sarah Fielding and Beaumont, then, are anxious to *use* the fairy tale as one more instrument in their repertoire of civilizing, educational tools. (As Mitzi Myers has pointed out, we shouldn't see the moral tale and the fairy tale as opposites.)[49] And both surround their fairy tales with carefully pointed dialogues that contain and further decontaminate them. Their dia-

logues reveal a turn not to the "romantic cult of 'sentimentalité and bonne
volunté'," as Warner has claimed,[50] but rather to Enlightenment belief in
sociability and conversation as the source of self-improvement and social
change. The dialogues might be seen as a juvenile version of the conversation
in "the authentic public sphere" that Habermas sees as the foundation of
bourgeois democracy[51]—but a version that requires a model, moral "governess" to guide and control them. (Alan Richardson calls such conversations
"monologic discourse disguised as dialogue.")[52] Enlisting the fairy tale in the
educational project requires the framing and domesticating gestures that the
dialogues provide. Both writers talk about their own tales (and others') as
potentially dangerous, echoing Locke's strictures about "Notions of *Spirits*
and *Goblings*" that might potentially trouble children's minds. (Beaumont's
later *Magazins*, designed for older girls, include no fairy tales at all.)

Public opinion seems to have turned more and more against the fairy tale;
as one writer for the *Monthly Review* said in 1788:

> we have little to say in their praise. Fairy tales were formerly thought to
> be the proper and almost the only reading for children; it is with much
> satisfaction, however, that we find them gradually giving way to publica-
> tions of a far more interesting kind, in which instruction and entertainment
> are judiciously blended, without the intermixture of the marvelous, the
> absurd, and things totally out of nature.[53]

Fairy tales were never the primary reading material for children before the
nineteenth century, but this reviewer is determined to banish them from
the child's library altogether. (Significantly, when the educational reformer
Martha Mary Sherwood revised Fielding's *The Governess* in 1820, she omitted both of Fielding's fairy tales, adding an anodyne and didactic one of her
own, as well as a lot of evangelical Christian commentary.) The fairy tale,
with its links to the supernatural and the romance, was increasingly seen as
an unstable, untrustworthy agent in the Enlightenment civilizing process.

III

As the suspicion of the fairy tale grew in enlightened, Dissenting circles at
the end of the eighteenth century, however, fairy tales had become a staple
of the chapbook. Looking back at his childhood reading, John Clare, the
"peasant poet"[54] born in 1793, remembered:

About now [when he was ten or twelve] all my stock of learning was gleaned from the Sixpenny Romances of 'Cinderella', 'Little Red Riding Hood', 'Jack and the bean Stalk', 'Zig Zag', 'Prince Cherry', etc and great was the pleasure, pain, or surprise increased by allowing them authenticity, for I firmly believed every page I read and considerd I possesd in these the chief learning and literature of the country . . . every sixpence thro the indefatigable savings of a penny and halfpenny when collected was willingly thrown away for them, as opportunity offered when hawkers offerd them for sale at the door.[55]

Clare loved and collected these "Sixpenny Romances," finding them an inexhaustible and exciting source of "knowledge." He retreated to the "woods and dingles of thorns in the fields on Sundays to read these things," hiding from other villagers who thought reading a "sure sign of laziness" and a waste of time. Even much later, when "Milton, Shakspear and Thompson" had become Clare's familiars, he continued to love the chapbook stories and ballads: "[N]ay I cannot help fancying now that cock robin babes in the wood mother hubbard and her cat etc are real poetry in all its native simplicity and as it should be."[56]

Only two of the chapbooks Clare mentions in his list above are based on English stories: "Jack and the Beanstalk" and "Zigzag."[57] The others—"Cinderella," "Little Red Riding Hood," and "Prince Cherry"—are all of French origin, either by Perrault (known as "Mother Goose" in England) or d'Aulnoy (often known as "Mother Bunch," a name adopted from an earlier tradition to parallel Mother Goose). "Prince Cherry," later translated by Andrew Lang as "Prince Charming," is one character in d'Aulnoy's "La princesse Belle-Étoile et le prince Chéri." In another passage Clare mentions more tales—"Jack and the Jiant," among them—but again most of the stories he remembers that we would now call fairy tales are not English.[58]

Other working-class autobiographers report their encounters with fairy tales in chapbooks as well. The title "Fairy Tales" appears over and over again; these were usually collections of two or three French tales, by Perrault or d'Aulnoy. (The most common seems to be one that included d'Aulnoy's "Blue Bird" and "Rosetta and the King of the Peacocks.") John Binns, born in Ireland in 1772, reports reading "the 'Arabian Nights Entertainments,' 'The Seven Champions of Christendom,' 'Don Bellianis of Greece,' 'The Irish Rogues and Repparees,' 'Fairy Tales,' and other such works."[59] Samuel

Bamford, born in 1788, tells about his yearning for the "numerous songs, ballads, tales, and other publications, with horrid and awful-looking woodcuts at the head."[60] About thirty years later, James Bowd (born ca. 1823) reports that his family managed to persuade him to be "leeched" for scarlet fever when he was seven by giving him a new "Halfpenney or Penney Book" each time: "I shall never forget the Impressions one of them left upon my mind the title of the Book was Blue Beard."[61]

Roger Chartier has rightly cautioned us against taking working-class autobiographies as typical: "Evidence of the sort . . . needs to be interpreted first as a presentation of oneself subject to the enormous social and cultural distance from one's origins brought by an exceptional career. Even if such life stories contain traits that are valid for all the self-taught, they tell us little about common uses of print and ordinary ways of reading."[62] Yet, however unusual their reading practices and the intensity of their engagement with their reading, these autobiographers do give us a good sense of the fairy tales that actually circulated in British chapbooks in the eighteenth and early nineteenth centuries. Far from giving access to "old native stories," these fairy tales came primarily from translations of French written, literary tales.

The "Fairy Tales" printed by Benjamin Tabart and by John Harris in the first decade of the nineteenth century (all in cheap editions that included one or more tales) were almost always French. Tabart's "Juvenile and School Library . . . where is constantly kept on Sale the largest Collection of Books of Amusement and Instruction in the World, from ONE PENNY to FIVE GUINEAS in price," specialized in sixpenny editions of tales from Perrault with colored plates—"Blue Beard, or Female Curiosity," "Little Red Riding Hood," and "Puss in Boots" among them. Later in the century James Catnach published many of the same tales, as well as "Toads and Diamonds" (the usual English translation of Perrault's tale "Les fées"), as "Large Halfpenny Books"; he also included English tales like "Tom Thumb," "Jack the Giant Killer," and "Jack and the Beanstalk" (though, as the Opies point out, no written edition of the last tale seems to have existed before 1807).[63]

What do we know about the history of these early English tales? Names and rhymes that appear in them clearly circulated before they were available in print in any form. For example, Tom Thumb's name and diminutive stature were well known before the first known chapbook edition of "The History of Tom Thumbe" in 1621 (fig. 11). This chapbook seems to be, as the

The History of *Tom Thumbe*, the *Little*, for his small stature surnamed, *King* ARTHVRS *Dwarfe*:

Whose Life and aduentures containe many strange and wonderfull accidents, published for *the delight of merry Time-spenders.*

Imprinted at London for *Tho: Langley*. 1621.

Fig. 11. Title page of chapbook, *The History of Tom Thumbe* (London: Thomas Langley, 1621). Courtesy of the Pierpont Morgan Library, New York. PML 45444.

Opies say, "the earliest extant printing of an English fairy tale" (36). The story of the minuscule hero is rambling, episodic, and already nostalgic for better and less hierarchical days: "In the old time, when King *Arthur* ruled this land, the World was in a better frame then it is now: for then old plainnesse and ciuill society were companions for all companies: then, an unguarded Plowman might come uncontroled to a Royal Princes presence" (41). Like all the British tales that have become part of our fairy-tale tradition, "Tom Thumbe" is set in the mythical time of King Arthur, has a male central character, and plays on the contrasts between very large (giants) and small (the two Jacks) or tiny (Tom Thumb). In "The History of Tom Thumbe" Tom's dress is described in minute and delicate detail:

> First, a Hat made of an Oken Leafe, with one feather of a Tittimouse tayle sticking in the same for a plume: his Band and Shirt being both sowed together, was made of a Spiders Cobweb, only for lightenesse and soft wearing for his body; his cloth for his Doublet and Hose, the tenth part of a dramme of Thistledowne weaved together: his Stockings the outward Rinde of a greene Apple: his Garters two little hayres pulled from his Mothers eyebrowes: as for his Shooes and Bootes, they were of a mouses skin, tan'd into Leather: the largenesse wherof was sufficient to make him twelue payre of Bootes, & as many shooes and Pantofles. (43)[64]

His gossamer dress and delicate limbs are always contrasted to the various giants' clumsy size and indelicate behavior. When he is swallowed whole by a giant, for example, "it little booted the Gyant to rest in quiet, for he thought the Diuell or his dam had plaide at Tennis in his paunch; therefore in a fury he hyed up to the toppe of his Castle wall where he disgorged his stomacke, and cast out his burthen, at least three miles into the sea" (51). This leads to a Jonah-like episode in which Tom Thumb is swallowed whole by a fish and ends up on King Arthur's dinner table. Tom is always in danger because of his size; his "history" is a history of falling into puddings and chimneys, being eaten by cows and fish, and stolen by birds. But he always saves himself by quick thinking or using his fairy godmother's magic gifts.

This may be one of the rare cases in which the French tradition borrows from the English, in Perrault's "Petit Poucet" of 1697. In England the story of Tom Thumb was told and retold, in chapbooks and penny histories, in farcical plays like Henry Fielding's *The Tragedy of Tragedies* (1730), in snippets in books for children like Newbery's *Tommy Thumb's Song Book* (1744). Swift extends the play of contrasts between huge and small in the first two books of *Gulliver's Travels* (1726). But, by the end of the nineteenth century, Andrew Lang omits "The History of Tom Thumb" from his canon-making *Blue Fairy Book* (1889) and substitutes Perrault's version as "Little Thumb," later often known as "Hop o' my Thumb." "General Tom Thumb" (the midget Charles Stratton) was a living figure and Barnum circus attraction in midcentury England and America.[65] Paradoxically, in Lang's eyes, Tom Thumb may have become too popular to be part of the fairy-tale tradition.

The first chapbook (now lost) that featured the entire "History of Jack the Giant Killer" was apparently printed in 1711. Versions of the threatening rhyme

Fee, fie, fo, fum,
I smell the blood
of an Englishman

were in circulation even before Edmund echoed it in Shakespeare's *King Lear* (ca. 1605). (A version also appears in the 1621 chapbook of "Tom Thumb.") Is it possible that the tale was constructed to incorporate the old rhyme and a few old legends about giants (some of them also present in "Tom Thumb")? As the Opies suggest, "the story of Jack the Giant Killer, as we know it, appears to consist of a number of classic anecdotes strung together by an astute publisher in the not-so-long-ago" (60). The mid-eighteenth-century chapbook version the Opies reprint is quite startlingly unlike the versions we now know. For example, the tale begins with a bawdy dialogue between the quick-witted Jack and the local parson:

A County Vicar, by chance one Day coming a-cross the Fields, called to *Jack*, and asked him several Questions; in particular, *How many Commandments are there?* Jack told him, *There were Nine.* The Parson replied, *There are Ten. Nay,* quoth *Jack,* Mr. Parson, *you are out; it's true there were Ten, but you broke one with your Maid Margery.* (64)

The dialogue continues with Jack's knowing and comic answer to the parson's catechizing, Blakean question about who made the oxen: "God made them Bulls, but my Father and his Man *Hobson* made Oxen of them" (64). Jack then outwits a series of Cornish and Welsh giants, each stupider and more voracious than the last. Only toward the end of the adventures he has sought out does he acquire the cloak of invisibility, cap of knowledge, rusty but trusty sword, and magic trumpet that aid him in his last conquests; his story is at bottom a story of human ingenuity conquering monstrous appetites. But the chapbook version registers a carnivalesque pleasure in the outrageous behavior and desires of the giants; the last giant's name, "Galigantus," echoes "Gargantua," hero of French chapbooks and Rabelaisian narratives (though without any of the learning or gentle wisdom he shows in Rabelais's version), and the boasting villain of "Tom Thumb."

Sarah Fielding may just possibly have known the tale, perhaps in the lost chapbook version of 1711 or in the oral versions that must have been circulating. Her story of "Barbarico and Benefico" also features a brutish and cowardly Welsh giant who is always "rolling his ghastly Eyes around in quest of human Blood" (21) and threatening to eat everyone he sees. As in the chapbook version, Fidus, the human hero, and Mignon, the dwarf, are aided in his defeat by reading a magic inscription. And the head of the giant also becomes an important prize—symbolizing the defeat of the giant's "gaping Maw" and inhuman appetites. But the contrasts are still more striking: in Fielding's didactic universe, even giants are capable of being *good*. Unlike the Grimms, she was able to imagine a civilized giant (see fig. 10 again). Benefico, mild, humane, and well proportioned, provides a physical and moral contrast with Barbarico, the possibility that he could have been other—or less "Other." Uncivilized behavior is not an inborn quality of giants in Fielding's tale, as it is in the chapbooks and most fairy tales, but apparently a moral choice. Her tale is not "for the delight of merry Time-spenders," like the 1621 chapbook of "Tom Thumb" (see fig. 11 again), but rather for the instruction of its earnest readers. Even the old chapbook giants could become models of deportment.

Like Sarah Fielding, many nineteenth-century retellers of "Jack the Giant Killer" carefully refined the tale. As Andrew Lang remarks in the preface to his *Blue Fairy Book* (1889), "a good version of this old favorite is hard to procure." In other words, it was difficult to find a version of "Jack the Giant Killer" without the bawdy and gory episodes that marked the chapbooks. Lang purifies and condenses the story, making "good" and "compact" what was initially bawdy and rambling. Many of the bloodiest details of the chapbook version have disappeared: a giant's favorite meal of men's "Hearts and Livers" with "Pepper and Vinegar"; the "Tripes and Trolly-Bubs" that fall out of a giant's belly; the "Devil's Lips" that a princess kisses to break an enchantment; the sword Jack runs "up to the hilt in the Giant's fundament." He has removed all the transgressive, scatological references to innards and orifices and filth that give the early versions their power.[66] In fact, even the barbaric old chant "Fee, fie, fo, fum" is missing. Lang retains some features like the captive ladies "tied by the Hair of the Head, almost starved to death" who have refused to "feed upon the Flesh of their murdered Husbands," in noble and civilized contrast to the appetites of the giants. But he abbreviates

the old story to conform to Victorian notions of decorum in children's literature and of the shape tales for children should take. As Alison Lurie pointed
out in 1971, folktales "are full of everything Lang leaves out: sex, death, low
humor, and female initiative."[67] Making the old tale a fairy tale (in our current
understanding of the term) meant stripping of it of most of its popular or folk
features, particularly its joy in the grotesque and in bawdy wit. "Jack the
Giant Killer" was not born a fairy tale but slowly became one, in a long
process of refinement.

IV

We have no evidence that anyone told what we would now call fairy tales in
nonliterate oral communities in England in the eighteenth century or earlier.
But this does not mean that there was no vigorous unofficial or "impolite"
culture, a culture that expressed itself in part in the many chapbooks that
were published and republished. (Hunter includes many other forms of print
in his elegy for the fairy tale and prehistory of the novel—newspapers, other
journalism, moral guides, travel books—but never mentions chapbooks.) As
Diane Dugaw has argued, "The longstanding insistence upon the orality of
folk tradition is a political idea whose oversimplifications have been in most
cases misleading at best. Attention to printed street literature forces us to
question a naïve view of the 'folk' and their 'oral tradition'; a fact which makes
it no accident that such materials have been dismissed as 'nontraditional.' "[68]
Cheap, commercial versions of stories like "Tom Thumb" and "Jack the Giant
Killer" circulated in the seventeenth and eighteenth centuries in England,
carrying on a tradition that may once have been oral but probably existed
only as scraps and rhymes. They were not transformed into or reinvented as
fairy tales until the nineteenth century. Then they joined what Katharine
Briggs has called "the foreign invasion"[69] from France, England, Scandina-
via, and the East, finally collected by people like Andrew Lang into the
gallimaufry of tales that we now think of as our "fairy-tale heritage."

Or, to say this another way, in the nineteenth century the discourses of
the chapbooks had to be purified before they could be elevated to canonical,
privileged status in the fairy-tale hierarchy. The rough magic of tales like
"Jack the Giant Killer" was smoothed out; their erratic narrative sequences
were made straight. Lang revised both the chapbook stories and the stories

by the *conteuses* into chaste and compact shapes like the ones the Grimms had popularized, or Walter Benjamin later described in his "Storyteller" essay. (The repeated words and phrases like "translated, or rather adapted," "condensed," and "abridged" in Lang's brief preface to the *Blue Fairy Book* suggest that he knew exactly what he was doing.) The "compact" forms invented by Perrault and the Grimms had won out; they had become *the* shape of what we now tend to think of as "the classic English fairy tale."

Once Again

> So I will tell you those stories, or possible stories, for many things may and do happen, stories change themselves.
>
> A. S. Byatt,
> "The Story of the Eldest Princess,"
> *The Djinn in the Nightingale's Eye*

As the tales of Perrault and the Grimms became naturalized in Britain, the belief that fairy tales must be compact and laconic took root and flourished. The nineteenth-century literary tales that are the most familiar to most readers—Oscar Wilde's "The Selfish Giant" or "The Happy Prince," Ruskin's "King of the Golden River," for example—tend to be short, told by an invisible and apparently impersonal third-person narrator, and modeled on the patterns that the earlier "collectors" had established. Less well known tales, many of them by women, were much more complex and layered narratives—tales by Anne Thackeray Ritchie or Julia Horatia Ewing, for example.[1] The comtesse de Ségur in France also invented long, complex tales that often look back to the models established by the *conteuses*.[2]

The recurrent revival of these strategies is really a literary version of the return of the repressed. Over the last two hundred years or so, even as the compact model has dominated most fairy-tale writing and research, some writers have looked for other ways to retell the old tales. Sara Maitland has described the advantages of retelling old stories:

[E]veryone knew them so the narrative could be stripped right down (saving lots of time) and they were filled with the reverberations of everyone's dreams; because there needed to be so little machinery it was easier to dive deep in them and find the rhythms.[3]

"Finding the rhythms" that structure and animate the tales, listening for the reverberations of common dreams, many writers in the later twentieth century have returned to the complex formal models that the *conteuses* relied on: elaborate framing techniques, embedded stories, transformations of old tales and motifs into new constellations. With startling frequency they turn out fiction that questions traditional fairy-tale patterns. As Karl Kroeber has observed, "all significant narratives are retold, and are meant to be retold—even though every retelling is a making anew."[4]

Some of these rewritings are simply *reversals*. As Maitland complains in the opening of her story "The Wicked Stepmother's Lament":

There's this thing going on at the moment where women tell all the old stories again and turn them inside-out and back-to-front—so the characters you always thought were the goodies turn out to be the baddies, and vice versa, and a whole lot of guilt is laid to rest: or that at least is the theory. I'm not sure myself that the guilt isn't just passed on to the next person, *intacta* so to speak.[5]

Since the characters in traditional fairy tales are often polarized—the wicked witch and the innocent princess, the selfish stepmother and the long-suffering stepdaughter, the wicked wolf and the compassionate hunter—reversal is quite easy. Early feminist rewritings often favored this technique, turning passive princesses into questing heroines, illuminating the motives or justifying the tactics of the wicked stepmother.[6] Their reversals do illuminate the patriarchal, often sexist systems that lie beneath most classic fairy tales. But, Maitland suggests, these simplistic reversals merely redistribute guilt and responsibility—and leave the existing punitive system of values more or less unchanged. Characters remain "unmixed," either purely good and naive, or thoroughly wicked, judged by conventional cultural codes.

Sometimes twentieth-century rewritings are *sequels* (or, very occasionally, *prequels*), imagining what might have happened before or after the traditional sequence of events, written either "before" or "beyond" the usual ending. In Maxine Kumin's poem "The Archaeology of a Marriage," for example, the romantic excitement is long over. Sleeping Beauty and the Prince have become an aging suburban couple, he worrying about his squash game and the firmness of their bed, she making jam of the blackberries he has collected from the brambles around their house:

> When Sleeping Beauty wakes up
> she is almost fifty years old . . .
>> Each evening she stands
> over the stewpot skimming
> the acid foam from the jam
> expecting to work things out
> awaiting, you might say, a unicorn
> her head stuffed full of old notions
> and the slotted spoon in her hand.[7]

Like her friend Anne Sexton, Kumin focuses on the inability of adult women to break out of earlier patterns, their thralldom to what Sexton calls "that story." Her Sleeping Beauty may momentarily question the old story and point out the way it has been repeated:

> Why, for that matter, should any
> twentieth-century woman
> have to lie down at the prick of
> a spindle etcetera etcetera.

But Kumin's sardonic "etcetera etcetera" highlights the repetitions in her older Sleeping Beauty's life as well, her daily skimming of "acid foam" from jam, her continuing half-sleep. Her sequel is a sad commentary on the persistence of fairy-tale expectations and "old notions." Such revisions extend the reach of classic fairy tales beyond their classic, misleading "happily ever after." By giving the characters in their fairy tales a history, a life beyond the usual contours of fairy-tale romance, Kumin and many others pry the old stories open, revealing their inadequacies and their silences.

Most contemporary tales also abandon the objective third-person narrator, telling the story in the first person or in an unreliable third-person voice. The traditional compact tale follows what Cristina Bacchilega has called "one of the narrative rules for fairy-tale production: an external or impersonal narrator whose straightforward statements carry no explicit mark of human perspective—gender, class, or individuality."[8] Complex tales, particularly those written recently, are usually told in a character's individual voice, often in a woman's voice. (Think again of the White Cat's version of her own history in d'Aulnoy's tale.) They depend for their effect on our ability to correct for the narrator's subjective vision, to imagine other readings of the events.

In her short story "Bluebeard's Egg," for example, Margaret Atwood gives us a new version of the old Bluebeard tale from the perspective of her central character, as the first sentence suggests: "Sally stands at the kitchen window, waiting for the sauce she's reducing to come to a simmer, looking out."[9] We see only what Sally sees as she "looks out" at her husband, her marriage, her own life, and a version of the Grimms' story "Fitcher's Bird" (*KHM* 46), but we gradually learn to second-guess her. Her perspective, unlike the apparently even vision of the anonymous storyteller, is clearly skewed and partial. Instead of presenting their stories as somehow immutable—one "true" version for all time—recent storytellers tend to stress the subjective unreliability of their narrators. Each new tale is only one version of the many possible versions. They encourage the reader to see the new telling as a *version*, as one, but not the only, way to tell the tale.

All these techniques—reversals, sequels and prequels, subjective narrators—have been staples of the rewritten fairy tale of the last twenty-five years. In the chapters that follow, though, I want to focus on two further narrative strategies: *reframing*, a technique that links contemporary rewritings with the work of the earliest literary fairy-tale writers, and *transliteration*, a new technique that depends on isolating and reinterpreting specific images from well-known fairy tales (though writers who "transliterate" still often rely on earlier strategies as well). When contemporary writers *frame* the tales they retell, they are acting in the spirit of a long fairy-tale tradition, as we will see in chapter 4. When they *transliterate* images from well-known tales, they are performing a new kind of framing operation, zooming in on one small detail that takes on new meaning in its new context, as we will see in chapter 5.

The history of the fairy tale, like most literary histories, is a history of continuity and change, of repetition and innovation. Contemporary writers have learned a great deal from their seventeenth-century predecessors, particularly their imaginative use of the frame as a way to direct our readings into new paths. Their complex, layered tales call into question the certainties of the compact tale, so often a repository of worn-out ideologies and myths. In their hands, the fairy tale becomes an agent for change: of minds, of hearts, of social arrangements. As A. S. Byatt says in the epigraph above, "stories change themselves." Or, more precisely, they *are changed*—by writers who want to challenge the narrative forms that have become tropes of or symbols for conventional ways of living in the world. Resurrecting old forms and inventing new ones, contemporary writers reach again and again for fairy tales to transform. Like Angela Carter, they force new wine into old bottles and hope for an explosion.

CHAPTER FOUR

New Frames for Old Tales

> The frame can provide another level of meaning
> . . . ; it can be both a commentary on the work
> and on itself.
>
> Wolfgang Kemp, "A Shelter for Paintings"

NEARLY ALL fairy tales are framed in some way. When we think of fairy tales, we think of them as bracketed between a "once upon a time" and a "happily ever after." (Perrault's prose tales and two of his verse tales begin with "Il estoit une fois," though the endings vary.) These framing gestures—and their equivalents in many European and non-European languages—tell us that we are entering and leaving a narrative world where the supernatural is commonplace, where the rules of our ordinary world do not apply, where wishes can come true. This world is rarely precisely fixed in time or in space, but the framing formulas make it clear that whatever happens, happens at a great remove from us. We peer into this world from a distance, often conscious of the difference between its enclosed space and the unfixed boundaries of our daily experience. A very small child may be terrified by Perrault's or even the Grimms' wolf; an older and more sophisticated child, however, knows that the wolf exists in a different world, a world that is not "real" and is far away, a world that exists only between the boundaries of "once" and "ever after."

This model—the "compact" or one-plot tale, framed only by the ritual opening and closing phrases—is the model we tend to associate with the fairy tale per se. It is the model made familiar by the prose tales Perrault wrote, each separate, bound together only by their existence in one volume. It is the model that the Grimms followed, publishing hundreds of discrete tales in the successive editions of their *Märchen*, from 1812 to 1857. And it is the model that Aarne and Thompson, the first to categorize and classify international tales into "tale-types," institutionalized as *the* form of the fairy tale. (In his study *Morphology of the Folktale*, Vladimir Propp also defines the folktale as an invariant sequence of events based on this model.)[1] Their search for the tale-type is also a search for the first or primary or "original" version of a tale; a search for the "underlying story, some deep structure, that is not itself a version."[2]

Many writers of fairy tales, however, have enclosed their tales within wider frames, what has been called "a series of oral storytelling events in which one or more characters in the frame tale are also narrators of the interpolated tales."[3] This structure was common as a narrative device from the Sanskrit *Panchatantra* to the *Thousand and One Nights* to Boccaccio's *Decameron* and Chaucer's *Canterbury Tales* (and continues to this day). We could call it an "exterior frame," an overarching theatrical proscenium that usually encloses all the tales. As Eberhart Lämmert points out, the characters in the frame-tale are usually waiting for something: for the plague to end in the *Decameron*, for the pilgrims to arrive at Canterbury in the *Canterbury Tales*. Sometimes, as in the *Thousand and One Nights*, where the stories are told to ward off Scherezade's death, tale-telling does not merely fill time up but extends it.[4] But the frames always locate the telling of the stories in a particular time and place, implicitly suggesting connections between the twice-told tales and the particular situation in which they are told. Like A. S. Byatt's fairy tales in her novel *Possession*, they are usually "a narrative within a narrative, *and* . . . part of that outer narrative."[5]

As we have seen, the *conteuses* deliberately set their work in this old tradition. They certainly knew Straparola's collection *Le piacevoli notte* (1550–1553), translated as *The Pleasant Nights*—and probably Basile's *Lo cunto de li cunti* (1634–1636) (The story of stories), better known as the *Pentamerone*.[6] Both of these early Italian collections are frame-tales. Straparola sets his varied stories, some that we would now consider fairy tales, in a carefully chosen discursive milieu: the conversations of a group of aristocrats, in a rented castle on an island off Venice, telling stories to amuse each other during "Caresme-Prenant" (the last three days of carnival before Lent). The storytellers, ten young women and two men, draw lots to determine the order; this underlines the somewhat random selection of tales and the aleatory character of the collection. But, in Straparola's case, the exterior frame sets the tales off from each other and gives them a reason, or at least an excuse, for being.

About fifty years later, Basile frames his collection with an overarching and self-referential fairy tale rather than the more-or-less realistic conversations that Straparola borrows from Boccaccio. But ultimately his frame-tale also introduces the "most expert and gossipy" lower-class crones who will tell the tales that follow. The princess Zosa, whose inability to laugh is the motivation for the elaborate carnivalesque antics of the frame, is persuaded to tell the last of the stories herself—a version of her own story that merges into the frame.[7] Like Straparola, Basile uses the frame to set up a simulated oral situation. The tradition of the written fairy tale in Europe, then, begins with tales framed in various conversational settings.

The *conteuses* of the 1690s, unlike Perrault, continue this nascent tradition. Many of the *conteuses'* tales are set within a longer narrative, or simply framed with an introductory dialogue, as we have seen. The *conteuses* rarely send a story naked into the world without the mediation of an exterior frame,

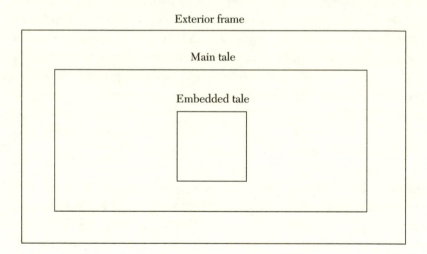

Diagram A

though these frames have often been omitted or forgotten in later published versions. Also common in their tales are other embedded stories—one reason their tales are so long. Many of their tales, already situated within an exterior frame, become the frames for other stories, often told by the characters in the central tale. This technique of embedded narratives or interpolated tales was common in the novels of the seventeenth century that the *conteuses* would have known well: Cervantes' *Don Quixote*, for example, or

Scudéry's *Grand Cyrus* (at sometimes tedious length), or Lafayette's *Princesse de Clèves* (much more economically). But in effect the *conteuses'* tales often have a Chinese-box or Russian-doll structure, tales embedded in tales that are embedded in a larger proscenium frame. Diagram A gives a rather oversimplified sketch of this structure. Many of the *conteuses'* tales take this form, with an introductory prologue or conversation leading into the main tale, which often includes at least one further embedded tale. (Think, for example, of Lhéritier's "Adroit Princess," which begins with a feigned conversation with Murat.)

The more traditional and extended structure, however, strings the various tales along like beads on a narrative chain, moving from frame-tale to tales told by the various characters in the frame—who often also embed further tales in their own. Diagram B, again oversimplified, represents the traditional structure. As we saw in chapter 2, in the discussion of the interplay

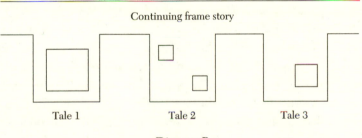

Continuing frame story

Tale 1   Tale 2   Tale 3

Diagram B

between d'Aulnoy's "La chatte blanche" and the comic story that surrounds it, "Le gentilhomme bourgeois," the embedded tales and the frame that joins them are always symbiotic, drawing life and sustenance even from their friction. The *conteuses'* complex narratives are bound up in a system of different discourses, discourses that tend to inform and inflect each other. Throughout the history of written fairy tales, there is often tension between the tales themselves and their more realistic settings. Framed narratives are embedded in a social context that may function as a clarification or as an ironic counterpoint; as Jeannine Blackwell says of the von Arnims' *Gritta von Rattenzuhausbeiuns*, the "Chinese box structure['s] nested narratives explain and deconstruct each other."[8]

Many, perhaps most fairy-tale writers who come after Straparola, Basile, and the *conteuses* enclose their tales in exterior frames. They do not write the simple tales, framed only by the opening and closing formulas (and occasional morals), that Perrault and the Grimms favored. These "compact," short narratives have dominated our conception of the fairy-tale genre and make it difficult for us to understand, appreciate, or perhaps even notice the more complex, nested narratives that have been part of its written tradition since the beginning. Jeannine Blackwell believes that women writers favor the framed tale, while male writers usually choose the simple model. But, though Perrault, the Grimms, and Andersen established the simple model, I think most male writers have continued to frame their tales, often placing them in exterior frames, sometimes including embedded stories. The simple, "compact," discrete tale seems to be the exception that has become the rule.

For example, when Goethe wrote the fairy tale he called simply "Das Märchen" (1795), he embedded it in his *Unterhaltungen deutscher Ausgewanderten* (Conversations of German refugees), a series of dialogues in a castle where a group of aristocrats have taken refuge during the French revolutionaries' occupation of the Rhine (first in 1792–1793, then again in 1795 while Goethe was writing his book). He gave "Das Märchen" to the oldest and perhaps wisest of the group to tell and used it as the closing enigma of a puzzling collection of stories. As he wrote to Friedrich Schiller in 1795: "Ich würde die Unterhaltungen [mit dem Märchen] schließen, und es würde vielleicht nicht übel sein, wenn sie durch ein Produkt der Einbildungskraft gleichsam ins Unendliche ausliefen"[9] (I would end the *Conversations* with the "Fairy Tale," and it would perhaps not be a bad idea if they opened out into the infinite at the end through a work of the imagination). Goethe establishes his frame only to break it at the end; there is no discussion after the "Märchen" in the text (though the bewildered critical discussion of the tale has gone on for two hundred years). The collection ends with the final strange vision of social harmony and order in the "Märchen" that may or may not persist into the present: "und bis auf den heutigen Tag wimmelt die Brücke von Wanderern, und der Tempel ist der besuchteste auf der ganzen Erde" (and even now the bridge swarms with travelers, and the temple is the most visited in the whole world).[10]

We could multiply examples throughout the nineteenth century. Goethe's younger contemporary Ludwig Tieck wrote a group of fairy tales in the 1790s, including his famous "Der blonde Eckbert" (1796–1797), that he published first as discrete tales. Later, however, he gathered them into a frame-tale called *Phantasus* (1812–1816), surrounding them with a series of discussions about the nature and function of fairy tales. Slightly later, in the 1840s, many German women writers of fairy tales gave them a local habitation, often introducing them as stories told by old women, as in the tales of Gisela and Bettina von Arnim. In England, slightly later still, Anne Thackeray Ritchie's *Fairy Tales for Grown Folks* (1867) and Christina Rossetti's *Speaking Likenesses* (1873) both use the framing convention of the down-to-earth older aunt figure who tells the tales to a listening audience. Though Andersen, Wilde, and others usually produced discrete, fairly compact tales, the tradition of the framing dialogue continued.

Many fairy tales written or rewritten in the twentieth century follow the simple, one-plot structure that has become normative—sometimes echoing, sometimes questioning their models. But often they are framed, in ways that suggest a familiarity with earlier framing techniques and with contemporary frame games. John Barth's witty "Frame-Tale," the first of the fourteen linked stories in his *Lost in the Funhouse* (1968), is perhaps the most extreme example of play with the frame (fig. 12). Its simple legend—"ONCE UPON A TIME THERE / WAS A STORY THAT BEGAN"—recalls the opening frames of thousands of fairy tales but varies it to emphasize its focus on narrative. If we follow his directions and twist the legend into a Möbius strip, it takes on all the characteristics of a shaggy-dog or "once on a stormy night" story, endlessly repeating itself, never ending. The "Frame-Tale" both places the following stories in the tradition of the framed collection and suggests the links between them—all concerned with the problems of narrative and with the relationship of the oral and the written. As Barth himself says in the "Author's Note," " 'Frame-Tale' is one-, two-, or three-dimensional, whichever one regards a Moebius strip as being. On with the story. On with the story."[11] But going on with the story isn't easy, given the various narrative traps Barth enmeshes us and his narrators in. The last exhausted words of the book, "Wrote it," suggest not so much an ending as a laying down the pen. The cycle of storytelling inaugurated by the "Frame-Tale" can never really be ended.

In *Lost in the Funhouse*, then, Barth inserts his fictions in the long tradition of framed narratives, playing with their possibilities and impossibilities, their dead ends, false floors, and distorting mirrors. As Cristina Bacchilega says, "Assuming that a frame always selects, shapes, (dis)places, limits and (de)centers the image in the mirror, postmodern retellings focus precisely on this frame to unmake the mimetic fiction."[12] Though Barth is playing with all narrative, not just the fairy tale, his "Frame-Tale" shows that the framed narrative is still alive and well, if transformed.

Sometimes, too, recent writers embed their fairy tales in longer narratives, just as the *conteuses* did. In her novel *Possession* (1990), for example, A. S. Byatt includes two complete fairy tales, "The Glass Coffin" and "Gode's Tale," and parts of several others. Many other strands of fairy-tale material run through the novel as well; the fictional nineteenth-century poet Christabel LaMotte's repeated return in her poetry and in her thoughts to the story of "Melusina"—originally told to her by her father, a nineteenth-century scholar of Breton folklore—is just one example.[13] These two tales, however, are set off in an almost discrete form, told, written, or transcribed by characters in the book as set pieces. In fact, Byatt later separated these stories from the novel and reprinted them in a collection of five unrelated fairy stories, *The Djinn in the Nightingale's Eye* (1994). She has given us an opportunity to see what happens when a tale is framed, and what is missing when the frame disappears.

"The Glass Coffin" is said to be one of Christabel LaMotte's stories in her *Tales for Innocents*, "which . . . were mostly rather frightening tales derived from Grimm and Tieck, with an emphasis on animals and insubordination."[14] The twentieth-century heroine of the book, Maud Bailey, has a first edition, bound in "scuffed green leather, with faintly Gothic lettering" (58) and with illustrations by Christabel LaMotte's equally fictional companion Blanche Glover. Byatt includes samples of the beginnings of two other tales from the Grimms in the book (38); Maud Bailey and Roland Mitchell, the twentieth-century hero, discuss a third, a story about a queen who gives birth to a child who is half hedgehog (a version of the Grimms' "Hans My Hedgehog," *KHM* 108). By the time we get to "The Glass Coffin," then, we know a great deal about its setting, its history, its author, and even its reader: Roland Mitchell, who reads it lying on "Maud's great divan" with its pristine white comforter and emerald sheets. Christabel LaMotte again creates a new version of one of the Grimms' tales, also called "The Glass Coffin" (*KHM* 163), a story about a poor tailor who rescues and marries a princess.[15] She, however, has transformed the story into an allegory about the integrity of the artist. Even after the tailor has married and is living happily ever after, he cannot stop making beautiful clothes:

FRAME-TALE

Cut on dotted line.
Twist end once and fasten
AB to *ab*, *CD* to *cd*.

(Continued)

ONCE UPON A TIME THERE

A   B   C   D

Fig. 12. John Barth, "Frame-Tale" from *Lost in the Funhouse*. © 1968 by John Barth, reprinted with permission of the Wylie Agency, Inc.

WAS A STORY THAT BEGAN

(Continued)

Only one thing was missing. A craftsman is nothing without the exercise of his craft. So he ordered to be brought to him the finest silk cloth and brilliant threads, and made for pleasure what he had once needed to make for harsh necessity. (76)

LaMotte refuses to let the tailor abandon his art. As Byatt says in her essay "Ice, Snow, Glass," "The story in *Possession* is told by Christabel LaMotte, woman and artist, who is deeply afraid that any ordinary human happiness may be purchased at the expense of her art."[16] The rewritten tale crystallizes some of Christabel LaMotte's fears and hopes, sexual as well as artistic; it also suggests that Maud Bailey could be an ice maiden too, that her apartment with its glittering green and white surfaces is a modern glass coffin that protects as well as confines her. In its context in *Possession*, the tale resonates with meanings. In *The Djinn in the Nightingale's Eye*, it seems simply an accomplished reworking of one of the Grimms' tales.

"Gode's Tale" is also deeply embedded in the text of *Possession*, told by a Breton housekeeper, Gode; retold in the 1859 *journal intime* of Sabine de Kercoz, Christabel LaMotte's young French cousin; discovered and photocopied by a twentieth-century French scholar; read by Maud Bailey and Roland Mitchell. Sabine de Kercoz emphasizes the mythical oral situation in which Gode tells her stories: "Gode's stories, even more than my father's, depend on the outer dark and the closeness, indoors, of tellers and listeners" (386). The tale, told by a servant (though without a distaff) at a *veillée*, has no analogue in the Grimms' tales but rather is influenced by Breton folktales. (Byatt herself says, "Its teller, Gode, the nurse, I took straight from Renan's account of his own Breton childhood and of his own old nurse, whose name was Gode. I owe a great deal to the Breton scholar Jean Markale, as well as to many nineteenth-century collections of legends.")[17] The tale focuses on the life and death of a proud young woman who refuses to acknowledge the attentions of a dashing young sailor but bears his child alone, probably commits infanticide, and then is haunted by "a tiny naked child dancing and prancing in front of her, round this way back widdershins, signing with little pointy fingers and with its hair like a mop of yellow fire" (390). After her death, the sailor, who has married another woman, is haunted by the child as well; finally, he dies listening to the child's cries and dancing that seem to come from another world, one that lies dangerously close to his own.

The story in isolation in *The Djinn in the Nightingale's Eye* is compelling and sad, an eerie echo of the many stories that surround the Baie des Tré-passés (the bay of the departed) in Brittany. Its language, rhythmic though quite plain and unadorned, is much more impressive than Sabine de Kercoz imagines:

> No, I have not told it like Gode. I have missed out patterns of her voice and have put in a note of my own, a literary note I was trying to avoid, a kind of prettiness or portentousness which makes all the difference between the tales of the Brothers Grimm and La Motte Fouqué's *Undine*. (392)

This kind of literary criticism is a running theme in the novel. Christabel LaMotte, for example, praises another of Sabine de Kercoz's attempts to tell an old tale, implying that she has been able "to keep alive, to polish, the simple clean forms of the tale which *must* be there" (379). But, in its context in *Possession*, the tale also shows Gode's deep and instinctive understanding of Christabel LaMotte's predicament, of her pregnancy, and of her determi-nation not to ask for any help. ("As Gode's story went on, I saw Christabel knit faster and faster, with her shining head bent over her work" [392].) It helps Sabine de Kercoz unravel the reason Christabel has sought sanctuary with her family. And it also acts as a false clue, since readers often assume until the end of the novel that Christabel's child is also dead, like the "little thing" in Gode's tale, and that she is haunted by it. Sexual and psychic reali-ties that cannot be spoken in Christabel's Victorian world are expressed in the "simple horror"[18] of Gode's tale.

At one point Sabine de Kercoz describes her own narrative technique:

> This piece of writing has come a long way, from its formal beginning, back in time, inward in space, to my own beginnings in a box-bed, inside the chamber inside the manor inside the protecting wall. (368)

This description would almost work for Byatt's technique in *Possession*, let-ters and diaries and narratives inside narratives inside narratives.[19] The most deeply inset narratives are her fairy tales, particularly "Gode's Tale," tales that send out ripples through all the Chinese boxes. Christabel LaMotte says, and Byatt clearly believes, that "all the old stories . . . will bear telling and telling again in different ways" (379). Byatt retells them in order to suggest the deep psychic undercurrents that run through the novel; their resonances inform our understanding of both the nineteenth-century and the twentieth-century characters, their deepest fears and wishes.

Byatt also has chosen an old technique to frame her tales, the technique her predecessors the *conteuses* often used. Like Basile's collection, *Lo cunto de le cunti*, and like Barth's *Lost in the Funhouse, Possession* is a story of stories, told in different voices. Perhaps, in fact, it is the late-twentieth-century obsession with, or possession by, narrative and narrative voices that has brought so many recent writers to frame their new versions of fairy tales. But often these writers suggest the power of the stories they frame to affect the outer narrative, to force us to reassess the complacencies of their own times. As Byatt has said, "whereas much post-modern self-reflexive narrative seems somehow designed to show that all narrations are two-dimensional and papery, that all motifs are interchangeable coinage, what I believe, and hope to have shown, is that the tale is always stronger than the teller."[20] In this chapter I will look at three very different kinds of twentieth-century fairy-tale frames: Joseph Cornell's mysterious shadow boxes, mostly from the 1940s; Anne Sexton's contemporary, pop-art frames in her *Transformations* (1971); and Emma Donoghue's interlocking, receding frames in her *Kissing the Witch* (1997). All three of these artists, despite their differences, concentrate on the ways new voices and new perspectives can inflect the old tales they retell. All of them are interested, like Byatt, in preserving the strength and psychic intensity of the old tales, even as they frame and transform them. While they reread and question some of the motifs of the tales, particularly their old conceptions of gender relations, they also pay homage to their continuing vitality and magic. As Karl Kroeber has said, "Narrative is the discourse most amenable to translative adaptations that permit simultaneous retention and revision of its peculiarities."[21]

I I

Joseph Cornell, the American artist who framed so many objects in fantastic visual conjunctions, seems to take pleasure in the way he can make fairy-tale narratives come to a stop or reflect themselves in a never-ending *mise-en-abyme*. Each fairy-tale box, as Dore Ashton saw, "with its fragments of printed materials, and its enumeration of suggestive objects, maintains a tension between the verbal and the visual. . . . Like the *Lied*, the Cornell box sojourns in a *terra incognita* between two art forms, the poetic and the plastic. Even the voice is in his work, for the voice is the instrument of poetry, and few of Cornell's works forsake the poem."[22] Cornell's frames, like most narrative framing techniques, explore the collision of different voices, of different ways to tell stories.

Throughout his life Cornell was inspired and haunted by the fairy tales he had read obsessively as a child: the tales of Hans Christian Andersen and the Grimms, the tales collected by Andrew Lang in the late nineteenth century in his rainbow series of *Fairy Books*. He often mentions tales in his notes and diaries, seeing a girl with long blonde hair in 1946 as a "Cinderella" or referring in 1967 to a matchbox from Shackman's toy store, "containing miniature rooms as from a Swiss or German cottage—Hansel & Gretel flavor."[23] Toward the end of his life he returns more and more often in his diaries to the tales of Perrault, from "Petit Poucet" to "Le Chaperon rouge" and "La belle au bois dormant," apparently savoring their role in a complex series of correspondences.

For Cornell any scene—even or perhaps particularly the most ordinary one—could become a fairy-tale scene. He noted, for example, the glow of a small house nearby in Flushing, where he lived: "fairy-tale aspect of the neighboring brick house lighted at night" (*Theater*, 365). He was particularly fascinated by the light at dawn and notes that "the new snow has prolonged the initial 'féerie' " (316). He associated fairy tales with a certain kind of radiance, the radiance that mysteriously transforms the everyday into something symbolic and magical, the "eterniday" (327), as he called it, with its "benedictory beauty" (220). He perceived these scenes as profoundly American and as otherworldly at the same time. The urban landscape around him often became the distant "fairyland" of his childhood, as light shimmered on the El or illuminated a store window.

He also tended to identify appealing, childlike young women as "fées" or fairies. Sometimes they were ballerinas, from the past (Fanny Cerrito, Marie Taglioni, Carlotta Grisi, Fanny Essler, and others) or from the present (Allegra Kent, "Zizi" [Renée Jeanmaire], Tamara Toumanova, Melissa Hayden). More often they were ordinary working girls he saw in the cafeterias and dime stores he loved or on the street: "la fée aux lapins" who sold stuffed rabbits at Woolworth's, girls passing his house on their bicycles, a movie-house cashier, a checkout girl at a drugstore, "Tina" (Joyce Hunter), who briefly lived at his house, stole boxes from him, and later was murdered. (Actresses and starlets like Hedy Lamarr and Lauren Bacall tended to be-

come "sybils" or "sylphides," though he notes making a collage for Yvette
Mimieux called "the Fairy.") Like the moments transfigured by light, the
"fées" help him crystallize his epiphanies: "Taking home the gift of light
precious light from former times: Garden Center—the diner (Dorothea [Tan-
ning] remembered)—fée aux lapins (secret again revealed of putting it down
while *in* it" (307). What might be merely erotic voyeurism becomes part of
his system for catching the moment in all its intensity and beauty, "putting
it down while *in* it." He frames his "fées" with the innocence and purity of
the remembered fairy-tale world. As Mary Ann Caws has said,

> Within the inexhaustible stream of girls or *grisettes* . . . , of fairies or
> sylphs and sisters and stars, each instance recalls and restores all the
> rest in a "jeu des fées" so that all are simultaneously present in each obses-
> sion. We can, through the diary, watch the accretion of each myth, the
> private construction of each obsession. On April 4, 1963, Cornell writes
> of "trying to catch the magic by which maiden becomes magical and
> the renewal so precious when it comes so authentically, so unsuspect-
> ingly. . . ." (*Theater*, 45)

Constructing myths, constructing boxes. During the 1940s and 1950s Cornell created many magical shadow boxes that also drew on his obsession with
fairy tales. His *Setting for a Fairy Tale* (ca. 1942) (fig. 13) and the many nearly
identical boxes that followed it (1942–1951) all focus on a huge Renaissance
building, usually colored pink or rose, surrounded by real twigs and tinsel
snow. The twigs eerily recall the ones that almost hide a china doll in his
disturbing box *Untitled (Bébé Marie)* of about the same time, but here they
glisten in the background, suggesting the magic aura around the castle that
Cornell wanted to create. The interior is usually framed with sparkling dots
of tinsel within the severe black outer frame of the box. Charles Simic calls
one box in this series, *Untitled (Pink Palace)* (ca. 1946–1948), "another oneiric
playhouse"[24]; the double frame enhances its dreamlike quality.

The building itself—so large in proportion to the tiny figures that gesticu-
late in front of it—is a cutout of a photostat from a 1576 book, *Les plus
excellents bastiments de France*. As Deborah Solomon reminds us, Cornell
often cut out the windows, too, and pasted the building on a mirror—so that
when we look at the building we see shards of ourselves reflected as well.[25]
It is as if we were part of the magic scene, both inside the multiple frames
that define its borders and outside looking in. Unable to remain invisible,

Fig. 13. Joseph Cornell, *Setting for a Fairy Tale*, 1942. © The Joseph and Robert Cornell Memorial Foundation/Licensed by VAGA, New York, NY. Box Construction. 11 9/16 × 14 3/8 × 3 7/8 inches (29.4 × 36.6 × 9.9 cm). Solomon R. Guggenheim Foundation, New York, Peggy Guggenheim Collection, Venice, 1976. 76.2553.125. Photograph by David Heald © The Solomon R. Guggenheim Foundation, New York.

we must acknowledge our paradoxical and disturbing presence in the dream-world of the castle. The mirrors both bring the castle into the present (Solomon suggests an affinity with the glimpses we catch of ourselves in city shop windows) and make the spectator part of its grand and glittering past. Cornell has recaptured the illusion of the classic fairy tale, bracketed in a timeless moment by the opening and closing ritual phrases ("Once upon a time. . . . happily ever after") and yet drawing its present readers and hearers in.

During the 1940s Cornell also became fascinated by the ways he could manipulate books—by cutting windows in them, by framing them in boxes, by using scraps of pages to edge or cover parts of larger boxes, by making them part of a "Stabile."[26] Several of his larger boxes—*Paul and Virginia* (ca. 1946–1948), *Les Trois Mousquetaires* (ca. 1948)—are homages to one book. Elaborately constructed, with doors that open to reveal tiny shelves with wrapped boxes, they are also in part collages, with printed pages (usually in French) and illustrations pasted on the boxes inside and out. Though these boxes are not usually identified as a group, they all reflect Cornell's fascination with the book as object and as doorway into the romantic past. (The exterior of the door of the *Paul and Viginia* box is of course a mirror: again a strategy that includes the spectator in the box.)

The most interesting box of this group is *Nouveaux Contes de Fées* (1948), sometimes called "Poison Box" (fig. 14). In a diary entry of January 24, 1947, Cornell records his delight in finding a myriad of objects and books that interested him or could become part of his constructions and souvenir cases:

> Took bus crosstown and lingered before appointment at *Vogue*, 4:00. Found Jenny Lind song sheet, La Sonnambula, and colored feathers in dime store. Boxes got good reception. Up to 59th St. Windfall of Bibliothèque Rose to cover étuis. Souvenirs containing good Gérard de Nerval (De Camp) an original colored Deveria of a standing oriental woman musician—two heroic sized forest prints for own boxes—unusual feeling of satisfaction and accomplishment, unexpected and more abiding than usual.
>
> Unexpected the "surprise" the conspiracy of events to produce this miracle of grace. (*Theater*, 139)[27]

Cornell's collecting habits are well known, though we tend to forget the "feeling of satisfaction and accomplishment" (of work well done, of serendipity, of mysterious affiliations and correspondences) that went with them. For Cornell, finding significant objects was always a "miracle of grace" that confirmed his notions about the mysterious underlying order of the world. But what I particularly want to note here is what he calls his "windfall of Bibliothèque Rose." One of the books he purchased that day may well have been Mme de Ségur's *Nouveaux contes de fées*, first published in the mid–nineteenth century, but reprinted in the Bibliothèque Rose, a series of illustrated popular books for children, in 1917.[28] This edition is full of black-and-white engravings by Doré and Didier, engravings that Cornell cut out and pasted all over the exterior of the box he made the next year (fig. 15). These illustrations—romantic, even chivalric in their tone—contrast sharply with the interior. Severely rectilinear, it has fifteen square compartments, each nearly filled with a cube wrapped in a page from the same Bibliothèque Rose edition of Madame de Ségur's tales. The tension between the fantastic figures and landscapes on the exterior and the Mondrian-influenced squares-within-squares on the interior

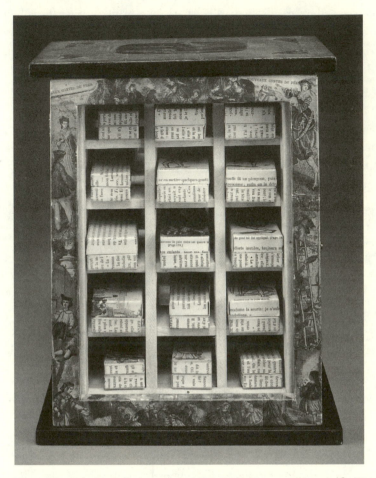

Fig. 14. Joseph Cornell, American, 1903–1972, *Nouveaux Contes de Fées* (called "Poison Box"). Painted, paper-covered, glazed, wooden box for a construction of wood, paint, velvet, mirror, paper-covered boxes, metal latches and hinges, 1948, 32 × 26 × 14.9 cm, The Lindy and Edwin Bergman Joseph Cornell Collection, 1982.1857 front view. Photograph © 1997, The Art Institute of Chicago. All Rights Reserved. © The Joseph and Robert Cornell Memorial Foundation/Licensed by VAGA, New York, NY.

reveals the strange symbiosis between the nostalgic and the timely, the old and the new, that characterizes much of Cornell's work.

In the 1940s Cornell was deeply influenced by Piet Mondrian's austere paintings and Marcel Duchamp's constructions. He notes in his diary of August 15, 16, 17, 1946:

Fig. 15. Joseph Cornell, *Nouveaux Contes de Fées*, side view no. 2. © The Joseph and Robert Cornell Memorial Foundation/Licensed by VAGA, New York, NY.

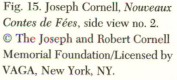

box with 35 identical 3/4″ *white* cubes [probably one of his "grid" boxes] remade box with grooves in cabinet style. . . . Mondrian feeling strong. Feeling of progress and satisfaction. Placed all of cubes before inserting into box an old volume in bright rich red embossed cover piled up like after dinner mints or sugar—near envelope containing popular old fashioned photos of dervishes Greek costumes, natural philosophy, etc. chromo birds. (*Theater*, 131)

Cornell was fascinated with the rigor of absolute whiteness and symmetry— but he was also often compelled to juxtapose it with the rich textures of old books and fragments from the "chromo" world. In the *Nouveaux Contes de Fées* he insists on the complex interplay between the squares-within-squares and the romantic, flamboyant illustrations; the dream of mathematical purity and the dream of a fairyland. The fragments of the text on the little cubes, with an occasional glimpse of a picture, are framed by the squares around them, which then in turn are framed by the extravagant illustrations on the larger box itself. As John Ashbery once said of Cornell's abstract, yet romantic boxes, "we are allowed to keep all the stories that art seems to want to cut us off from, without giving up the inspiring asceticism of abstraction."[29] "Keeping the stories," Cornell forces us to contemplate the world of the fairy tale caught in the grid of an apparently alien regime. He plays with the text as text, as printed on the wrappers of his cubes, but also with the text as the source of an imaginative world.

A. S. Byatt suggests the complex magic of Cornell's boxes in a sentence she wrote about the Grimms' tale "The Glass Coffin": "A fabricated world in a glass case gives a delight an ordinary castle doesn't."[30] Cornell's glass cases, even at their most geometric and rigid, heighten the wonder that was one of his characteristic attitudes toward the world. The worlds he fabricates evoke all the mystery he found in the everyday, precisely because of the ways he frames them. Cornell sometimes suggests that his encapsulated boxes were based in part on narrative forms:

> 6/4/67
>
> "Fairy tale of Nature"! Indeed! Well and good.
>
> But what of great teeming glory of the unfolding tale within—within domicile & in chambers of imagery. (*Theater*, 371)

In this late diary entry, Cornell constructs a model of the nested narrative, a narrative that "unfolds" in interlocking rooms within a "domicile" or larger structure. The fairy tales he tells or retells, the "chambers of imagery" he constructs, depend on their frames for their effect. The boxes' "uncanny magic" (a phrase I borrow from Mark Rothko)[31] is the magic of the miniature, an enclosed theatrical space, protected by wood and glass from the contamination of flux and change.[32] The tension between the rigid, geometrical frames and the evocative, mysterious objects they contain—most evident perhaps in *Nouveaux Contes de Fées*—is a new version of the tensions that inform the old narrative framing practices.

III

Like Joseph Cornell, and like many other late-twentieth-century poets, Anne Sexton returned to the Grimms' fairy tales repeatedly. And, like Cornell, she

had known them since childhood, when her great-aunt read them to her. As
Maxine Kumin says, "they were for her, perhaps, what Bible stories and
Greek myths had been for other writers."[33] In her late collection *Transformations* (1971), she chooses seventeen of them (apparently her daughter Linda's
favorites) to reframe and meditate on. One—a very short tale called "The
Gold Key," the two hundredth and last in the final edition of the Grimms'
collection, if we exclude the "Children's Legends"—introduces her collection and becomes its exterior frame. In her version of the tale, Sexton transforms the Grimms' dispassionate, nearly invisible third-person narrator into
a speaker whose angry and sardonic perspective on her midcentury American world determines the shape of the whole collection:

> The speaker in this case
> is a middle-aged witch, me—
> tangled on my two great arms,
> my face in a book
> and my mouth wide,
> ready to tell you a story or two.
>
> > (*T* 1; *CP* 223)[34]

Like the figures in many of the *conteuses'* frontispieces, this tale-teller is
both looking at a book and speaking to an audience; she sets herself in a
written tradition of textual transmission and in an oral one at the same time.
She orders her audience to "draw near," to listen, to give her "attention," as
if they were in the room, and still emphasizes that she is both working from
and writing a book. Unlike the *conteuses'* figures, however, she is not a sibyl
or fée or goddess, but a "middle-aged witch," a witch whose powers may or
may not be benign.

As several critics have pointed out, Sexton tended to begin her public
readings with an early poem, "Her Kind," from *To Bedlam and Part Way
Back* (1960); her daughter calls it her "signature poem."[35] (It was also part of
the name she gave her chamber rock group, "Anne Sexton and Her Kind.")
In this poem, too, she figures herself as a witch:

> I have gone out, a possessed witch,
> haunting the black air, braver at night;
> dreaming evil, I have done my hitch
> over the plain houses, light by light:

lonely thing, twelve-fingered, out of mind.
A woman like that is not a woman, quite.
I have been her kind.   (*CP* 15)

This earlier witch is deformed ("twelve-fingered"), isolated ("lonely thing"), simultaneously mad and neglected. (We can take "out of mind" to mean both "out of *her* mind" and forgotten, as in "out of sight / out of mind.") She has "done her hitch" in the witchy flying business; she hovers over the night-world, reinterpreting. She is "a woman who's not a woman, quite," liminal, on the margins, the better to criticize, my dears. As she says in a letter to Paul Brooks, her editor at Houghton Mifflin, "of course I am a witch, an enchantress of sorts and have already been worshipped and hung and in the same order."[36]

Like her predecessor in "Her Kind," the speaker of *Transformations* is "tangled on her two great arms," outsize, grotesque, faintly menacing. Her mouth is not just open but "wide," ready to tell terrible tales or to devour. And she is now "middle-aged"—both like and unlike the apparently serene, upper-middle-class, middle-aged woman we see smiling in a wicker chair on a sunporch in the photo of Sexton on the back cover of the paperback edition of *Transformations*. "Dame Sexton," as she calls herself in "The White Snake" (*T* 11; *CP* 229) with a chilling echo of New England witchcraft, seizes the power to speak, to disturb, to narrate, and to reframe.

At the end of the introductory frame-poem, Sexton shows the Grimms' boy-hero (an Everyman who is "each of us. / I mean you. / I mean me") turning the gold key that should reveal all the secrets. In the Grimms' tale, we never learn what is inside the chest that the key miraculously fits, "and now we must wait until he has quite unlocked it and opened the lid, and then we shall learn what wonderful things were lying in the box" (*KHM* 200). Sexton, however, moves this tale to the beginning; the "wonderful things" the key reveals are her own "transformed" tales:

Presto!
It opens this book of odd tales
which transform the Brothers Grimm
Transform?
As if an enlarged paper clip
could be a piece of sculpture.
(And it could).   (*T* 2; *CP* 224)

Throughout the series, Sexton refers to pop-art icons like Andy Warhol's Brillo boxes and Campbell's soup cans ("There stood the parson, / rigid for a moment, / as real as a soup can," as she says in "The Little Peasant"[*T* 30; *CP* 241]) or Claes Oldenburg's blown-up baseball bats and hamburgers, monumental versions of commonplace twentieth-century objects that "make strange" by their very size. Sexton does not "rewrite" the tales she has chosen, change their contours or (usually) their endings. Rather, she makes them into pop images, etched with the corrosive acid of American consumer culture. As many critics have pointed out, her language in *Transformations* is blunt, colloquial, full of references to 1960s brand names and trademarks ("Duz," "Bab-O," "Sanforized," "Muzak," and many more). If her versions of the Grimms' tales are "enlarged paper clips," oversized and overcharged, they derive their aesthetic power from their new contexts. She constructs ironic, self-consciously contemporary prologues or frames that cannot quite contain them, openings that bring them "up-to-date" in new and often horrifying ways.

Sexton, in an interesting reversal, often spins golden fairy-tale motifs into straw. In "Hansel and Gretel," for example, Sexton begins with the frightening little monologue of a mother who finds her son so adorable that

> I want to bite,
> I want to chew,
> I want to eat you up.   (*T* 101; *CP* 286)[37]

She repeats common terms of endearment: the child is a "little plum" and "chicken biddy," his neck "as smooth as a hard-boiled egg," his cheeks like pears. But in the middle of the monologue the mother suddenly reveals the possible horror, the potential for cannibalism behind these terms:

> I have a pan that will fit you.
> Just pull up your knees like a game hen.
> Let me take your pulse
> and set the oven for 350.   (*T* 101; *CP* 287)

Here Sexton's household know-how—setting the oven at the roasting temperature sanctioned by "Mrs. Rombauer" (the author of *The Joy of Cooking*, referred to in "Self in 1958" [*CP* 155])—is hideously transformed into a sinister witch's technique. She emphasizes the startling correspondences between the American housewife, the heartless mother or stepmother of the

Grimms' tale, the witch become threatening mother, and Gretel herself. Like the mother in the prologue, the witch tells Gretel

> how her brother
> would be better than mutton;
> how a thrill would go through her
> as she smelled him cooking;
> how she would lay the table
> and sharpen the knives
> and neglect none of the refinements.
>
> (*T* 104; *CP* 288–89)

Gretel, too, imitates the mother in the prologue:

> [She] shut fast the oven,
> locked fast the door,
> fast as Houdini,
> and turned the oven on to bake.
>
> (*T* 104–5; *CP* 289)

Sexton reveals the narrow boundary between mother love and engulfment by the mother; we think back to the middle-aged witch's mouth gaping voraciously "wide" in the opening frame-poem.

Even at the end, when Hansel and Gretel return home and the family is reconstituted (without the evil mother/stepmother, of course), they think again of the witch's fiery death in the oven:

> Only at suppertime
> while eating a chicken leg
> did our children remember
> the woe of the oven,
> the smell of the cooking witch,
> a little like mutton,
> to be served only with burgundy
> and fine white linen
> like something religious.
>
> (*T* 105; *CP* 290)

The chicken leg takes us back to the "chicken biddy" and game hen of the prologue, the smell of the witch to her own salivating as she thinks of roasting

Hansel. Every character in Sexton's version of the tale (with the possible exception of the father) is a potential cannibal; the children's meal at the end becomes a perverted sacrificial meal and unholy ritual. We can watch Sexton as she pushes the implications of the Grimms' tale further and further, blowing it up to expose its fundamental horrors, the barely repressed murderous impulses in the heart of the nuclear family, and the terrifying interchangeability of its characters.[38] The witch with the oven is not alone.

And witches multiply throughout the sequence. The wicked stepmother in "Snow White"

> danced until she was dead,
> a subterranean figure,
> her tongue flicking in and out
> like a gas jet.
>
> (*T* 9; *CP* 229)

The stepmother's fiery death is the kind of violent retribution the Grimms favored—yet at the end of the poem Sexton implies that Snow White has more than a trace of her stepmother in her:

> Meanwhile Snow White held court,
> rolling her china-blue doll eyes open and shut
> and sometimes referring to her mirror
> as women do.
>
> (*T* 9; *CP* 229)

Many women, Sexton warns in the opening, "will dance the fire dance in iron shoes" (*T* 5; *CP* 225). Again the characters become similar; the polar oppositions fade: we all have a witch within us.

Briar Rose, after she wakes up, sees herself as the thirteenth, evil fairy if she closes her eyes:

> a faltering crone at my place,
> her eyes burnt by cigarettes
> as she eats betrayal like a slice of meat.
>
> (*T* 111; *CP* 293)

Her insomnia is due in part to her recovered memories of incest, but also to her pained recognition that she and the baleful fairy are interchangeable, that the penalty for leaving her trance is aging, losing, "faltering." Like Snow

White's stepmother with her gas-jet tongue, she must "eat" her anguish and her guilt.

Sexton also transforms the Grimms' witch, Mother Gothel, in her "Rapunzel." No longer the threatening, malevolent, and selfish figure the Grimms drew, she is the emotional center of the poem—an aging woman who loves a much younger one. Like Rumpelstiltskin, she wants a child; unlike Rumpelstiltskin, she gets one—a child who becomes her mirror, her other self, her lover. The child Rapunzel is lured away by the prince's dazzling "dancing stick" and eventually they marry:

> They lived happily as you might expect . . .
> The world, some say,
> is made up of couples.
> A rose must have a stem.
>
> (T 42; CP 249)

But, with the phrase "some say," Sexton undercuts the pat ending, the apparent confirmation of the heterosexual romance pattern that the Grimms and most earlier versions of the tale take for granted. Her poem ends with Mother Gothel and her grief:

> and only as she dreamt of the yellow hair
> did moonlight sift into her mouth.
>
> (T 42; CP 249)

In many other poems in the series Sexton stresses the similarities between the romance ingenue and the stepmothers or evil fairies. Here she stresses the human side of the witch, her capacity for love, her complex longings. Most interpretations of the story stress the witch's power and her selfishness, her desire to keep Rapunzel away from the world. (See Bruno Bettelheim's comment, for example: "Having acted foolishly and selfishly, the sorceress loses out—but since she acted from too much love for Rapunzel and not out of wickedness, no harm befalls her.")[39] But Sexton underlines the conventional predictability and emptiness of the usual ending by framing it with the witch's story. She suggests that the happiness of Rapunzel and her prince is another version of Cinderella and hers:

> Cinderella and the prince
> lived, they say, happily ever after,

like two dolls in a museum case . . .
never getting a middle-aged spread,
their darling smiles pasted on for eternity.
Regular Bobbsey twins.
That story.

(*T* 56–57; *CP* 258)

Both Rapunzel and Cinderella live out the fantasy of an unchanging, ever-lasting relationship, false and frightening with its "pasted on" smiles. Though Sexton usually retains the outlines of conventional tale conclusions, with their weddings and promises of never-ending bliss, she always manages to make them look sterile and static. The exterior frame, with its witch narrator, and the framing prologues, with their deadpan but cutting contemporary edge, always undercut and slice away the usual meanings of "that story."

After *Transformations* was essentially ready for publication, Sexton asked the poet Stanley Kunitz for his opinion. He suggested "switching the pro-logues and making them epilogues," but she found that she couldn't do it:

> With about four or five of [the poems] it was a stroke of genius. With about five of them it's so-so. With eight of them it destroys. The poems seem to grow out of the prologue[s] to, as it were, take root in them and come forth from them.[40]

Just as Cornell's boxes frame and transform the objects within them, Sexton's prologues make the Grimms' tales new. She has transplanted them into ap-parently alien, even contaminated soil, where they "take root" and send out new and unexpected shoots. The supermarkets, parking lots, cocktail parties, and mental institutions of her prologues—so far from the Grimms' villages and dark woods—become the modern matrix for her "small, funny, and hor-rifying"[41] versions of the old stories. Without these deeply ironic introduc-tions, her tales would lose their tensile roots in contemporary American cul-ture.

IV

Recently a young Irish writer, Emma Donoghue, has published her versions of traditional tales in *Kissing the Witch: Old Tales in New Skins*. Though mysteriously marketed for "young readers," this is a book that both depends on an intimate acquaintance with the Grimms' and Andersen's tales and calls all the old stereotypes into question. Like Sexton, Donoghue reframes the tales, placing them in a receding series of frames, creating something like a Quaker Oats box effect. She is also interested in "rehabilitating the witch," speaking in the voice of a witch who is both human and vulnerable, contesting the ways the witch has been represented in generations of tale-telling.[42] She insists on the possible links between the best-known tales and the system of gender relations that they reveal. Unlike Sexton, however, she does not bring the tales up-to-date or make them "very contemporary."[43] Rather, she retains the apparently timeless settings and simple language that we associate with tales.

The first tale, "The Tale of the Shoe," is a version of "Cinderella." In Donoghue's retelling, however, Cinderella is not abused by her stepmother and stepsisters (who in fact do not appear) but rather is driven by her own self-hatred to scrub and sweep:

> Nobody made me do the things I did, nobody scolded me, nobody punished me but me. The shrill voices were all inside. Do this, do that, you lazy heap of dirt. . . . I listened for my mother, but I couldn't hear her among their clamor.[44]

Like the Grimms' Aschenputtel (*KHM* 121), she is paralyzed by her grief over her mother's death: "Ever since my mother died the feather bed felt hard as a stone floor" (1). And, as in the Grimms' tale, she finds the spirit of her mother in a hazel bush. But Donoghue's tale is really the tale of the relationship between the Cinderella speaker and the fairy godmother, a human incarnation of the Grimms' little white birds or a relic of Perrault's version of the tale. Even the prince, who "seemed like an actor on a creaking stage" (6), plays only a very minor role. As the speaker says toward the end, "I had got the story all wrong. How could I not have noticed she was beautiful?" (7). Like Sexton, Donoghue calls "that story" into question, persistently suggesting new versions for us to deal with, changing the endings: "This was a strange story, one I would have to learn a new language to read, a language I could not learn except by trying to read the story" ("The Tale of the Rose," 39). Most of her speakers, all women, think of themselves and their own lives as worthless; like her Cinderella, they are redeemed not by the traditional marriage plot but by the possibility of romantic love between women.

Perhaps the most startling innovation of Donoghue's book, however, is the way she frames and links the tales. A character in each tale becomes the narrator of the following tale. For example, the fairy godmother in "The Tale of the Shoe" tells the story of her previous life in the next, "The Tale of the Bird." The tales are all connected by a linking, italicized question and answer, framed typographically on a page of its own:

> *In the morning I asked,*
> *Who were you*
> *before you walked into my kitchen?*
> *And she said, Will I tell you my own story?*
> *It is a tale of a bird.* (9)

This question and answer, a new version of the conversations that link the tales in collections from Straparola to the *conteuses*, is echoed over and over again in the book. Each tale becomes a prequel, a first-person story that tells the story that led up to the preceding tale.

"The Tale of the Bird" is a much-muted version of Perrault's "Bluebeard" or the Grimms' "Fitcher's Bird" (*KHM* 46). The husband's only cruelty is forbidding his young pregnant wife to go out in the sun. No bloody chamber, no murdered wives, no stained key or egg, no dramatic rescue. The narrator, like the Cinderella figure in the previous tale, is obsessed with her own unworthiness: "I would be a stain on my husband's line. . . . I was always to keep in mind the tiny smoky image of what an insignificant creature I had been before he honored me with his gaze" (17). At the beginning of the tale, the speaker takes on shape and weight only because her husband, rich and powerful, has singled her out, created her with his privileged gaze. But, like Jane Eyre, the narrator finds that she cannot live a life, luxurious though it is, that is restricted to a narrow compass: "In their smooth leather, my feet itched for the stubble of the open fields, and my eyes strained for a far horizon" (19).[45] The injured bird she nurses back to life, over her husband's objections and incomprehension, and then releases becomes a symbol of her determination to escape and her love of freedom: "I could have kept it beside me, a silk-tethered plaything, but what would have been the use of that?" (23).

In this tale, as in the first one and in most of the linked tales that make up the book, the narrator chooses freedom instead of security, self-possession (a word we have diminished by overuse) instead of marriage. In "The Tale of the Handkerchief," for example, the princess turned goose girl decides that she prefers her simple life, that being a princess is a burden, while the false princess realizes that her marriage is precarious in spite of the true princess's promise not to reveal her secret. In "The Tale of the Apple," Snow White decides to return to her stepmother in the castle. In "The Tale of the Voice," Andersen's little mermaid decides to leave the unfaithful prince and return to her sisters. Donoghue links the tales not only with the repeated question-and-answer frames but also with their common concern for female independence.

This concern surfaces even in "The Tale of the Cottage," a startling revision of the Hansel and Gretel story. The narrator, described in the previous tale as "slow in the head" (121), tells the tale in blunt, half-formed prose. As the previous narrator says, "sentences seemed too much for her" (121); she struggles to find words for her experience: "I once had brother that mother say we were pair of hands one fast one slow" (133). Her stepfather, the "huntman," abandons them in the woods over her mother's objections, reversing the genders in the Grimms' version. (One of Donoghue's aims is clearly to revise our image of the monstrous older stepmother/witch who haunts their tales.)[46] She and the cleverer Hansel are taken in by a friendly witch, but when Hansel has "hair chin instead of smile" (139), he begins asking the witch for kisses and lifting her skirts. Only then is he imprisoned in the cage. The loyal Gretel figure releases him but refuses to leave with him: "Home not home if mother not mother" (140). Our knowledge of this intellectually limited Gretel, her goodness and her loyalty, is deepened as we recall her role in the previous story as a Rumpelstiltskin figure exploited by a selfish spinner who has never even dreamed of asking her name or thinking of her as a person. Just as this Rumpelstiltskin/Gretel claims the child she has been promised and has cared for in "The Tale of the Spinster," she clings to the witch who has sheltered and warmed her in "The Tale of the Cottage." Donoghue uses one tale to frame the next, in part to stress continuities of behavior, in part to undermine the gender stereotypes we tend to bring to fairy tales. Rumpelstiltskin, usually portrayed as a malevolent male "helper figure,"[47] can also be a self-sacrificing woman, emotionally whole if intellectually limited.

"The Tale of the Kiss" is the last story in the collection and the only one that is not a reworking of a "classic" fairy tale, though it is reminiscent of Virgil's myth of the cave-dwelling Sibyl and Breton tales about a cliff-dwelling wisewoman. The speaker is an aging witch who both revels in and fears the power she has, "power that came not from my own thin body or my own taut mind, but was invested in me by a village" (213). She has left the village community because of her barrenness yet realizes only later in her life that "perhaps it is the not being kissed that makes her a witch; perhaps the source of her power is the breath of loneliness around her" (226). She meets a rebellious young girl, red-haired like herself and just as uninterested in being a "good" daughter or wife, who makes her want to renounce the power that her separation from the human community has given her, to acknowledge human need and love. Her renunciation echoes Prospero's at the end of *The Tempest,* his refusal of "this rough magic"—but we know from the previous tale that, unlike Prospero, she has ended up in another cave above another village, still dispensing what passes for magic, now looking like the witch we expect: "a stoop, a stick, a wart on her nose, a whisker on her chin" (189).

We never know what has driven her to another cave, "half a year away" (207). She refuses to reveal the middle of her story: "And what happened next, you ask? Never you mind. There are some tales not for telling . . ." (228–29). Unlike Donoghue's other first-person narrators, she acknowledges a gap between the story she tells and the previous story in which she plays a part. The narrative chain is broken; the receding planes dissolve.[48] Like Shakespeare in the masque or the chess game in *The Tempest,* Donoghue blurs the edges where illusion and reality meet, breaking the theatrical frame that has linked her stories in sequence. The beautiful red-headed girl never tells her story; rather, the witch turns to her audience (the little mermaid? the readers? both? neither?) and brings the collection to a close by saying: "This is the story you asked for. I leave it in your mouth" (228). The direct address (to "you," whoever it is) abruptly halts the sequence and ruptures its framing illusions. Not all stories are linked to others; not all stories can be told.

Donoghue's framing strategy, then, includes its own dissolution. The repeated framing gesture disappears; the sequence seems to end. Or perhaps this is a way to suggest that the series continues indefinitely, that the ending is an invitation to the reader to tell her own story (a version of what Roland Barthes calls the "writerly text," a text demanding that the reader become a "writer"). Like Goethe's "Märchen" at the end of the *Unterhaltungen deutscher Ausgewanderten,* Donoghue's last tale gestures toward an infinitely receding sequence of tales and unknown continuations: "I leave it in your mouth." The frame dissolves or vanishes; the reader's voice carries on.

Donoghue's imaginative reworking of the tales, then, is a play for voices. Each tale is told by a different voice; no two voices are alike. Sexton frames all her tales with the sardonic, vulgar voice of the storytelling witch, the witch who speaks American slang and knows all the brand names, the witch who speaks ironically from a perspective that is outside cultural limits, all too knowing about sex and human psychology—this startling voice framing tales told in the usual third person: "Once there was a lovely virgin / called Snow White" (*T* 3; *CP* 225). Donoghue transforms the tales into first-person narratives, each linked to the others, yet different in style and in perspective. To use a phrase from John Barth's "Author's Note" to *Lost in the Funhouse*, all these framed tales are "composed for 'printed voice.' "[49] Simulation of narrative voices, a feature of fairy tales from their earliest written beginnings, continues in these late-twentieth-century versions of the frame. Sexton, Donoghue, even—though perhaps paradoxically—Cornell, all retell old stories in new voices, varying them, asking questions about them, placing them in new frames that alter their meanings.

CHAPTER FIVE

The Art of Transliteration

> I am a woman committed to
> a politics
> of transliteration, the methodology
>
> of a mind
> stunned at the suddenly possible
> shifts of meaning
>
> Olga Broumas, "Artemis"

WHAT COULD Olga Broumas mean by "a politics of transliteration"? Greek-American, she is adept at transforming the characters of one alphabet into the alien characters of another. But clearly here she means much more than that. To "transliterate" for Broumas is to invent a language for the experiences that cannot be caught in any language that already exists; as she says, in the same poem, "we must / find words / or burn."[1] Her quest is urgent: there is no time to lose. Her poetic "methodology" takes her back to her personal history, to Greek mythology, and to fairy tales. She "transliterates" or re-forms the old stories, omitting some elements, emphasizing others, to make them part of her new and dangerous vision of the world.

Here we could return to one of Emma Donoghue's sentences: "This was a strange story, one I would have to learn a new language to read, a language I could not learn except by trying to read the story" ("The Tale of the Rose," 39). Many of the women who have recently revised or rewritten fairy tales have created "a new language" for them, a language that reimagines what William Carlos Williams once called "the syntax of things." They transform the old fairy-tale sequences, the repetitive plots, into new and unexpected patterns. The "Story Template" caricatured by Roz Chast (see fig. 1 again) is no longer adequate, or perhaps even relevant. Writers who "transliterate" tend to ignore or elide the old didactic patterns. They play, rather, on our memory of salient images, often apparently peripheral details, transforming them into new centers of meaning.

We might take Lisel Mueller's poem "Immortality" as an example of trans-literation. She bases her poem on the Grimms' version of "Sleeping Beauty," but she does not focus on its usual elements: the long-awaited birth, the fairy's curse, the prick of the spindle, the long sleep, the coming of the prince, or the awakening. Instead, she remembers what caught her attention as a child: the Grimms' image of the fly, caught in midflight for a hundred years, finally waking up:

> and the fly, arrested mid-plunge
> above the strawberry pie
> fulfills its abiding mission
> and dives into the sweet, red glaze.[2]

The Grimms treat this scene only fleetingly in "Dornröschen" (*KHM* 50); they focus much more sharply on the cook who finally boxes the scullery boy's ear than on the fly itself. And Mueller knows that her interpretation of the scene has changed:

> As a child I had a book
> with a picture of that scene.
> I was too young to notice
> how fear persists, and how
> the anger that causes fear persists,
> that its trajectory can't be changed
> or broken, only interrupted.
> My attention was on the fly:
> that this slight body
> with its transparent wings
> and life-span of one human day
> still craved its particular share
> of sweetness, a century later.

Now she knows that fear and anger persist as well as sweetness, that their trajectories are just as immutable. The fragile fly, its wings still intact, still yearns for the strawberry; the cook's temper has not improved. But, by isolating this tiny image from the well-known tale, she has reconceived the tale's trajectory as well. No longer a powerful myth about the princess's long sleep that can be broken only by the coming of the right man, it becomes in Mueller's language a meditation on what immortality might be, or what can remain through the passing of time. And she suggests that, even as a child, she was not fixed on the conventional plot. The tale had not deformed her sense of herself and of the possible roles she could play; rather, what caught her attention was a scene that might seem peripheral, not central to "that story."

In the great feminist fairy-tale debates of the 1970s, all the participants assumed that tales have a direct effect on women's lives and dreams, presenting "romantic paradigms that profoundly influenc[e] women's fantasies and the subconscious scenarios for their real lives."[3] Even Alison Lurie, who sparked the debates with her 1970 article "Fairy Tale Liberation," assumed a direct relationship between women's lives and the tales they read or were fed. She argued that "the traditional folk tale" offered women—as heroines and as storytellers—active roles and powers that the everyday Dick-and-Jane stories of her childhood denied them: "To prepare children for women's liberation, therefore, and to protect them against Future Shock, you had better buy at least one collection of fairy tales."[4]

But other feminist literary critics would have none of this. They argued that most popular fairy tales, like "Cinderella" and "Snow White" and "Sleeping Beauty," had heroines who were passive, apparently dead or sleepwalking, dependent on the arrival of the prince for any animation and for entry into a real life—though a real life that never was given any contours after the obligatory royal wedding. As the earliest feminist critics of fairy tales all agreed, women in the best-known tales were either beautiful, slumbering young girls or powerful, usually wicked and grotesque older women. Though there might be a muted tradition of tales in which women were admirable, active, clever, and self-assertive participants, the dominant tradition (particularly the tales popularized by Andrew Lang in his rainbow fairy-tale series and later adopted by the Disney industry) prescribed harmful roles for women that little girls could not help but imitate. As Vivian Gornick says in a recent essay, "We were in thrall to passive longing, all of us—Dorothea [Brooke, from *Middlemarch*] and Isobel [Archer, from *Portrait of a Lady*], me and my mother, the fairy tale princess. Longing is what attracted us, what compelled our deepest attention."[5] Rather than design a life for themselves, the women "in thrall" to fairy-tale patterns wait for male rescue, or at least for something to happen. They half-consciously submit to being male property, handed from father to suitor or husband without complaint or volition. And it is the gender economy of the often-repeated fairy tales that has betrayed them. As one of Margaret Atwood's characters replies to her own question " 'Did you believe that stuff when you were little? . . . I did, I thought I was really a princess and I'd end up living in a castle. They shouldn't let kids have stuff like that.' "[6]

In 1975, in the thick of the fairy-tale debates, Hélène Cixous wrote in "Sorties":

> *Il était une fois . . .*
>
> De l'histoire qui suit on ne peut pas encore dire: "ce n'est qu'une histoire." Ce conte reste vrai aujourd'hui. La plupart des femmes qui sont réveillées se souviennent d'avoir dormi, *d'avoir été endormies.*
>
> *Il était une fois . . . et encore une fois . . .*
>
> Les belles dorment dans leurs bois, en attendant que les princes viennent les réveiller. Dans leurs lits, dans leurs cercueils de verre, dans leurs forêts d'enfance comme des mortes. Belles, mais passives; donc désirables: d'elles émane tout mystère.[7]

> (*Once upon a time . . .*
>
> One cannot yet say of the following history "it's just a story." It's a tale still true today. Most women who have awakened remember having slept, *having been put to sleep.*
>
> *Once upon a time . . . once . . . and once again,*
>
> Beauties slept in their woods, waiting for princes to come and wake them up. In their beds, in their glass coffins, in their childhood forests like dead women. Beautiful, but passive; hence desirable: all mystery emanates from them.)

Cixous uses these fairy-tale patterns as one focus of her attack on the binary organization and hierarchy of gender in the West. She believes it is precisely the repetition of the "once upon a time"s that has helped create women who cannot value themselves, who are most themselves precisely and paradoxically when they are absent or not themselves, "the same story repeating woman's destiny in love across the centuries with the cruel hoax of its plot."[8] As Lurie pointed out in her second article, "Witches and Fairies," in 1971, the heroines of novels from Gwendolen Harleth to Lady Chatterley to Nicole Warren in Fitzgerald's *Tender Is the Night* all fit this type; we could multiply the literary examples endlessly. But people who argued that fairy tales are dangerous for girls and women, as well as people who argued that fairy tales are essential reading, focused on the power of their "images of woman" to shape or deform real lives, as did most feminist critics of the time. Lurie sums up this belief in her offhand, Wildean remark about "real life, which as usual imitates art."[9]

Women's autobiographies, however, often suggest more oblique and complex responses to the tales that supposedly govern our lives. Though many writers testify to the power certain patterns and roles continue to have, others show that fairy tales have symbolic resonances that work against, or even contradict, the dominant models. The formation of the female subject, if such a thing exists, takes place in many indirect and mediated ways.[10] Many autobiographies assume that there is an "essential self" that the autobiography as mirror can reflect. As Felicity Nussbaum has suggested, the ideology of the genre traditionally demands a stable "I": "In first-person narrative, the 'I' arbitrates reality through cultural codes to make 'experience' intelligible and to place it in a familiar framework."[11] But many modern autobiographers, from Gertrude Stein to Roland Barthes, have avoided or elided the "I," deliberately thwarting our desire for a unified subject we can recognize and reiterated cultural codes that help us make it make sense.

In the pages that follow, I will often refer to *Mirror, Mirror on the Wall*, edited by Kate Bernheimer, a recent collection of essays by various contemporary women writers who were asked to reflect on the function of fairy tales in their childhood, "how fairy tales affected their thinking about emotion, the self, gender and culture."[12] Their wildly different answers suggest some of the multiplicity of ways fairy tales can mirror and form versions of the female self. But I will focus on Christa Wolf's autobiographical meditations on her Nazi childhood, *Kindheitsmuster* (1976), and on Carolyn Kay Steedman's innovative double biography/autobiography, *Landscape for a Good Woman* (1986), both shot through with fairy tales. Neither text presents a stable and coherent self. In both books, fairy tales become what Steedman calls "interpretative devices," stories to think with, stories that do not necessarily determine lives but can give children (and adults) a way to read and to understand them. As Walter Benjamin says, in his review of a book called *Alte vergessene Kinderbücher* (Old, forgotten children's books) (1924), "Children are able to manipulate fairy stories [*Märchenstoffen*, or tale elements] with the same ease and lack of inhibition they display in playing with pieces of cloth and building blocks."[13]

I I

Christa Wolf calls her autobiographical text *Kindheitsmuster: Ein Roman* (Patterns of childhood: a novel—the subtitle is omitted, significantly, in the English translation).[14] The difficulty of making contact with her childhood self is one of the themes and problems of the text; Wolf refers to this self as "Nelly," never as Christa, and only in the third person. She does not pretend to be able to breach the distance between them, to claim that the "auto" in "autobiography" represents a continuous and stable self, or to avoid the sentimental nostalgia of what she calls "der Tourismus in halbversunkene Kindheiten" (14) ("the tourist trade in half-buried childhoods" [6]). She further complicates the problem of the continuous self by interweaving scenes from her childhood during the Nazi era and the Allied occupation (from roughly 1933 to 1947); from a trip she makes with her husband, brother, and fourteen-year-old daughter to her hometown, now in Poland, in 1971; and from her meditations on current events (the Vietnam War, for example) during the writing of the book from 1972 to 1975. She consistently refers to her adult self as "du" or "you," stressing her own distance even from the self that is experiencing and writing in the present. Only in the last few paragraphs does Wolf use the pronoun "I" instead of the second-person "you"—and there it is the "I" of the writer looking back on what she has written.[15] The subtitle "Ein Roman" suggests the impossibility of bringing her selves together, even at the end:

> Und die Vergangenheit, die noch Sprachregelungen verfügen, die erste Person in eine zweite und dritte spalten konnte—ist ihre Vormacht gebrochen? Werden die Stimmen sich beruhigen?
> Ich weiß es nicht. (519)
>
> And the past, which can still prescribe rules governing speech, which can still split the first person into a second and third—has its supremacy been broken? Will the voices be still?
> I don't know. [406])

Early in the book, Wolf stresses the inauthenticity of her attempts to recapture her childhood self. Like Lisel Mueller, she is unable to remember; as Mueller says, "I tried to go home again. I stood at the door of my childhood, but it was closed to the public."[16] There are a few moments when Wolf seems to begin to be able to approach the child doing childlike things:

> Da hättest du es also. Es bewegt sich, geht, liegt, sitzt, ißt, schläft, trinkt. Es kann lachen und weinen, Sandkuten bauen, Marchen anhören . . . (13–14)

> (You've got it, then. She moves, walks, lies down, sits, eats, sleeps, drinks. She can laugh and cry, dig holes in the sand, listen to fairy tales . . . [7])

But this list of the child's activities is strangely mechanical, almost like an advertisement for a doll with many talents (accentuated in the German by the neuter pronoun "es" for "das Kind"). This child can do the things any three-year-old can do—and one of those things is to listen to fairy tales, as any good German child should. References to the Grimms' tales run throughout the book: snakes who might be fairy princes, frog princes, "Hänsel and Gretel," the hedge of thorns around Sleeping Beauty's castle. When her father returns, wizened and unrecognizable, from a Russian prisoner-of-war camp, "Nelly" has half-expected his transformation:

> Merkwürdigerweise hat Nelly es geahnt. Märchen bereiten uns von klein auf darauf vor; Der Held, der König, der Prinz, der Geliebte wird in der Fremde verwunschen: als ein Fremder kehrt er zurück. (507)

> (Strangely enough Nelly had foreseen it. Fairy tales prepare us for it from childhood on: The hero, the king, the prince, the lover, falls under a spell in foreign lands; he returns as a stranger. [398])

Fairy tales often provide "Nelly" with a way of reading and even predicting the world, like Steedman's "interpretative devices."

But, though the Grimms' tales are one ground of her existence, she also constantly plays variations on them. She mentions the hedge of thorns around Sleeping Beauty's castle, but she never sees herself as the sleeping princess. Snow White ("Schneewittchen") becomes the name of a witch; the story of Hänsel and Gretel's parents plotting their deaths becomes a reason to try to overhear her own parents' conversations about politics; when she and her brother act out "Mary's Child" (*KHM* 3), she refuses to confess to opening the forbidden thirteenth door as the truthful child of the tale does. Living in a broken-down castle at the end of the war makes her think "sie

würde nie wieder in einem Märchen lesen können: 'Und er nahm sie mit
auf sein Schloß . . . ,' ohne laut lachen zu müssen" (425) ("she'd never again
be able to read a fairy tale which said: 'And he brought her home to his castle'
without bursting out laughing" [336]). Often "Nelly" finds herself acting in
opposition to the tales she knows, refusing to act out their plots "wie vor-
geschrieben" (152) ("according to the script" [116]). These refusals, in fact,
become dry runs for her instinctive opposition to some (though certainly not
all) Nazi political doctrines, like the expectation that all young girls should
be happy to bear Aryan children for the fatherland. Fairy tales provide scripts
for living, but they can also inspire resistance to those scripts and, in turn,
to other apparently predetermined patterns.

Very early "Nelly" begins to object to the happy endings of fairy tales:

> Es war dieselbe Irritation, die sie von den Märchenschlüssen her kannte,
> wenn sich der Befriedigung, daß alles sich so wohl gefügt . . . doch, kaum
> eingestanden, ein kleines bißchen Enttäuschung beimengte, spätestens
> bei der Schlußbemerkung: Und wenn sie nicht gestorben sind, so leben
> sie heute noch. . . . Wer war sie, an den Schlüssen der Märchen herumzu-
> mäkeln? (118)

> (It was the same irritation that came over her at the end of fairy tales,
> when the satisfaction that everything had turned out all right . . . was none-
> theless mixed with a barely admitted touch of disappointment, especially
> at the conclusion: And they lived happily ever after. . . . Who was she to
> find fault with the endings of fairy tales? [89])

The traditional German ending is even more pat and irritating than the English: literally, "and if they haven't died, they're living still." Yet Wolf's early
resistance to that ending suggests that children don't always accept fairy
tales as a package, or as packaged. Throughout her book she stresses the
tension between the richness of some elements of the tales and the sham
finality of their closure. Shattering the usual conventions of autobiography,
she also breaks fairy tales into parts. Just as her text becomes a collage of
scenes and thoughts from different eras of her life, a "novel" rather than an
"autobiography," so the fairy tales she remembers are fragmented and woven
apparently at random into her text. They do not have the compelling force
of coherent myths but rather provide scattered models for resistance and for
interpretation.

III

Steedman's book, published ten years later, is an attempt to tell the stories of the lives she and her mother made for themselves, stories that contest the existing templates for narratives of British working-class life and of female psychological development. She is the daughter of Lancashire parents who migrated to London in the mid-1930s, looking for better work and opportunities, fleeing family and perhaps other threats in the North. Her mother's mother was a weaver and a weaver's daughter, precariously self-sufficient after her husband's death at the Somme; her father's parents had once owned, and lost, a corner sweetshop. Only when Steedman is an adult, after her father's death, does she discover that her parents had never married, because her father already had a wife and child. Her illegitimacy becomes a confirmation of her continuing sense of exclusion from dominant, middle-class British culture. Her book is an attempt to trace the *"development* of class consciousness (as opposed to its expression) . . . as a *learned position*, learned in childhood, and often through the exigencies of difficult and lonely lives."[17]

Much of Steedman's book focuses on the life of her mother, whose stories and dreams disrupted and deformed Steedman's own: "stories designed to show me the terrible unfairness of things, the subterranean culture of longing for that which one can never have" (8). Like the women and fictional characters Gornick talks about, Steedman's mother longed for things that she half-knew were unattainable, and yet longed for them all the same: "a New Look skirt, a timbered country cottage, to marry a prince" (9). The New Look skirt would have taken far too many yards of material to make in postwar Britain; the timbered country cottage was always just out of reach, in spite of the thousands of pounds she saved in building-society funds; the prince never came. In one of the more amusing as well as telling passages in the book, Steedman's father describes how difficult it was to live with her mother during the abdication crisis of 1936: "Mrs. Simpson was no prettier than her, no more clever than her, no better than her. It wasn't fair that a king should give up his throne for her, and not for the weaver's daughter" (47).

As Steedman sees it, her mother believed what fairy tales like the Grimms' "Goose Girl" (*KHM* 89) told her: that if she were good and patient and long-suffering, a prince would recognize her worth and carry her off, off into a different social world, a world that was "fair." She is never the dependable emotional center of the home, as working-class "Mums" are supposed to be, but always off-center, yearning for a life that is denied her.

And yet, like many interpreters reading the story of Cinderella, Steedman never mentions one basic fact about the goose-girl story: that the goose girl is the true princess in disguise, displaced by a scheming maid. As Joyce Carol Oates reminds us, "In a crucial sense fairy tales work to subvert romantic wishes, for they repeatedly confirm 'order' and redress dislocations of privileged birth while leaving wholly unchallenged the hierarchical basis for such privileging."[18] Steedman believes that her mother has been betrayed by the false hope that fairy tales like "The Goose Girl" give, but she (and perhaps her mother) have misread the story or tailored it to fit other, perhaps more compelling patterns. As Oates and many others have pointed out, there are very few stories of heroic adventure for women in the usual fairy-tale repertoire; only male characters like Dick Whittington, Jack the Giant-Killer, or Tom Thumb rise from rags to riches through their own ingenuity and courage. Most of the stories that seem to point to such social movement for women are actually reaffirmations of social status and enactments of Freud's "family romance": "My real parents were a king and queen; I was really always a princess."

Trying to articulate her mother's longings, then, Steedman reaches for a fairy-tale pattern that actually undermines them, reaffirms their impossibility. She attributes conventional hopes and fairy-tale expectations to her mother, confirming her continuing estrangement from her. In the last scene in the book, returning to her childhood home for the first time in years, she sees her mother as a witch who looks just like the witch in illustrations for "Hänsel and Gretel": "[She] opens the door of the gingerbread house; she stands there; you look at her face: she is like my mother" (140). Again Steedman places her mother in a conventional, polarized role.

When she talks about her own life, however, she chooses different patterns, usually from Andersen's tales that she read over and over early in childhood. Rather than see herself as the central female figure of the tales, she oscillates from identification to interpretation of symbolic structures. Emphasizing her middle name, Kay, a name she doesn't use in signing her other books, she insists on the parallels between herself and the "Kay" of Andersen's "Snow Queen," a boy who is emotionally frozen by the shards of a broken mirror: "Kay was my name at home, and I knew that Kay, the boy

in 'The Snow Queen,' was me, who had a lump of ice in her heart" (46).
She also repeatedly returns to Gerda, in many ways the active heroine of
Andersen's tale—the faithful girl who searches for Kay throughout the world
and finally redeems him from the powerful and icy Snow Queen. The little
robber girl Gerda meets, who will not sleep without her knife, becomes a
central image in Steedman's interpretations of her parents' life together:

> Each had a knife, sharp-edged with a broad yet pointed blade, and what
> they did with the knife, what the grown-ups did, was cut each other. . . .
> Downstairs I thought, the thin blood falls in sheets from my mother's
> breasts; she was the most cut, but I knew it was she who did the cutting.
> I couldn't always see the knife in my father's hand. (54)

This bloody scene becomes the key to her understanding of her parents,
their relationship to each other and to their children. Her mother uses the
knife primarily to hurt herself, "displaying to my imagination the mutilation
involved in feeding and keeping us" (82). Her father lacks the phallic power
of the knife, the power of the father to name, to give laws, and to control. As
Steedman says, "the fairy tales always tell the stories that we do not yet
know" (55).

Throughout the book, Steedman stresses the ways in which her family
constellation differs from the dominant middle-class fairy-tale and Freudian
norms. Middle-class women have a "central relationship to the culture. The
myths tell their story" (17):

> In the fairy-stories the daughters love their fathers because they are
> mighty princes, great rulers, and because such absolute power seduces.
> The modern psychoanalytic myths posit the same plot, old tales are made
> manifest: secret longings, doors closing along the corridors of the bour-
> geois household. (61)

Excluded from the world of dominant fathers and big houses, Steedman
cannot love or fear her absent and powerless father: "He did know some
rules, but he didn't embody them: they were framed by some distant authority outside himself" (57). She also knows that her feelings for her mother are
a tangled mixture of resentment and guilt. Unlike her mother, or at least
unlike the mother she has created in her autobiography, she does not long
for the unattainable, as expressed in "The Goose Girl," or attempt to insert

herself into the dominant fairy-tale framework. Rather, she reinterprets the tales and case studies she reads to explain her own childhood on the social margins.

Another tale by Andersen, "The Little Mermaid," becomes talismanic for Steedman's understanding of her own emotional life. Though in this case she sees both her mother and herself as the central mermaid figure, rather than as the witch who advises her or the emotionally distant prince, she does not make either the heroine of a romance plot. Both she and her mother are little mermaids, but neither is in thrall to conventional longings:

> The Little Mermaid was not my mother sacrificing herself for a beautiful prince. I knew her sacrifice: it was not composed of love or longing for my father, rather of a fierce resentment against the circumstances that were so indifferent to her. She turns me into the Little Mermaid a few years later, swimming round and round the ship, wondering why I was not wanted, but realizing that of course, it had to be that way. (55)

The Little Mermaid removes herself from the world of her sisters, who are at home in the water, but is never at home in the human world on the land. The tale becomes a metaphor for emotional dead ends and repetitions, the mermaid's voicelessness a sign of inability to speak in way that might change things.[19] Her mother's circumstances remain unaltered; both her parents remain distant and essentially unavailable.

For Steedman herself the tale is also a lesson in enduring suffering: "I knew that one day I might be asked to walk on the edge of knives, like the Little Mermaid, and was afraid that I might not be able to bear the pain" (46). The knives, so prominent in her renderings of her parents' lives, here are turned against her, crippling her emotionally. (It was only after reading Steedman that I began to notice how often knives figure in Andersen's tales, all their repressed violence rising momentarily to the surface.) Like her mother, she chooses a kind of self-mutilation, violently cutting herself off from meaningful human contact.

Very early Steedman begins to feel distanced from herself as well. She sees herself in an old photograph when she was about four, and remembers that "things were wrong; there was a dislocation between me and the world; I am not inside myself (51)." The shift into the present tense here (from "was" and "were" to "I am") suggests her continuing self-estrangement. Like Wolf, Steedman splits her "self" into various "selves": the academic self from the working-class self; the self skilled in Freudian analysis from the emotionally frozen self; the childhood self from the self who is trying to remember, interpret, and understand. Writing an autobiography, combining her autobiography with a biography of her mother, is part of her attempt to see continuities between those selves, to "compose" a self for herself, to reunite the observing eye and the feeling "I." Her readings of Andersen's tales, as well as of "The Goose Girl," are part of that complex and often fragmentary project. At the end, again like Wolf, she must acknowledge "the irreducible nature of all our lost childhoods" (144). There is no existing narrative structure that can contain her particular story, no existing "structure of political thought" that can recognize "all these secret and impossible stories" (144). The meaningful fragments of fairy tales can only suggest some of those nearly inexpressible secrets.

As A. S. Byatt says, "These stories are riddles, and all readers change them a little, and they accept and resist change simultaneously."[20] Some fairy tales do fall into repetitive patterns, as their early feminist critics saw: tracing the longings of a goose girl or a mermaid for an apparently unattainable prince, freezing heroines in glass coffins to wait for his arrival. These repetitive plots can be reframed, as Sexton, Donoghue, and others have handled them, changing their significance by placing them in new and contrasting contexts. But their sharply etched images (a rose, a transformation, a knife, a mirror) open them up to other readings, other ways to understand them. In women's recent autobiographical writing, these images are refracted in the splintered forms of the narratives themselves. One conventional form, one unambiguous mirror cannot contain them.[21]

Cristina Bacchilega has recently argued that "the tale of magic's controlling metaphor is the *magic mirror*, because it conflates mimesis (reflection), refraction (varying desires), and framing (artifice)."[22] One could say that the controlling metaphor of recent women's autobiographies is the *broken mirror*, the mirror that does not pretend to reflect subjectivities or lives as unified wholes. As Wolf says, "Im Idealfall sollten die Strukturen des Erlebens sich mit den Strukturen des Erzählens decken" (345) ("Ideally the structures of experience should match the structures of narrative" [272]). Autobiography, as we have long understood it, should be a serene and accurate reflection of a life. But even the complex layering of narrative levels that makes up Wolf's text cannot reproduce or match what she calls the "verfilztes Geflecht" (345) ("tangled mesh" [272]) of her experiences. All she can do is attempt to reproduce the reflections in the broken shards of the autobio-graphical mirror.

Steedman's repeated references to Andersen's "Snow Queen" suggest the importance of the image of the broken mirror for her understanding of her autobiographical project. At the beginning of Andersen's tale, as we have seen, a splinter of a wicked magician's mirror pierces Kay's heart. And at the end Gerda finds Kay in the Snow Queen's ice-palace, working "the ice-puzzle of reason," attempting to fit fragments of ice together. In the story the fragments finally cohere, forming the word "eternity," when Gerda, in tears, sings a song about the child Jesus, recalling Kay to the warmth of human relationship and Christian belief. But Steedman avoids any mention of Andersen's optimistic and typically rather saccharine ending. Rather, she focuses repeatedly on the splintered mirror and on the icy power of the Snow Queen to lure Kay to her cold and colorless kingdom: "The mirror breaks, just as the clock strikes five, and a lump of ice is lodged in the heart" (97).[23] The broken mirror is a metaphor throughout for Steedman's feelings of emo-tional isolation and exclusion, but it also reflects the difficulty she has in creating a narrative form for her experiences. She finds it necessary to begin before the beginning, to see how her mother's stories of her life shaped her own and how their stories are interwoven; her book is "about the experience of my own childhood, and the way in which my mother reasserted, reversed and restructured her own within mine" (8). There is no single story of indi-vidual growth and development, but rather a tangle of stories caught up, like Wolf's, in cultural currents and political realities that have yet to be de-scribed in any way that can contain or explain them.

Neither Wolf nor Steedman pretends that she has solved the problem of competing, even conflicting selves, selves woven out of different material exigencies and discursive possibilities. Both accept the continuing mystery of the Chinese puzzle of identity, rejecting the false solutions and happy endings that fairy tales and traditional autobiography provide. Fractured identities demand fractured forms, a momentary self glimpsed in a remem-bered scene—or in a fragment of a fairy tale.

I V

These fragments, carefully selected, help Wolf and Steedman shape their sense of themselves as gendered subjects in this world. We could call this one kind of "transliteration," a "methodology" that permits them to "keep the old stories," as Joseph Cornell did, and yet simultaneously retell them in a new context. Their autobiographies suggest the continuing force of the images and constellations of fairy tales, but also their malleability.

In the group of seven fairy-tale poems that end *Beginning with O* (1977), Olga Broumas shows just how protean the tales can be. Though inspired in part by Sexton's *Transformations*, she further transforms the tales she chooses. Her homage to Sexton begins earlier in the book in the poem "Demeter," an act of homage to all her literary "foremothers":

> Anne. Sylvia. Virginia.
> Adrienne the last, magnificent last.[24]

Like Sylvia Plath, Virginia Woolf, and Adrienne Rich, Sexton has shown her a path to follow, tentative steps toward finding the "tiny fragments / [that] survive, mangled into our language" ("Artemis," 23–24). Broumas does not frame her tales in any of the ways that Sexton does; she doesn't begin the sequence with a frame-tale or start each tale with an ironic contemporary prologue. But she consistently transposes the traditional images of the tales she choose into a new and often unfamiliar key.

Broumas's version of "Rapunzel" is deeply influenced by Sexton's "Rapunzel" and begins with an epigraph from Sexton's poem:

> *A woman*
> *who loves a woman*
> *is forever young.* (59)

Like Sexton, Broumas focuses on the relationship between the older woman/ witch and Rapunzel; like Sexton, she sees it as life-giving. Unlike Sexton, however, she elides the heterosexual romance plot almost completely: there is no seductive prince with his "dancing stick" (*T* 41; *CP* 248) in this Rapunzel's story. Broumas does refer to other women who

> grew to confuse greed
> with hunger, learned to grow thin on the bitter
> root, the mandrake, on their sills. (59)

Throughout the poem she transforms Sexton's surprisingly delicate, even timid sketches of the sexual bonds between Rapunzel and the witch into intense evocations of lesbian passion, into what Stanley Kunitz calls in his foreword "the alphabet of the body" (xii). Sexton's poem reproduces the vision of the older witch, abandoned; Broumas's speaker is the younger woman, who traces their sexual encounters with abandon:

> I'll break the hush
> of our cloistered garden, our harvest continuous
> as a moan, the tilled bed luminous
> with the future
> yield. Red
>
> vows like tulips. Rows
> upon rows of kisses from all lips.   (60)

This Rapunzel's rapt evocation of sexual ecstasy shatters the cloistered "hush" that still surrounds it in Sexton's version. Broumas plays with the metaphorical links between "tilled" garden beds and other beds, on the aural connections between "tulips," two lips, and "all lips."[25] Unlike the bleak and bitter encounters she sketches in the middle of the poem, this one fulfills deep feminine yearnings for "our lush perennial" (59). Broumas rewrites as profoundly natural sexuality that has been written off as "unnatural" or perverse.

For her "Cinderella" Broumas again chooses an epigraph from Sexton's work, this time from "Welcome Morning" in Sexton's posthumous volume *The Awful Rowing toward God* (1975):

> . . . *the joy that isn't shared*
> *I heard, dies young.*   (57)[26]

Broumas's Cinderella, like Sexton's in the last lines of her Cinderella poem, is isolated from other women in the house of the prince, frozen in place in a glass bell:

> I am the one allowed in
>
> to the royal chambers, whose small foot conveniently
> fills the slipper of glass.   (57)

But, unlike Sexton's Cinderella, she is not a mechanical doll or an eternal Bobbsey twin; she can still make choices and reject her privileged and isolated status:

> Give
> me my ashes. A cold stove, a cinder-block pillow, wet
> canvas shoes in my sisters', my sisters' hut. Or I swear
>
> I'll die young
> like those favored before me, hand-picked each one
> for her joyful heart.
>
> (58)

Cinderella's wish for "wet canvas shoes" to replace the icy and fragile glass slipper is part of her longing to rejoin her "sisters," whatever rough world they may inhabit. Though adept at "cracking / the royal code" (57), the official tongue men speak as "their fathers' language" (57), she seems to be attempting to find or bring to consciousness a different language, one that will reconnect her with other women. Her versions of "Snow White" and of "Rumplestiltskin [*sic*]" chronicle this attempt: "How to describe / what we didn't know / exists . . . Approximations. / The words we need are extinct" ("Rumplestiltskin," 65).

Another poem that searches for these "extinct" words is Broumas's startling version of "Little Red Riding Hood." Sexton reframes the tale as a story about deception and deceivers; Broumas reconceives it as a drama of birth and return to the mother. She boldly recasts the well-known images and dialogue of the tale:

> Dressed in my red hood, howling, I went—
>
> evading
> the white-clad doctor and his fancy
>   claims: microscope,
> stethoscope, scalpel, all
> the better to see with, to hear,
> and to eat—straight from your hollowed basket
> into the midwife's skirts.
>
> (67)

Little Red Riding Hood's red hood becomes a "mantle of blood" (67) surrounding the newborn; the basket she is usually given by her mother becomes her mother's womb or pelvis. And the wolf with his palaver is transformed into a frightening male obstetrician with his shiny instruments, an obstetrician who is not allowed to intervene between the mother and the midwife. (In her poem "Demeter" Broumas speaks of "the terror / of new-borns" [22].) This child moves directly from one woman to another, as she does later in her life. She takes the mother's admonition to stay on the path and watch out for wolves, prominent in many versions of the tale, as a warning to avoid all men:

> I kept to the road, kept
> the hood secret, kept what it sheathed more
> secret still. I opened
> it only at night, and with other women . . .
>
> (68)

The red hood is transformed again in the course of the poem: at first the mother's blood that envelops the newborn, it now becomes the hood of the clitoris, the sheath that guards the source of her sexual pleasure. Throughout the sequence, Broumas re-forms images from the best-known fairy tales that haunt the Western imagination—extracting them from one set of narrative patterns and shaping them into new forms in another. Her fairy-tale poems do not end with a wedding ceremony or even with the familiar stasis but rather, as in "Little Red Riding Hood," with pity for the "lost, flower-gathering sisters" (68) who have not been taught to evade the dangerous wolves. As Mary J. Carruthers says, "she takes the stance of an 'archaeologist,' discovering the fragments and remnants of a lost . . . language"[27] This is particularly true of her poems that go back to Greek myth, but it is true as well of her revisions of fairy tales. Like Mueller, Wolf, and Steedman, Broumas isolates and transforms the iconic images we all recognize into letters of an unfamiliar language. As she says, "to use words that have never been used to describe our lives *to* describe our lives makes those words ours."[28] Her transliterations demand that we read the images in a new cultural framework, a framework that not only questions the traditional patterns of what Sexton calls "that story" but creates new patterns for stories women can tell.

V

In one sense, creating new stories out of fragments of other stories is nothing new. As Angela Carter has said, in her introduction to *The Old Wives' Fairy Tale Book*,

The chances are, the story was put together in the form we have it, more or less, out of all sorts of bits of other stories long ago and far away, and has been tinkered with, had bits added to it, lost other bits, got mixed up with other stories.[29]

Every tale we now know as a fairy tale or "old wives' tale" has probably been pieced together from various narrative sources and fragments. Each teller splices those story threads together for his or her own purposes.

But the projects that Mueller, Wolf, Steedman, and Broumas have been engaged in (fortunately they're all still alive as I write this) are a special instance of this ancient practice. They all reinterpret the powerful images that crowd the tales, sometimes turning the tales inside out. They do not discard the tales that the early feminist critics found so threatening, but rather show us how to use them. As Salman Rushdie said of Angela Carter, "She opens an old story for us, like an egg, and finds the new story, the now-story we want to hear, within."[30] Their transliterations transform the tales into powerful "now-stories."

Carter's own collection of stories based on fairy tales, *The Bloody Chamber* (1979), is a particularly compelling instance of this practice. Sometimes her transformations of old tales are subtle and delicate, as in "The Courtship of Mr. Lyon." In this version she keeps the outlines of the traditional tale of "Beauty and the Beast," first written down by Gabrielle de Villeneuve as part of her novel *La jeune Amériquaine, et les contes marins* (1740), much condensed by Beaumont in her *Magasin des enfants* (1756). Beauty's father, still a ruined merchant, spends the night in the Beast's castle (after his ancient car breaks down), steals a rose to bring back to his daughter, and is forced to promise her to the Beast in exchange for his release. The Beast is as usual transformed into a man through Beauty's faithfulness and love.[31] The details of Carter's version are subtly twentieth-century (the car, whiskey and soda, a garage, a photograph, a shrilling telephone), but most of the tale takes place in an enchanted landscape, nearly frozen in time: "a miniature, perfect, Palladian house that seemed to hide itself shyly behind snow-laden skirts of an antique cypress" (*BC* 42; *BB* 144).[32]

Throughout the tale, Carter refers to other stories, not only to earlier written versions of "Beauty and the Beast," but to Carroll's *Alice in Wonderland* and, perhaps surprisingly, to the tales of the *conteuses*. Beauty "browsed in a book she had found in the rosewood revolving bookcase, a collection of courtly and elegant French fairy tales about white cats who were transformed princesses and fairies who were birds" (*BC* 46; *BB* 148). Beauty does not find these tales absorbing: "she . . . found herself yawning; she discovered she was bored" (*BC* 46; *BB* 148). Like her predecessors, the *conteuses*, Carter alludes to other tales in the tradition; like the *conteuses*, she often subtly mocks them.[33] And yet she derives many of the details of this story from their tales, particularly from d'Aulnoy's "The White Cat": Beauty is waited on by "an army of invisibles," and "all the natural laws of the world were held in suspension" (*BC* 47; *BB* 150). This revision of "Beauty and the Beast" is both mockery of and homage to the Frenchwomen who wrote earlier versions of the tales. Carter's imagination is always set in fascinating motion by earlier writers; she both needs and transforms them.

As she said in the "Afterword" to her earlier collection of tales, *Fireworks* (1974),

> I'd always been fond of Poe, and Hoffman—Gothic tales, cruel tales, tales of wonder, tales of terror, fabulous narratives that deal directly with the imagery of the unconscious—mirrors; the externalized self; forsaken castles; haunted forests; forbidden sexual objects. . . . [The tale] interprets everyday experience through a system of imagery derived from subterranean areas behind everyday experience. (*BB* 459)

Literary fairy tales tend to explore the same realms of psychic experience as Poe's and Hoffmann's tales; they often deal with the repressed and the forbidden. Throughout *The Bloody Chamber*, Carter both acknowledges and goes beyond the tales she knows.

For example, in her second version of "Beauty and the Beast," "The Tiger's Bride," Carter rings startling changes on the traditional tale. Again she borrows details from the "Beauty and the Beast" tradition: for example, the heroine often gazes into a magic mirror that shows her her father, this time in all his greed and self-absorption. As in "The Courtship of Mr. Lyon," Carter depends on our knowledge of the many earlier version of the tale for her effects. But "The Courtship of Mr. Lyon," for all its subtle revisions, could almost be called a "duplicate" in Jack Zipes's terms. In "The Tiger's Bride," however, Carter reworks the tale we know completely. The father recklessly, callously loses his daughter to the Beast at cards; at the end the daughter does not transform the Beast into a man but is herself transformed into an animal with "beautiful fur" (*BC* 67; *BB* 169).[34] As the tale draws to a close, she begins to see herself not as a human being at all but as a "mechanical doll," mirrored and travestied by a "clockwork twin" or "simulacrum" of herself who is sent to wait on her (*BC* 60; *BB* 162). To be human is to be a selfish machine without a heart; to acknowledge her animal nature and her sexual desire for the Beast in all his natural "beastliness" is to be transformed.

As Cristina Bacchilega points out, both of Carter's Beauties are still entrapped in a rather narrow set of narrative possibilities; both, in spite of their moments of agency, or the exercise of "will[s] of their own" (*BB* 148), are still handed from father to male partner as the traditional narrative framework demands.[35] Though the ending changes, the narrative premises remain the same. We might remember here the ending of d'Aulnoy's tale "Le Mouton": the ram or "Beast" dies at the end because Beauty has been too busy being reconciled with her father to remember to save him. But this dystopic, unhappy ending also reinforces the paternal authority that d'Aulnoy often tries to undermine.[36] Carter's "happy" endings, however different, both still participate in the "traffic in women," that old plot that regulates the economics of the sexual exchange from father to husband.[37]

In "The Bloody Chamber," however, the title story of the collection, Carter imagines a different plot. Drawing on the tangled skein of tales that form the Bluebeard tradition, she sets her tale at the turn of the last century in Paris. The innocent heroine's father is dead. She and her mother have lived in poverty, eking out a living through her mother's inventive courage and the heroine's talent for playing the piano. Her mother has sold her jewels, "even her wedding ring" (*BC* 13; *BB* 117), to pay for her daughter's musical education, trading one of the last tokens of her apparently happy marriage to help her daughter forge an independent career. But her daughter sells herself—half-knowing what she is doing—to a much older libertine, who delights in late-nineteenth-century decadent pornography and has chosen her as his innocent, sacrificial Saint Cecilia, his "virgin of the arpeggios" (*BC* 36; *BB* 139). After their marriage, they go to his family castle by the sea in Brittany, where all at first goes more or less as the traditional versions of the tale do: his departure, her use of the forbidden key, and her discovery of the chamber with the bodies of his three previous wives, "that private slaughterhouse of his" (*BC* 30; *BB* 133). He returns and realizes at once that she has disobeyed him; he then orders her to prepare to be executed. But here Carter changes the pattern, for the heroine is rescued at the last moment not by her brothers or by her sister, as in most earlier ver-

sions of the tale, but by her mother—who has divined by what Carter calls
"maternal telepathy" (*BC* 40; *BB* 143) that she must come to her rescue.
The rescue is melodramatic, even stagy; Carter explicitly compares it to
"those clockwork tableaux of Bluebeard that you see in glass cases at fairs"
(*BC* 40; *BB* 142). Her mother erupts like a Verdi opera into the Wagnerian
Liebestod of the execution scene; as Mary Kaiser points out, "she is woman-
as-avenger on a grand scale."[38] Like Broumas, Carter stresses the return to
the mother: at the end of the tale, the heroine lives not only with her new
husband, the blind piano-tuner from the castle, but with her mother too. But
Carter also troubles this return by suggesting its theatrical excess and magical unreality.

The peace in which the three live at the end is not untroubled, either.
When her Bluebeard husband learns that she has entered the forbidden and
bloody chamber, he presses the traditional stained key on her forehead,
where it leaves a permanent heart-shaped mark, "like the caste mark of a
Brahmin woman. Or the mark of Cain" (*BC* 36; *BB* 139). This stain reflects
her half-conscious complicity in her own near-destruction, the guilt that re-
sides within her apparent sexual innocence. It is the visible sign of her terrible self-knowledge that comes even before their marriage: "[F]or the first
time in my innocent and confined life, I sensed in myself a potentiality for
corruption that took my breath away" (*BC* 11; *BB* 115). Carter returns to the
stain in the last paragraph:

> No paint nor powder, no matter how thick or white, can mask that red
> mark on my forehead; I am glad he [the blind piano-tuner] cannot see it—
> not for fear of his revulsion, since I know he sees me clearly with his
> heart—but, because it spares my shame. (*BC* 41; *BB* 143)

In this tale Carter plays with two feminine stereotypes: the passive young
woman as stainless innocent, the active older woman/mother as rescuer out
of some heroic epic, as aging martial maid or turn-of-the-century, petrifying
Medusa. But throughout, and particularly at the end, she returns to the heroine's clear-eyed acknowledgment of her own susceptibility to sexual perver-
sion, her not unwilling participation in her first husband's sadomasochistic,
theatrical scripts: "I clung to him as though only the one who had inflicted
the pain could comfort me for suffering it" (*BC* 18; *BB* 121).[39] He praises her
"thin white face, with its promise of debauchery only a connoisseur could

detect" (*BC* 20; *BB* 123). Like the white lilies that are ever-present in the story, both in their bedroom and in the bloody chamber itself—even like her husband, who is white and identified with the lilies—she is both white and darkly sensual, ready to fester. Though some feminist critics have singled out this story for praise because it ends with the intervention of and a return to an active, heroic mother, its final implications are far more disturbing.[40] Carter examines and questions the sentimental, essentialist notions that women are, can be, or should be sexually "pure" and that there is a special kind of communication between mother and daughter. In rewriting the Bluebeard story, she challenges us to acknowledge that the virtuous victim does not, cannot exist; that the heroic, avenging mother is a fantasy, too, only to be expressed in the overblown language of heroic rescue; that even the blind piano-tuner, sensitive and nurturing though he is, is really a nonce figure, composed and fictionalized as the husband's opposite, not as a possibility in the real world. She uses romance figures to refuse romance; as she once said, "I'm in the de-mythologising business."[41]

To demythologize for Carter is in part to cite different versions of each myth—gathering bits and pieces from various versions of the tales, echoing fragments from the European literature of the past. It is also to site each story in a particular time and place, often in *The Bloody Chamber* mysterious rooms of decaying buildings in the late nineteenth or early twentieth century. Citing and siting, she welds the fragmentary pieces into startling new wholes. All of her stories in *The Bloody Chamber* transform well-known tales, in her many virtuoso voices and narrative styles. But since the last story, "Wolf Alice," is in many ways a reversed, wavering mirror image of the first story, "The Bloody Chamber," it seems a good place to end.

"Wolf Alice" tells the stories of a solitary feral child who gradually discovers her womanhood, and of a solitary necrophiliac Duke who acts out the mythic role of the ghoulish werewolf or Dracula figure. Neither seems fully human; both are eventually transformed, like Lewis Carroll's Alice, by a looking glass. The tale is not really a "Little Red Riding Hood" story, like the two tales that precede it in *The Bloody Chamber*: "The Werewolf" and "The Company of Wolves." Rather, as in many of her other tale transformations, Carter plays with shards of fairy tales and other stories in order to suggest the narrow boundaries between the beastly and the human and the importance of acknowledging our animal nature. As she says,

the wolves had tended her because they knew she was an imperfect wolf;
we secluded her in animal privacy out of fear of her imperfection because
it showed us what we might have been. (*BC* 122; *BB* 224)

As always, Carter's choric "we" underscores the conventional, inhumane
thought patterns of the human society that excludes the feral child. Unlike
the wolves, "we" are unable to nurture a child who threatens our belief in
what we are. Part of Carter's project in *The Bloody Chamber* is to investigate
this "we"'s certainties or "the social fictions that regulate our lives—what
Blake called the 'mind-forged manacles.' "[42]

As the child gradually becomes more human, however, she retains the
generosity and accepting nature of the wolves. When the Duke is injured
by a villager whose bride's corpse had been desecrated, she instinctively
undertakes to heal him:

> Then, she was as pitiful as her gaunt grey mother; she leapt upon his bed
> to lick, without hesitation, without disgust, with a quick tender gravity,
> the blood and dirt from his cheek and forehead.
>
> The lucidity of the moonlight lit the mirror propped against the red
> wall; the rational glass, the master of the visible, impartially recorded the
> crooning girl. . . . [and], as if brought into being by her soft, moist, gentle
> tongue, finally, the face of the Duke. (*BC* 126; *BB* 227–28)

Though dressed in a wedding dress she has found in the castle, now a mirror
image of the dead bride, the feral woman has not forgotten her wolfly pity
and gentleness. And it is her animal instincts that bring the Duke back into
the visible world, that restore or bring him back into his human self. At the
end of "The Tiger's Bride," Beauty feels herself losing "all the skins of a life
in the world" and gaining "a nascent patina of shining hairs" (*BC* 67; *BB*
169). At the end of "The Company of Wolves," the Red Riding Hood figure
sleeps "sweet and sound . . . in granny's bed, between the paws of the tender
wolf" (*BC* 118; *BC* 220). In all three stories, Carter points out that many of
our fairy tales insist on the separation of man and beast, and on the necessity
of remetamorphosis from beast figure to man. Part of her project is to question that separation, to show the inhumanity of our wish to ignore our animal
nature. Though critics have often insisted that this only means acknowledging our primal, earthy sexuality, Carter goes beyond this simple equation. She both questions the meaning of "human" and stresses the complex

Blakean beauty of the tiger. As Margaret Atwood once said, "she does have a yen for tigerhood."[43]

The life-giving, transforming mirror of "Wolf Alice" redeems, or at least gives us an alternative for, the dozens of mirrors in "The Bloody Chamber" that cruelly reflect and multiply the desires of the monstrous husband and his supposedly innocent bride. Carter suggests that it is the site or position of the mirror that matters, and that the Duke's moldering castle is finally a more human and humane place than the lush, decadent, highly civilized bedroom of the Bluebeard Marquis. Though neither the feral Wolf Alice nor the Duke ever speaks, their mute sympathy questions our easy belief in the healing powers of the word and the primacy of language. Carter is a mistress of the word, but her linguistic virtuosity "provokes unease" ("Afterword to *Fireworks*," *BB* 459) even as it compels our admiration. For Carter, "transliteration" means in part creating structures that call the primacy of the word and the letter into question. Often—as she and Broumas and Donoghue all point out—the language she needs does not exist; she can approach it only by negation, by "provoking unease" about the linguistic structures that surround us.[44]

Twice-Told Tales

> In Colcha embroidery, I learn,
> women use ravelled yarn from old wool blankets
> to trace out scenes on homespun woollen sacks—
> our ancient art of making out of nothing—
> or is it making the old life serve the new?
> Adrienne Rich, "Turning the Wheel"[1]

IN HER recent essay called "Fairy Stories," A. S. Byatt comments on the dazzling possibilities of the literary fairy tale:

> The literary fairy tale is a wonderful, versatile hybrid form, which draws on primitive apprehensions and narrative motifs, and then uses them to think consciously about human beings and the world. Both German Romantic fairy tales and the self-conscious playful courtly stories of seventeenth-century French ladies combine the new thought of the time with the ancient tug of forest and castle, demon and witch, vanishing and shape-shifting, loss and restoration.[2]

Both Byatt and Carter (in her story "The Courtship of Mr. Lyon") place themselves explicitly in this long hybrid tradition. Fabulous fabulists, they both recognize the power of the strategies earlier writers (Straparola, Basile, the *conteuses*) used to transform the tales and scraps of tales they knew in order "to think consciously about human beings and the world." Following their predecessors, the *conteuses*, they know that artifice, verbal magic, and old, powerful images can help them excavate the psychic truths and social horrors beneath traditional twice-told tales, "through a system of imagery derived from subterranean areas behind everyday experience," as Carter puts it.[3]

Like Byatt and Carter, many other late-twentieth-century writers have returned to the fairy tale, mined its imagery, questioned its usual pieties.

Most of them, consciously or not, have produced versions that do not hark back to the strategies of writers like Perrault and the Grimms; their tales are not "distressed" to seem ancient, timeless, or in some way authentic. Rather, they draw on the "other tradition" of the fairy tale, the tradition I've tried to describe and understand throughout this book. Writers as different as Donald Barthelme, Robert Coover, Jeanette Winterson, Margaret Atwood, Monique Wittig, Caryl Churchill—writers I could have included here—all have chosen fairy-tale plots and recurring motifs as the ground for variation, experimentation, and transformation.[4] They present their tales as versions of versions, framing them in new ways, transliterating their language and images into new constellations. In one sense we could call their work postmodern, a parodic and often self-parodic play of mirrors and frames, as Cristina Bacchilega has.[5] But I want to stress their connection to the tradition of the literary fairy tale (which may in fact be the only tradition of the fairy tale we actually have), its complex forms and strategies. All these writers know that they are retelling old stories, and that each retelling is both a new version of an old tale and, simultaneously, a new beginning.[6]

One of the most powerful recent versions of an old story, "The Goose Girl" (KHM 89), is Adrienne Rich's title poem in her 1984 collection *The Fact of a Doorframe*. In this poem, written in 1974, Rich celebrates the solidity of wooden doorframes, arches, portals: "something to hold / onto with both hands" in times of trouble and suffering. In the middle stanza of the three-stanza poem, she recalls the central image of "The Goose Girl," the horse's head that speaks:

> *I think of the story*
> *of the goose-girl who passed through the high gate*
> *where the head of her favorite mare*
> *was nailed to the arch*
> *and in a human voice*
> If she could see thee now, thy mother's heart would break
> *said the head*
> *of Falada.*[7]

Rich frames the story of Falada in the center of her poem, in a context of human despair and suffering. (In this formal move, she echoes the framing techniques that the *conteuses* and her contemporaries have used to give tales new significance, as we saw in chapter 4.) Falada's voice intensifies the misery of the goose girl, a princess betrayed by her serving maid—but, at the same time, Falada's repeated speech eventually leads to her rescue from servitude. The wooden arch, framed in the poem, also frames both Falada's head and the goose girl.

Rich then goes on to make the wooden archway and, implicitly, Falada's faithful, repeated voice itself an image for the making of poetry:

> Now, again, poetry,
> violent, arcane, common,
> hewn of the commonest living substance
> into archway, portal, frame
> I grasp for you, your blood-stained splinters, your
> ancient and stubborn poise
> —as the earth trembles—
> burning out from the grain.

To write poetry is to shape the "commonest living substance"—wood or words—into a frame for human experience. These frames are always imperfect, splintered, bloodstained, torn by suffering—but also poised, stable, something to grasp. Both "common" and "arcane," familiar and unfamiliar, poetry reframes the old words and the old stories, transliterating images we all know into a new language.

Like many of her contemporaries, then, Rich finds in fairy-tale images a source of power and of transformation. Rather than simply retell the story of "The Goose Girl," she focuses on one central iconic moment, a moment that her readers will certainly remember, but places it in a new context and reads it in a new way. Falada's speech is no longer merely the voice of a faithful and articulate animal, so common in our fairy-tale tradition, but has become a representation of the language of poetry.

As an introduction or portal to her collection, printed facing the title page, the poem suggests Rich's continuing struggle to find words for her complex social vision. Lesbian, feminist, social activist, she writes poetry that continually questions existing social beliefs and practices—and acknowledges the pain inherent in such questioning. Like many of her contemporaries, she finds a resource and a stimulus in fairy-tale imagery, from "The Snow Queen" to "The Goose Girl." Sometimes, early in her career, she apparently tried to avoid the painful realities that fairy tales make evident: "Unspeakable fairy tales ebb like blood through my head," rarely acknowledged in the smooth and sanctioned surface of her verse, "ebbing" and disappearing as they were suppressed.[8] More recently, however, she figures herself as

> a woman's voice singing old songs
> with new words, with a quiet bass, a flute
> plucked and fingered by women outside the law.[9]

Making new out of old, finding new words for old melodies, singing "outside the law" that tends to restrict and misinterpret such singing, Rich's work could stand for the generations of women, from the 1690s to the 1990s, who have rewritten fairy tales in order to reinterpret and reorder the world. Like Angela Carter, they turn the old stories into new stories that are "now-stories," in Salman Rushdie's phrase, stories that refract and criticize the world they find both enchanting and unbearable.[10] They make "the old serve the new," as the Colcha weavers do in my epigraph from another of Rich's poems. Just as d'Aulnoy, Lhéritier, and Bernard mocked and subverted the apparently immutable sex roles and marriage practices of their day in their *contes de fées*, Rich and her contemporaries use fairy tales to question the social patterns and often the heterosexual expectations of our own. Telling tales twice (or thrice, or four times), they all force us to reconsider the pieties of our time. They reveal the cracks and fissures in the old bottles, and sometimes—as Angela Carter hoped—make them explode.

We may now have "machines to do our dreaming for us," as Angela Carter once complained.[11] But the sea of fairy tales that surrounds us—in collections of tales, cartoons, movies, advertisements, sayings—remains a vast reservoir of well-known images, characters, and plots. Fairy tales are the stories we still have in common, stories we know others know. Though most allusions are chancy in contemporary culture, allusions to tales like "Snow White" or "Beauty and the Beast" or "Sleeping Beauty" or "Cinderella" or "Little Red Riding Hood" are a sure thing. We can refer to these stories and expect to be understood. As Karl Kroeber has said, "each retelling of a story permits the articulation of deeper possibilities that exist because they were *not* expressed in the original telling."[12] As they retell the fairy tales we all know, contemporary writers fill in gaps, reverse traditional situations, and imagine ways the stories could have been otherwise. As they contemplate the cultural forms older versions reflect, they see what needs to be seen again and seen afresh—and show it to us.

 NOTES

INTRODUCTION
ONCE, NOT LONG AGO

1. Shuman and Briggs, "Introduction," 112–13. Cristina Bacchilega, in her *Postmodern Fairy Tales*, has made good use of their points.

2. See Susan Stewart, "Notes on Distressed Genres" in *Crimes of Writing*, particularly 66–70 and 84–86.

3. I find it sad, but significant, that a recent collection of fairy tales edited by Maria Tatar—*The Classic Fairy Tales*, a Norton Critical Edition that appeared in 1999—includes no tales by the women writers who wrote tales at the same time as Charles Perrault in France in the 1690s, even though they have been much studied in the last ten years. Tatar includes Beaumont's condensed version of "Beauty and the Beast" (1756), but she pays virtually no attention to the many tales written by Frenchwomen that preceded it. Just as this book was going to press, however, Norton published another Critical Edition—*The Great Fairy Tale Tradition*, edited by Jack Zipes—that includes a good selection of tales by the *conteuses*.

4. Tatar, *The Hard Facts*, 33.

5. Jacob and Wilhelm Grimm, *Kinder- und Hausmärchen*, no. 12. All citations of the Grimms' tales in the text will use the abbreviation *KHM* and a tale number keyed to the final 1857 edition. Quotations from the preface to the Grimms' collection are based on the Rölleke and Marquardt edition listed in the bibliography.

6. Lüthi, *Once upon a Time*, 119.

7. The most accessible discussions of these theories are in Tatar's *Hard Facts*, particularly 62–72, and Peter Brooks's *Reading for the Plot*, particularly 11–23. Brooks uses the Grimms' tale "Allerleirauh" (All kinds of fur) as the paradigm for his investigation of nineteenth-century narrative. See, however, Susan Winnett's sharp feminist critique of Brooks's narratology as based on Freud's descriptions of male physiological erotic experience and "what men want" ("Coming Unstrung")

8. Todorov, *The Fantastic*, 163. Vladimir Propp's sketch of the form of the tale or "skaz" in *Morphology of the Folktale* begins with villainy or lack and ends in equilibrium. (See Nancy Canepa's discussion in *From Court to Forest*, 20.) But there is always an implied equilibrium or at least stasis in the opening paragraphs. See also Anny Crunelle-Vanrigh in "The Logic of the Same and *Différance*": "Fairy tales are informed by closure, a movement from change to permanence. Their plots move from

an initial, pernicious metamorphosis to a stable identity that must and will be reached or recaptured" (116–17).

9. The essay is most readily available in English in a collection of Benjamin's essays called *Illuminations*, ed. Hannah Arendt, 83–109. My in-text references are to this edition. In German it appears in his *Gesammelte Schriften*, vol. 2, pt. 2, pp. 438–65. For specific discussions of the essay, see particularly Hans-Heino Ewers, "Erzählkunst und Kinderliteratur," and Zipes, "Revisiting Benjamin's 'The Storyteller,' " in *Happily Ever After*, 129–42.

10. In this passage Benjamin uses the word *Märchen*, which Zohn translates as "fairy tale," Zipes in "Revisiting Benjamin's 'The Storyteller' " as "folk tale," and Ruth Bottigheimer in *Grimms' Bad Girls and Bold Boys* as "fairy or folk tale." When Benjamin translated his own storyteller essay into French, he used the word *conte* ("tale" or "story") for *Märchen* (see *Schriften*, vol. 2, pt. 3, p. 1304). But when Benjamin speaks in that same passage of the traditional ending "und wenn sie nicht gestorben sind, so leben sie heute noch" (and if they're not dead, they're living still—a German concluding formula like our "and so they lived happily ever after"), he seems to me to be thinking of the *Märchen* brought together and popularized by the Grimms and now known in English as fairy tales—so I have decided to retain Zohn's translation.

"The Storyteller" essay grew out of Benjamin's long fascination with the *Märchen* as a form, though earlier, in his review of a book called *Alte vergessene Kinderbücher* (1924), he spoke of it in less reverent terms as "a waste product [*Abfall*]—perhaps the most powerful to be found in the spiritual life of humanity: a waste product that emerges from the growth and decay of the saga." *Selected Writings*, vol. 1 (1923–1926), 408. See also passages in Benjamin's letters of 1925 to Gershom Scholem and Hugo von Hofmannsthal (*Briefe*, 1:383–84, 388–89, 394–95).

11. Tolkien, "On Fairy Stories." See also Jacqueline Rose, *The Case of Peter Pan*, for discussion of the persistent association of childhood with cultural infancy, particularly 9 and 56–57.

12. For comments on the relationship of this essay to Benjamin's whole cultural and messianic project, see Susan Buck-Morss, *The Dialectics of Seeing*, 336–40. For a mordant and sometimes devastating critique of Benjamin's postlapsarian assumptions about modernity, see Leo Bersani, *The Culture of Redemption*, 47–63. As Bersani points out, Benjamin's "thought is full of pairs—with one term referring to something inauthentic but familiar, the other to something authentic but lost" (49). Thanks to Martin Harries for suggesting I read this book.

13. Marcia Lieberman's " 'Some Day My Prince Will Come' " (1972), a reaction to Alison Lurie's more sanguine assessment of the effect of fairy tales on women's expectations, was one of the first to point out the ideology behind many of the Grimms' and Andersen's tales. Madonna Kolbenschlag's *Kiss Sleeping Beauty Good-Bye* (1979) and Colette Dowling's *The Cinderella Complex* (1981) popularized the feminist critique of fairy tales. Bottigheimer's "Tale-Spinners" (1982) examines the "faint cries of distress and fatigue" she hears in some of the Grimms' tales. Zipes's anthology *Don't Bet on the Prince* (1987) includes many feminist retellings of tradi-

tional tales, as well as a critical preface and several important articles, among them Lieberman's and another early one by Karen Rowe called "Feminism and Fairy Tales" (1979).

14. Nancy Walker, *The Disobedient Writer*, 4.

15. The poet Adrienne Rich wrote an essay in 1972 that clarifies this process of "re-vision": "When We Dead Awaken: Writing as Re-vision," now collected in her volume of essays *On Lies, Secrets, and Silence*, 33–49.

16. See Bate, *The Burden of the Past and the English Poet* (1970), and Bloom, *The Anxiety of Influence* (1973).

17. The classic book in this vein is Sandra Gilbert and Susan Gubar's *The Madwoman in the Attic* (1979), a book that uses the figures of Snow White and her deadly mother/stepmother as images for the impossible choices the canon offers women writers. For early and influential articles that outline critical approaches to the process of canon revision, see Annette Kolodny, "A Map for Rereading: Or Gender and the Interpretation of Literary Texts" (1980) and "Dancing through the Minefield: Some Observations on the Theory, Practice, and Politics of a Feminist Literary Criticism" (1980), both handily reprinted in *The New Feminist Criticism*, ed. Elaine Showalter, 46–62 and 144–67.

18. Zipes, *Fairy Tale as Myth / Myth as Fairy Tale*, 9.

19. In *Retelling Stories, Reframing Culture*, John Stephens and Robyn McCallum define the process of revision this way: "The ideological effect of a retold text is generated from a three-way relationship between the already-given story ["the pretext"], the metanarrative(s) which constitute its top-down framing, and its bottom-up discoursal processes" (4). Even if we could visualize this abstract and confusing process, I think their formulation relies too heavily on the idea of *one* given story, an urtext or original. As Barbara Herrnstein Smith has pointed out in her article "Narrative Versions, Narrative Theories," our conception of narrative tends to be dualistic, particularly so when we talk about "original" narratives and revisions: "[W]hat narratologists refer to as the basic stories or deep-plot structures of narratives are often not abstract, disembodied, or subsumed entities but quite manifest, material, and particular retellings—and thus versions—of those narratives" (218). Or, as Nelson Goodman puts it, "When I speak of several versions of the same or virtually the same story, I am by no means conceding that there is some underlying story, some deep structure, that is not itself a version" ("The Telling and the Told," 801).

20. Bacchilega, *Postmodern Fairy Tales*, 146, 23.

21. Canepa, "Basile's Quest for the Literary Fairy Tale," 40.

22. See Bakhtin, *The Dialogic Imagination*, particularly the chapter "From the Prehistory of Novelistic Discourse," 41–83, and the glossary.

23. My thanks to John Connolly, colleague and dean, for this thought-provoking question after an informal talk I gave at Smith in the "Liberal Arts Lunch" series in 1996.

24. I might have used the terms "primary" and "secondary," echoing the division in the theory of the epic between epics that have oral and traditional roots and epics

that are literary imitations and reworkings of earlier oral material. But this would reinforce some of the distinctions that I want to argue against—between older and newer forms of the fairy tale, between traditional or "folk" versions and newer versions rooted in the written record. (Given recent research, the distinction may not actually be valid for the epic, either.)

25. Molly Hite, *The Other Side of the Story*, 4. I have omitted the adjective "feminist" at the end of the second sentence ("for the reading and writing of feminist narrative") because "complex" tales are not all feminist by any means. Basile's often misogynist tales, or Donald Barthelme's *Snow White*, or Robert Coover's *Briar Rose* are good examples.

26. See his essay "From Work to Text," in *Image—Music—Text*, particularly 160: "The intertextual in which every text is held, it itself being the text-between of another text, is not to be confused with some origin of the text: to try to find the 'sources,' the 'influences' of a work, is to fall in with the myth of filiation; the citations which go to make up a text are anonymous, untraceable, and yet *already read*: they are quotations without inverted commas." His term "stereophonic" seems very much like Bakhtin's term "heteroglossia."

27. See Lewis Seifert, *Fairy Tales, Sexuality, and Gender*, 8. Seifert also comments on the ways Perrault's tales had become the model for "the" fairy tale by the nineteenth century (228–29 n. 21).

28. Certainly most tales have elements that come from folklore. But, as Michel Butor said in his 1973 essay "On Fairy Tales," "to address oneself immediately to the peasant oral tradition is a way of evading the problem that these tales raise for us" (349). I believe that we need to look first at the tales we know themselves and their relationships with other tales, rather than delve primarily into what Butor calls their folklore elements or "substructure."

29. I have not tried to deal with the many wonderful examples of Victorian fairy-tale telling, partly because some, like the comtesse de Ségur's 1853 *Nouveaux contes de fées pour les petits enfants*, were designed expressly for children (though no less imaginative and even subversive on that account), partly because Nina Auerbach and U. C. Knoepflmacher have dealt with many British ones so well in their collection *Forbidden Journeys*. Knoepflmacher has extended their investigations more recently in his *Ventures into Childland*; he gives splendid examples of tales as reinventions of earlier stories, poems, and novels.

30. For groundbreaking work on these writers in English, see Jeannine Blackwell, "Fractured Fairy Tales" and "Laying the Rod to Rest," and Shawn Jarvis, "The Vanished Woman of Great Influence" and "Trivial Pursuit?"

31. *Shame: A Novel*, 68. In spite of his subtitle, Rushdie persistently refers to his book as a fairy tale or fairy story.

32. I borrow this term from Meaghan Morris, *The Pirate's Fiancée*, 3; there she defines it, quoting Anne Freedman, as the study of "the production of a speaking position, with respect to discursive material that is both given and foreign." Elspeth Probyn's formulation in *Sexing the Self* has also been useful: "The possibility of the

self rests within a filigree of institutional, material, discursive lines that either erase or can be used to enable spaces in which 'we' can be differently spoken" (4). I am interested in the ways women writers have worked with the various discourses of the fairy tale, "both given and foreign," in order to articulate their own place in its history.

33. Warner, *From the Beast to the Blonde*, xxiii.

34. For the uses of the term "negotiation" for feminist literary criticism, see my colleague Ann Rosalind Jones's introduction to her book *The Currency of Eros*.

CHAPTER ONE

FAIRY TALES ABOUT FAIRY TALES: NOTES ON CANON FORMATION

1. DeJean, *Ancients against Moderns*, ix.

2. Showalter, "Toward a Feminist Poetics," in *The New Feminist Criticism*, 129.

3. Guillory's book has had a strange effect on the discussion of the canon; in fact, it has nearly stopped it (except in the popular press). Though it would seem to have a real and negative impact on many of the ongoing projects of feminist literary criticism, few feminist critics have responded to it. I find it surprising, for example, that Lillian Robinson, in her 1997 collection of essays and talks, *In the Canon's Mouth*, makes no reference to Guillory's work, though he mentions an early essay of hers. (She does discuss, at some length, Gilbert and Gubar's satire *Masterpiece Theater*, which appeared two years later, in 1995). The only feminist critic who seems so far to have engaged Guillory's argument in depth is Elizabeth Hanson in "Boredom and Whoredom," particularly 169–72.

I see Guillory's book as an example of so-called postfeminist theory, which, while acknowledging the work of feminist critics, effectively invalidates much of it by denying the existence of, or at least the importance of, the gendered subject (for comments on this move, see Teresa de Lauretis, *Technologies of Gender*, 24) or by arguing that other factors (class, in Guillory's case) have a greater explanatory power than does gender. This is most evident in Guillory's second chapter, a study of what we might call the "coming into canonicity" of Gray's "Elegy in a Country Churchyard" and its pastoral repression of class issues. In the course of the chapter, he has occasion to refer to "one 'Mrs. Barbauld,' a writer no one would regard today as canonical" (103). The patronizing "one," the following reference, and the reiteration of the phrase "Our Poetess" from a quotation all suggest that Guillory himself considers the eighteenth-century canon immutable, and women writers immutably (and perhaps correctly) excluded from it. A look at the "high academic" writers and theorists he treats in the book—from Gray to the New Critics and T. S. Eliot to Paul de Man—tends to confirm this impression.

4. Guillory, *Cultural Capital*, 15.

5. See Margaret W. Ferguson, "Renaissance Concepts of the 'Woman Writer,'" 152–56.

6. Guillory, *Cultural Capital*, 349.

7. Joan DeJean has described the way seventeenth-century novels by Frenchwomen were denied classic status in the course of the eighteenth and nineteenth centuries; their fairy tales were subject to many of the same processes. See particularly DeJean's last chapter, "The Origin of Novels: Gender, Class, and the Writing of French Literary History" (159–99), and a footnote about fairy tales (255–56) in *Tender Geographies*.

8. See Florence Howe, "Introduction: Eliot, Woolf, and the Future of Tradition," in *Tradition and the Talents of Women*, 5: "To write women out is, of course, to be profoundly anti-historical."

9. Gubar, "What Ails Feminist Criticism?" 885 n. 12.

10. For the German text of the Grimms' introduction, see the Rölleke and Marquardt edition of the *KHM*, 1:xvi. All translations from German and from French are mine, unless otherwise indicated in the notes. Here I have modified Tatar's translation of the introduction in Appendix B to *The Hard Facts*, 209.

11. See Susan Stewart, *On Longing*: "Nostalgia is a sadness without an object, a sadness which creates a longing that of necessity is inauthentic because it does not take part in lived experience. . . . Nostalgia, like any form of narrative, is always ideological: the past it seeks has never existed except as narrative, and hence, always absent, that past continually threatens to reproduce itself as a felt lack" (23). Her comments about the temporality of nostalgic narrative are particularly relevant to the Grimms' conception of fairy tales.

12. Rey Chow gives a lucid formulation of this recurring complex of ideas in *Primitive Passions*, 22–23. As she says, these ideas tend to become prominent at times of cultural crisis—as the Napoleonic era certainly was for the Grimms.

13. Stewart, "Scandals of the Ballad," in *Crimes of Writing*, 102–3. Eric Hobsbawm, in his introduction to a collection of essays called *The Invention of Tradition*, makes much the same point. See also Peter Burke, *Popular Culture*: "In this sense the subject of this book was discovered—or is it invented?—by a group of German intellectuals at the end of the eighteenth century" (8). Raymonde Robert has interesting things to say about the construction of the image of a "folk" tale-telling situation, though she does not distinguish between the model Perrault and the Grimms followed and the very different model the women writers constructed (*Le conte de fées littéraire*).

14. The Grimms' opinion has been the dominant one until very recently. In 1975 Jacques Barchilon continued to call them the feminine imitators of Perrault (*Le conte merveilleux français*, 63); in 1985 Volker Klotz dismissed them in a few pages as "the writing beauties at court"(*Das europäische Kunstmärchen*, 79–87); even Zipes claimed in 1983 that these women "followed" Perrault (*Fairy Tales and the Art of Subversion*, 15). Only Zipes's 1991 edition of French fairy tales, *Beauties, Beasts and Enchantment*, Warner's *From the Beast to the Blonde*, and Warner's edition, *Wonder Tales* (a collection of six fairy tales of the 1690s, "done into English" by very well known translators and writers) have really begun to bring these women's tales out of their long obscurity, at least in the Anglo-American world.

15. Villiers, *Entretiens*, dedication. As Gabrielle Verdier says in a note in her article "Figures de la conteuse" (485), "les femmes font les frais de cette affirmation de solidarité masculine" (women pay the price for this affirmation of masculine solidarity).

16. Villiers, *Entretiens*, 109.

17. See particularly Tatar's chapter " 'Teaching Them a Lesson': The Pedagogy of Fear in Fairy Tales," in *Off with Their Heads!*, 22–50. Psychologists still tend to see fairy tales as primarily pedagogical and disciplinary; Bruno Bettelheim's *The Uses of Enchantment* and Cashdan's recent *The Witch Must Die* (which includes a deadpan guide for parents recommending tales to read to a greedy child, to a lazy one, and so on) are good examples.

18. Showalter finds the same motifs in nineteenth-century British criticism of women's writing; see *A Literature of Their Own*, 39–40, 75. Gilbert and Gubar have described similar tropes in vol. 1, *The War of the Words*, of *No Man's Land*, particularly in chapter 3, "Tradition and the Female Talent," 125–62.

19. Villiers, *Entretiens*, 286–87. See Susan Noakes, "On the Superficiality of Women," for an overview of the persistence of this motif, from medieval tracts to the present.

20. Villiers, *Entretiens*, 278–79.

21. See Seifert, *Fairy Tales, Sexuality, and Gender in France*, 86–87, for helpful comments on some of these same passages.

22. For a full exploration and critique of the gendered cultural standards developed in the seventeenth century, see Timothy J. Reiss, *The Meaning of Literature*, particularly chapter 7: "Cultural Quarrels and the Argument of Gender." As Reiss says, "Ideal consumers of high culture, admitted producers of subordinate cultural artifacts [short novels, fairy tales, letters], women now had their role essentially set for a long time to come" (217). Women were not excluded from the cultural sphere but rather were regarded as second-class citizens within it—as they were in the political sphere. For the quarrels about women writers in the 1690s in France, see DeJean, *Ancients against Moderns*, particularly 66–73.

23. Herder, "Von Ähnlichkeit," 557.

24. Wieland's *Die Abenteuer des Don Sylvio von Rosalva* (The adventures of Don Sylvio of Rosalva, 1764) is a loving mockery of d'Aulnoy's tales, just as Cervantes both parodies and celebrates the prose romance of the previous century in *Don Quixote* (1605–1615). Goethe himself refers to the mysterious disembodied hands in d'Aulnoy's tale "La Chatte blanche" in his *Werther* (1774).

25. Walckenaer seems to have been influenced by Germaine de Staël's distinctions between Mediterranean and Northern literatures in her *De la littérature* (1800). Warner rather uncritically repeats some of Walckenaer's derivations and links the "fées" to wisewomen of earlier times, from the queen of Sheba to the Sibyl to Saint Anne. Though the women who wrote fairy tales tended to represent themselves as "fées" or sibyls or Greek goddesses, I believe they did this to distinguish themselves from Mother Goose or the illiterate female teller of tales.

26. Walckenaer, *Lettres*, 33. Further page numbers will be given in the text.

27. Here Walckenaer is quoting Villiers, *Entretiens*, 74.

28. See Tatar's discussion of various imitations of this scene in Germany and England in the nineteenth century, and the accompanying illustrations (figs. 8–14) in *The Hard Facts*, 106–14. She notes that the middle-class grandmother replaced the lower-class nurse in later illustrations, and that she is sometimes represented then as reading from a book. *Caveat*: The frontispiece of Warner's book *From the Beast to the Blonde* is said to be the frontispiece of the first edition of Perrault's prose *Contes* (1697). But it is misidentified; it must be from a later edition.

29. Quoted in Gilbert Rouger's introduction to Perrault's *Contes*, xix.

30. Rouger, introduction to Perrault's *Contes*, xix.

31. See Soriano, *Les contes de Perrault*, 362–63.

32. Ed. Jacques Barchilon (New York: Pierpont Morgan Library, 1956). The provenance and authenticity of this manuscript has been questioned.

33. Perrault, *Contes*, xxx–xxxi. Further page numbers, based on this edition, will be given in the text.

34. See Wendy Wall, *The Imprint of Gender*, chapter 1, for a fascinating discussion of the way sonnet writers toward the end of the sixteenth century in England manipulated codes and "staged" their writing to take advantage of the possibilities inherent in both manuscript and print transmission.

35. See Gerard Genette, "Introduction to the Paratext" and *Seuils*, particularly chapters 1 and 2.

36. Alain Viala, in his 1985 book *Naissance de l'écrivain*, pays almost no attention to the women writers who were also involved in creating the literary sphere and the profession of writer in France—though his conclusions about the way writers formed and marketed themselves are consistently provocative.

37. Though I originally read d'Aulnoy's tales in early editions, all page references and quotations to her tales are keyed to the new and much more accessible, slightly modernized Société des Textes Français Modernes edition, *Contes*, ed. Barchilon and Philippe Hourcade.

38. Murat, *Histoires sublimes et allégoriques*, 216.

39. Auneil, *La tiranie des fées détruite*, 206–7.

40. For most translations of the *conteuses*, I have consulted Zipes's versions in *Beauties, Beasts and Enchantment* but have often modified them. For d'Aulnoy's "La chatte blanche" and "Le serpentin vert," I have usually followed the translations by John Ashbery and A. S. Byatt in the volume *Wonder Tales*, ed. Warner, but have sometimes made small changes.

41. Both tales are easily accessible in French in Rouger's Classiques Garnier edition of Perrault's *Contes*, in English in Zipes's *Beauties, Beasts and Enchantment*. Rouger believes that Bernard's uncle or mentor Fontenelle may have been involved in the production of the tale; though this is not impossible, it does seem typical of the continuing effort of literary historians to show that women in the seventeenth century did/could not write alone. (See DeJean, *Tender Geographies*, 128–29.)

42. Jeanne Roche-Mazon ("De qui est Riquet à la houppe?") claims that Bernard's came first, but her argument is not really convincing. Warner gives no reasons at all for her assumption that Perrault's is a "rebuttal" of Bernard's version (*From the Beast to the Blonde*, 253–55). Dates of publication are not a reliable indicator of priority, since the tales probably circulated in oral form first.

43. I borrow this phrase from Rachel Blau DuPlessis's *Writing beyond the Ending*, though she confines her analysis to twentieth-century women's texts.

44. Compare Lhéritier's tale "Les enchantements de l'éloquence." In the first sentence of the story proper she is deliberately vague about the time the story took place and then goes on to say, "[I]l y avoit un gentilhomme de grande considération qui aimoit passionément sa femme (et c'est ce qui fait encore que je ne puis deviner quel temps c'était)" (Once upon a time there was a distinguished gentleman who loved his wife passionately [and it is this fact that makes it impossible for me to guess when this could have taken place]). (See Lhéritier's *Oeuvres meslées*, 165–66, and the modernized version included in Rouger's edition of Perrault's *Contes*.) The *conteuses* are often mordant about the romance/fairy-tale conventions that have to do with marriage.

45. Zipes, *Fairy Tales and the Art of Subversion*, 34–36. His opinion seems to have changed, however; see his introduction to Bernard's tale in *Beauties, Beasts and Enchantment*, 93–94.

46. Zipes, *Fairy Tales and the Art of Subversion*, 23.

47. It would be possible to argue that Bernard undercuts this interpretation by having a particularly unattractive and jealous character tell this tale in *Inés de Cordoüe*. (I will in fact argue in the next chapter, "Voices in Print," that we ignore the frames of the *conteuses'* tales at our peril.) But the counterideological force of the ending of the tale seems unmistakable.

48. See Tatar's *Hard Facts*, particularly chapter 1, for a study of the changes the Grimms made in the tales in *Kinder- und Hausmärchen* between 1812 and 1857, and Zipes's description of the petrification of tales into myth in the introduction to *Fairy Tale as Myth / Myth as Fairy Tale*, as well as his earlier *Fairy Tales and the Art of Subversion*.

49. Though many recent critics have wanted to see late-seventeenth-century fairy-tale writing as an active intervention on the side of the Moderns in the Quarrel of the Ancients and Moderns, d'Aulnoy's work is not good evidence for that claim.

50. Seifert, "Female Empowerment and Its Limits," 24.

51. Aarne and Thompson, 402. Folklorists and fairy-tale scholars use AT plus a number to refer to Aarne and Thompson's classifications of tales in their invaluable *Motif-Index of Folk-Literature*.

52. See Calvino, *Italian Folktales*, 43–44 (Tale no. 14).

53. This may be a sly reference to the portraits of women hung in the castles built by Catherine de Gonzague and Marie de Médicis, later owned by female leaders of the Fronde. (See Faith Beasley, *Revising Memory*, 226 and 271 n. 53.) Like Madame

de Lafayette's princesse de Clèves at Coulommiers, d'Aulnoy's White Cat is situated in a milieu that emphasizes her connection with an illustrious female history.

54. Did Christina Rossetti know d'Aulnoy's "White Cat"? D'Aulnoy's description of the fruit is a strange anticipation of Rossetti's fruit in "Goblin Market," in its excess, its odd animation, and in the jumbling of fruits that ripen at different times. In both d'Aulnoy's tale and Rossetti's poem, the fruit is the object of obsessive and dangerous female desire.

55. Seifert likens these tiny, apparently worthless objects to the whole tale, and to the *conteuses'* other tales: "When the reader . . . breaks open the seemingly worthless shell of the fairy tale, s/he too discovers a hidden interior that reveals the unsuspected power of an underestimated creator" ("Female Empowerment and Its Limits," 26). But another way to interpret this repeated motif would be to see it as a validation of the *conteuses'* technique of placing stories within stories, the more valuable the more deeply embedded. See also Patricia Hannon, *Fabulous Identities*, 87— though she refers only to the embedding of d'Aulnoy's first fairy tale, "L'île de la félicité," in her novel *Histoire d'Hypolite, comte de Duglas.*

56. Calvino, *Italian Folktales*, 44.

57. For the uses of excess in d'Aulnoy's tales, see Hannon, *Fabulous Identities*, 207–9, 213–14.

58. Seifert, "Female Empowerment and Its Limits," 27.

59. Lang, *The Blue Fairy Book*, 159. He also includes—and ruins—d'Aulnoy's "The Yellow Dwarf" and "The Story of Pretty Goldilocks," an almost unrecognizable version of d'Aulnoy's "La belle aux cheveux d'or." I will discuss the impact of Lang's collections more thoroughly in chapter 3.

60. Lang, *The Blue Fairy Book*, 173.

61. Guillory, *Cultural Capital*, 349.

62. Jane Tompkins's argument in *Sensational Designs*, about nineteenth-century American fiction, is relevant here: "We are always making choices, and hence value judgments, about which books to read, teach, write about, recommend, or have on our shelves. The point is not that these discriminations are baseless; the point is that the grounds on which we make them are not absolute and unchanging but contingent and variable" (193). Though I am not convinced by her specific judgments about nineteenth-century texts, just as some readers will not be convinced that the *conteuses'* tales are "any good," her central points are crucial for any discussion of aesthetic value.

CHAPTER TWO
VOICES IN PRINT: ORALITIES IN THE FAIRY TALE

1. Karen E. Rowe explores the history of this connection, beginning with the story of Philomela, in her essay "To Spin a Yarn."

2. Thanks to my colleague Ann Rosalind Jones for bringing these images to my attention. (Restaurants called "Silent Woman," with a headless female torso as their

logo, still existed in Maine and California in the 1970s; one advertised regularly in the *New Yorker*.)

3. Warner, *From the Beast to the Blonde*, 34. Warner concentrates on the fear of woman's speech and mentions the "headless woman" motif in her third chapter, "Word of Mouth: Gossips II," 27–50.

4. Quoted by Warner, *From the Beast to the Blonde*, 52. Warner details the connections among storks, geese, donkeys, and women at some length.

5. Carter, introduction to *The Old Wives' Fairy Tale Book*, xi.

6. Propp, "The Nature of Folklore," in *Theory and History of Folklore*, 14. Katie Trumpener's analysis of this passage in *Bardic Nationalism* brings out its crucial characteristics: "Folklore, in Propp's description, becomes the mother and prehistoric nurse, and literature the son who suckles himself in infancy on the folkloric but who eventually must leave his mother's arms to follow his destiny" (341 n. 9). Her whole fifth chapter, "The Old Wives' Tale," is a telling deconstruction of German and Anglo-American romantic myths about the nurse figure.

7. Trinh, *Woman, Native, Other*, 121. Trinh's last chapter, "Grandma's Stories," is a remarkable treasure trove of myth about female storytelling; see, for example, these lines: "Salivate, secrete the words. No water, no birth, no death, no life. No speech, no song, no story, no force, no power. The entire being is engaged in the act of speaking-listening-weaving-procreating" (127). Warner repeats a version of it, linking mother's milk and vernacular language, in *From the Beast to the Blonde*, 169–70.

8. See Dégh's *Folktales and Society*, particularly chapter 6, and Schenda's doubts about the association between fairy tales and middle- or lower-class mothers in *Von Mund zu Ohr*, chapter 5.

9. Catherine Velay-Vallantin, "Tales as a Mirror," 130, and see 95–97 and 128–32. Louis Marin's analysis of the frontispiece, in "Les enjeux," also suggests the ways it plays into Perrault's literary strategies in designing his collection.

10. Velay-Vallantin, "Tales as a Mirror," 132.

11. Gabrielle Verdier, in her excellent article "Figures de la conteuse," has studied this frontispiece and others in later editions of d'Aulnoy in order to show that she rejects the model of the storytelling woman with the spindle in favor of a Sibyl-like figure. But her contention that these frontispieces show women writing seems too simple. (They often seem to be writing and speaking at the same time.) And she does not discuss the traces of salon conversation and practices that are present in the tales written by women.

12. Occasionally, as in the volume of tales by La Force in the same edition, the publishers use Perrault's frontispiece for tales by the *conteuses*. It seems impossible to determine who chose the frontispieces—publisher or author—and why. Perrault's frontispiece may have become a kind of default position: when printers were unable to find another frontispiece, they slapped Perrault's on any collection of tales. The other, more unusual frontispieces I have discussed above were consciously selected to show a different kind of tale transmission.

13. DeJean, *Tender Geographies*, 233n.

14. On words "in costume" and the effects of the materiality of print in literature for children, see Jeffrey Mehlman, *Walter Benjamin for Children*, 6.

15. Murat, *Histoires sublimes et allegoriques*, iii.

16. See Seifert's discussion of this passage in *"Les Fées Modernes*,*"* 142–43, and in *Fairy Tales, Sexuality, and Gender*, 90–91. In his article, he emphasizes Murat's celebration of "a distinctively gendered literary enterprise" and the rarity of dedications to other writers. Hannon in her *Fabulous Identities*, 185–86, talks about the way Murat ridicules not only the ancient fairies but the kind of story told by Perrault.

17. Murat, *Histoires sublimes et allegoriques*, iii–iv.

18. Perrault, *Contes*, 75, and Lhéritier, *Oeuvres meslées*, 163–64 (also reprinted in Perrault volume, 239).

19. Guillory, *Cultural Capital*, 24.

20. See Dundes's essay "Who Are the Folk?" in *Interpreting Folklore*, and Roger Chartier's analogous redefinitions of "popular culture."

21. See Jan M. Ziolkowski's penetrating discussion of these issues in folklore research in his article "A Fairy Tale from before Fairy Tales."

22. In his essay "Latin Language Study as a Renaissance Puberty Rite," Ong makes it clear that "oral memory skills" and Latin were taught almost exclusively to boys. But, as far as I can tell, he does not see how narrow—and by the seventeenth century, how un-oral—his definition of "orality" is.

23. Ong, *Orality and Literacy*, 159–60.

24. DeJean, *Tender Geographies*, 47.

25. Chartier, "Texts, Printing, Readings," 170. Marc Fumaroli, in "Les enchantements de l'éloquence," argues that both Perrault and the *conteuses* use a language that is based on worldly conversation, rather than the language of the schools (184–85). See also Ruth Finnegan in *Oral Poetry*: "In practice, interaction between oral and written forms is extremely common, and the idea that the use of writing *automatically* deals a death blow to oral literary forms has nothing to support it" (160). She gives examples from British and American balladry, Irish songs, and American cowboy laments, as well as from modern Yugoslavia.

26. Sévigné, *Correspondance*, 516.

27. The neologism "mitonner" derived from cookery, where it means to simmer slowly. (It is related to the word "mie," the soft part of a loaf of bread, the noncrusty part—a word that was also used in seventeenth-century France for a governess, though that is usually thought to be short for "amie.") The word tends to have connotations of flattery, buttering someone up so that that person will do something for you. (Examples Furetière gives in his *Dictionnaire* of 1693 include "This nephew *mitonne* his uncle, so that he will make him his heir," and "This cavalier *mitonne* the old woman, so that she will give him her daughter in marriage.") But the word here seems to have slightly different connotations: the storytellers at court seem to be treating their audience, the ladies of Versailles, as governesses treat spoiled children, catering to their wishes (perhaps in order to get into their good graces).

28. These include Erica Harth's *Cartesian Women* and Mary Vidal's *Watteau's Painted Conversations*. Benedetta Craveri summarizes their efforts and others' in "The Lost Art."

29. Harth, *Cartesian Women*, 17.

30. See Robert, *Le conte de fées littéraire*, 330–35, and chapter 1 of Seifert's *Fairy Tales, Sexuality, and Gender*. Armine Kotin Mortimer, "La clôture féminine," also emphasizes the frame primarily as a representation of a closed and exclusive society. For a recent discussion of d'Aulnoy's use of the frame, one that is closer to my emphasis on literary form and play (though I first read it after this chapter was completed), see Anne Defrance, *Les contes de fées et les nouvelles de Madame d'Aulnoy*, 31–91.

31. Lhéritier, *Oeuvres meslées*, 229–30.

32. For a stimulating account of the sources and principles of "simplicité naïve" in Perrault's work, see Fumaroli's "Les enchantements de l'éloquence," particularly 156–60.

33. Zipes, "Origins of the Fairy Tale," in *Fairy Tale as Myth / Myth as Fairy Tale*, 21.

34. See Seifert's *Fairy tales, Sexuality, and Gender*, 76–78, for a very interesting discussion of salon interaction and the stylistic principle of *négligence*.

35. Quoted by Hannon, *Fabulous Identities*, 184. The manuscript, written after Murat was exiled from court, is in the Bibliothèque de l'Arsenal, 3741.

36. See Stewart, *On Longing*: "The exchange value of language, a value we see at work in oral genres even in modern society (e.g., the reciprocity of puns, the joke-swapping session) is replaced by a form of what we might, in analogy, call surplus value. Literary discourse is performed not within the ongoingness of conversation but in the largely private production and apprehension of the text . . ." (5). The conversational frames of the *conteuses'* tales could be seen as an attempt to preserve or replicate the "exchange value" of tale-telling in the salons.

37. See DeJean, *Tender Geographies*, 22–24, 71–77. For a brief account of the way these practices affected the transmission of fairy tales, see Zipes's introduction to *Beauties, Beasts and Enchantment*, particularly 2–4, and his "Origins of the Fairy Tale," in *Fairy Tale as Myth / Myth as Fairy Tale*, 20–23. Renate Baader (*Dames de Lettres*) also is helpful in elucidating the role fairy tales played in the salons.

38. Bernard, *Inés de Cordoüe*, 6–7. Further page numbers from this edition will be given in the text.

39. This may be a camouflaged reference to the function of the salons in the late years of Louis XIV's reign, when he was increasingly influenced by the puritanical practices of Mme de Maintenon. See Dorothy R. Thelander, "Mother Goose and Her Goslings," for a discussion of the "muffled aristocratic disaffection" (493) that these tales reveal.

40. See Hannon, *Fabulous Identities*, 202.

41. Robert, *Le conte de fées littéraire*, 207.

42. Hannon mentions this interruption in "A Politics of Disguise" but does not discuss the way the interruption and the frame itself form a further *mise-en-abyme* in the complex layering and generic instability of the tale.

43. Michele Farrell has shown the importance of the inscription of women's desires and agency in this tale in "Celebration and Repression of Feminine Desire"; but, though she discusses the tale within the tale told by the White Cat about her family's past, she misses the function of the larger comic frame and its naive readers.

44. Lhéritier, *Oeuvres meslées*, 312–13.

45. "Lettre à Mme D* G*," *Oeuvres meslées*, 305–6.

46. As Hannon has pointed out in *Fabulous Identities* (184), Murat also claims priority in the use of this material in her preface: "La seconde chose que j'ay à dire, c'est que mes Contes sont composez dés le mois d'Avril dernier [note that the royal permission or Privilege for this volume is April 1699], & que si je me suis rencontrée avec une de ces Dames en traitant quelques-uns des mêmes sujets, je n'ay point pris d'autre modele que l'original, ce qui seroit aisé à justifier par les routes differentes que nous avons prises" (The second thing I want to say is that my tales were composed last April, and if I have treated some of the same subjects as one of the other ladies, I have taken no model but the original, which would be easy to prove by the different paths we have taken). Though Murat sees herself as a member of a group, she is also eager to assert her priority in the use of material from Straparola (in her tale "Le Turbot") over d'Aulnoy (in her tale "Le Dauphin"). As she says, she has an "amour de père" (fatherly love) for her work ("Avertissement" to *Histoires sublimes et allegoriques*). Hannon argues that "the *conteuses* worked together to establish a collective identity which, significantly, did not preclude the stirrings of a desire to claim individual authorship" (178).

47. Certeau, "The Scriptural Economy," in *The Practice of Everyday Life*, 134.

48. Fumaroli, "Les enchantements de l'éloquence," 180. As Fumaroli points out, both Perrault and his niece Lhéritier fashioned their prose following the "style coupé," the style that since Montaigne had been opposed to the rhetoric of the schools. But Perrault's prose in his *Contes* is at the simpler end of this stylistic continuum, while Lhéritier's (and the other *conteuses'*) is far more complex.

49. On the *Bibliothèque bleue* in France in the seventeenth and eighteenth centuries, see Robert Mandrou, *De la culture populaire*. He makes a convincing case for its dissemination throughout all social classes.

50. Warner claims in *From the Beast to the Blonde* that Mother Goose was d'Aulnoy's "assumed persona, the lowclass older woman, her very opposite in social class and age and privilege" (166). But, though d'Aulnoy became identified with a Mother Goose or Mother Bunch figure during the eighteenth century in England, this certainly was not the persona she constructs in any of her tales.

51. As Rowe says in "To Spin a Yarn," often "a male author or collector attributes to a female the original power of articulating silent matter. But having attributed this transformative artistic intelligence and voice to a women, the narrator then reclaims for himself . . . the controlling power of retelling, of literary recasting, and of dissemi-

nation to the folk" (61). Jeannine Blackwell characterizes the ideological work of Herder and the Grimms in a similar way: they "essentially transferred the frame of narrative authority from the fictional female storyteller to themselves, yet retained her as a silenced, illustrative icon in the frontispiece: a source, a peasant informant who need not have her own narrative strategies, who provides raw materials for the collector, or who submerges and rechannels her female voice" ("Laying the Rod to Rest," 29–30).

CHAPTER THREE
THE INVENTION OF THE FAIRY TALE IN BRITAIN

1. Kroeber, *Retelling/Rereading*, 2. Kroeber attributes this belief to modernism's contempt for "story" itself. But its roots go back at least to the late eighteenth century, as we saw in chapter 1.

2. For the recent origin of many British "traditions," see *The Invention of Tradition*, ed. Eric Hobsbawm and Terence Ranger.

3. See J. Paul Hunter, "Looking Backward: A World Well Lost?" in *Before Novels*, particularly 141–63.

4. Edwin Muir, *Collected Poems 1921–1958*, 262. This poem, probably written between 1955 and 1958 and published posthumously, was brought to my attention in Spufford, *Small Books and Pleasant Histories*, 1.

5. The best discussions I know of this eighteenth-century impulse are Stewart's "Notes on Distressed Genres" and "Scandals of the Ballad," in *Crimes of Writing*, 66–131.

6. Quoted in Alan Richardson, "Wordsworth, Fairy Tales, and the Politics of Children's Reading," 34.

7. This belief is one of the animating forces in Benjamin's "Storyteller" essay. Traces of it still surface in Kroeber's *Retelling/Rereading*: "Especially with the advent of printing, the primacy of the teller linking then to now has been usurped by an author presenting a new story, legitimated by its immediate impact rather than its previous existence" (37).

8. William Empson, *Some Versions of Pastoral*, particularly 6. But see also his brief analysis of the political assumptions behind Gray's "Elegy in a Country Church-yard," 4–5.

9. Jochen Schulte-Sasse, "Art and the Sacrificial Structure of Modernity," 102.

10. See Stewart, "Notes on Distressed Genres," in *Crimes of Writing*, 69: "Of course the novel, with its fantastic capacity to represent, its necessarily incomplete ambition toward totality, becomes here both the antithesis of the 'distressed' genre and the logical consequence of the distressed genre's claims."

11. Spufford, *Small Books and Pleasant Histories*, 32.

12. In *The Cheese and the Worms* Carlo Ginzburg bases his reconstruction of the mental life of Menocchio, a late-six-century Italian miller from Friuli, on the interaction between the oral culture he grew up immersed in and the books he read: "The

almanacs, the songsters, the books of piety, the lives of the saints, the entire pamphlet literature that constituted the bulk of the book trade, today appear static, inert, and unchanging to us. But how were they read by the public of the day? To what extent did the prevalently oral culture of those readers interject itself in the use of the text, modifying it, reworking it, perhaps to the point of changing its very essence?" (xxii).

13. Preface to vol. 1 of the first edition of the *Kinder- und Hausmärchen* (1812), translated by Tatar, *The Hard Facts*, Appendix B, 205.

14. See Karen Seago, "Some Aspects of the English Reception," 56n, on the history of the Grimms' tales in England.

15. Calvino, "Introduction" to his *Italian Folktales*, xvi. As Bacchilega says in *Postmodern Fairy Tales*, "Like the Grimms', Calvino's approach . . . supports a humanistic and nation-building project" (20). Like the Grimms, Calvino too is caught up in what Schenda calls "five-minutes-before-midnight" thinking, the belief that the collector has rescued tales just in the nick of time, before their final disappearance (*Von Mund zu Ohr*, 151). See also Shelly Errington in *The Death of Authentic Primitive Art*: "Authentic primitive art is not being produced anymore, the story goes, because the cultures that produced it are 'dead' " (118).

16. Moses Gaster, "The Modern Origin of Fairy-Tales," 339–40.

17. Schenda, "Telling Tales—Spreading Tales," 75. Though Schenda's essay has often been cited, the truly radical nature of his questions has been overlooked. See also Richard Bauman, "Conceptions of Folkore": "[T]o identify a particular oral text as traditional is to highlight its place in a web of intertextuality that, far from placing it apart from written literature, unites it with written literature still more firmly" (16).

18. See also Albert Wesselski, *Theorie des Märchens*, 84: "Schon aus diesen wenigen Beispielen erhellt, daß das Märchen nicht immer als Märchen entsteht, sondern oft erst duch Uberwindung von Raum und Zeit zum Märchen wird" (Even these few examples show that the fairy tale does not always begin as a fairy tale but rather often becomes a fairy tale as it moves through space and time).

19. Schenda, *Von Mund zu Ohr*, 46. Fumaroli also emphasizes the interaction of the oral and the written throughout all classes of society in the seventeenth century in France: "Selon Marc Soriano, l'art populaire est essentiellement oral, l'art savant relevant de l'univers écrit et imprimé. Il est cependant notoire que, pour s'en tenir à l'exemple des *Contes* de Perrault, plusieurs d'entre eux remontent à des récits imprimés antérieurement. . . . Il pourrait s'agir moins d'une antinomie que d'un développement en fugue des deux modes de tradition" (According to Marc Soriano popular culture is essentially oral. But it is notorious that, to give only the example of Perrault's tales, many of them have their sources in earlier written stories. . . . It could be a question less of an opposition than of a fugal development of the two modes of tradition) ("Les enchantements de l'éloquence," 155).

20. See my colleague Nancy Mason Bradbury's book *Writing Aloud*. Bradbury emphasizes the way written texts became part of oral practice in late medieval England, as well as the way written texts echoed oral performance.

21. Manfred Grätz in fact asserts that there were no tales we would now call "Volksmärchen" circulating in the eighteenth century: "Eine volkstümliche, orale Märchentradition ist allerdings weder für Frankreich noch für Deutschland bislang nachgewiesen" (No one has yet demonstrated the existence of an oral folk tale tradition in either Germany or France) (*Das Märchen in der deutschen Aufklärung*, 266). This is true for England as well; the fairy tales known as such in the eighteenth century were mostly adopted from the French salon tradition, as were the German ones. While Grätz may have overstated his case, his doubts are an important corrective to the predominant view of the history of fairy tales. His argument that tales became shorter and simpler in Germany toward the end of the eighteenth century because they were beginning to be marketed for children, not because of a return to actual oral material, certainly seems convincing.

22. Darnton, "Peasants Tell Tales," 17–18. Darnton also tries to show that fairy tales reflect national histories, social situations, and *mentalités*, comparing tales in French and German. Steven Swann Jones's "On Analyzing Fairy Tales" (a useful critique of some of Darnton's "ethnographic" methods), Elliot Oring's critique of some of Jones's points ("On the Meanings of Mother Goose"), and Jones's reply are all in the same 1987 issue of *Western Folklore*. Darnton's book also provoked a lively discussion in France: see Chartier's "Texts, Symbols and Frenchness" and the debate among Pierre Bourdieu, Darnton, and Chartier: "Dialogue à propos de l'histoire culturelle."

23. Jones, "On Analyzing Fairy Tales," 99.

24. For a brief discussion of the survival of this conception in much twentieth-century writing about fairy tales, see Richardson's fine essay "Wordsworth, Fairy Tales, and the Politics of Children's Reading," particularly 46–48. Ziolkowski's arguments about the dangers of giving priority to oral traditions over written versions ("A Fairy Tale from before Fairy Tales") also seem to me compelling.

25. Geoffrey O'Brien, "Recapturing the American Sound," 48.

26. Tatar, *Off with Their Heads!*, xxi.

27. See Stewart, *On Longing*, 43: "The invention of printing coincided with the invention of childhood, and the two faces of children's literature, the fantastic and the didactic, developed at the same time in the miniature book."

28. See Spufford, *Small Books and Pleasant Histories*. Most of the chapbooks she catalogs and discusses still circulated in the eighteenth century, with the addition of a number of French fairy tales. I disagree with Spufford's blanket dismissal of these chapbooks as "useless" (249), but her work is essential to an understanding of their early history and distribution.

29. See Spufford, *Small Books and Pleasant Histories*, 74–75, on Johnson, Boswell, and Burke. (Boswell's ambivalent memory of his reading is clear in his description of the chapbook "histories" as "my old darlings.")

30. Summerfield, *Fantasy and Reason*, xv.

31. All page references in the text are to Fielding, *The Governess, or, Little Female Academy*, with an introduction by Mary Cadogan, in the Pandora Mothers of the

Novel series. The 1968 Oxford facsimile edition, edited by Jill E. Grey, is harder to find, and the texts are identical.

32. See Richardson's brief discussion of the novel in *Literature, Education, and Romanticism*, 135–36.

33. See Arlene Fish Wilner, "Education and Ideology in Sarah Fielding's *The Governess*," particularly 308–9.

34. For a good overview of the translations, which included many tales written by other *conteuses* and the chevalier de Mailly, see Nancy and Melvin Palmer, "English Editions of French *Contes de Fées* attributed to Mme d'Aulnoy."

35. See Victor Watson, "Jane Johnson," particularly 37–40.

36. On the exhibition and significance of supposed "freaks," see Stewart, *On Longing*, particularly 104–11; on the grotesque in eighteenth-century England, see Peter Stallybrass and Allon White, "The Grotesque Body and the Smithfield Muse: Authorship in the Eighteenth Century," in *The Politics and Poetics of Transgression*, 80–124.

37. A Freudian would probably point out the sexual symbolism of the grove, "so well secured from an Invader, by the thick Briars and Thorns, which surround it, having no Entrance but thro' that tender Jessamine" (73).

38. In this connection it would be interesting to compare *The Governess* with Sarah Scott's 1762 *Millenium Hall*, a representation of a group of women who have had some (usually sad) experience in the world and have retired to a female community (that is, however, mediated through the gaze of two male visitors).

39. *Female Spectator*, 2:121, quoted in Rachel Carnell, "It's Not Easy Being Green," 203.

40. Villeneuve's version is most easily available in English in Zipes's collection *Beauties, Beasts and Enchantment* (1989). Unfortunately he was forced to cut it from the second edition of the collection, *Beauty and the Beast and Other Classic French Fairy Tales* (1997), because of its length.

41. Betsy Hearne reproduces the title page and the first page of the 1783 edition of *The Young Misses Magazine*, as well as Dialogue V (which contains "Beauty and the Beast") in her *Beauty and the Beast*, 189–203. But she cuts off the conversation that follows Mrs. Affable's reading of the tale.

42. *Magazin des enfans* (1756), xiv–xv. I have translated this myself, since I haven't been able to consult a full copy of the original English edition of 1757 or any later edition.

43. For a detailed comparison of her "Beauty and the Beast" and Villeneuve's, see Robert's invaluable *Le conte de fées littéraire*, 146–53. She stresses in particular the way Beaumont mutes all of Villeneuve's erotic innuendos.

44. *Magazin des enfans*, 4:13.

45. For a good discussion of the differences between the two versions of the tale, see Zipes, "The Origins of the Fairy Tale," in *Fairy Tale as Myth / Myth as Fairy Tale*, 29–41.

46. Hearne, *Beauty and the Beast*, 66.

47. One of the pupils, Lady Molly, makes the following analogy, now difficult to read: "Je crois que me serois accoutumée à la voir [la Bête] comme la *Belle*. Quand Papa prit un petit garçon tout noir, pour être son laquais, j'en avois peur, je me cachois quand il entroit, il me paroissoit plus laid qu'une Bête. Eh bien! petit-à-petit j'm'y suis accutumée: il me porte, quand je monte dans le carosse, & je ne pense plus à son visage"(*Magazin des enfans*, 1:83) (I believe I would have become accustomed to seeing the Beast as well as Beauty. When Papa engaged a little black boy to be his valet, I was afraid of him, I hid when he entered, he seemed to me uglier than a Beast. But little by little I have gotten used to him: he lifts me up, when I get into the carriage, and I don't even think of his face any more). This is further evidence, if we need any, of the construction of the black as Other, and that Other as bestial.

48. Warner, *From the Beast to the Blonde*, 294.

49. Myers, "Romancing the Moral Tale," particularly 97–99.

50. Warner, *From the Beast to the Blonde*, 293.

51. See Jürgen Habermas, *The Structural Transformation of the Public Sphere*, particularly 1–56.

52. Richardson, *Literature, Education, and Romanticism*, 69.

53. Quoted by Samuel Pickering in *John Locke and Children's Books*, 40. For a useful discussion of late-eighteenth-century British critiques of the fairy tale, see Pickering's second chapter. Surprisingly, however, he mentions neither Sarah Fielding nor Beaumont.

54. On the stability of and ideological assumptions behind this term, see Morag Shiach, " 'Peasant Poets' 1730–1848: Consistency in Difference," in *Discourse on Popular Culture*, 35–70.

55. "Sketches in the Life of John Clare," in *John Clare's Autobiographical Writings*, 5–6. The spelling and punctuation are Clare's.

56. "Autobiographical Fragments," in *John Clare's Autobiographical Writings*, 57.

57. Eric Robinson, the editor of Clare's *Autobiographical Writings*, claims that "Zig Zag" was a story called "The Man with a Long Nose" that included the rhyme "Did you see a maid running zigzag / And in her hand a long leather bag" (165 n. 8). But I think it is much more likely to have been *Some account of old Zigzag, and of the horn which he used to understand the language of birds, beasts, fishes, and insects*, often added to a collection of stories called *The valentine's gift*, originally published by John Newbery in 1765 and reprinted many times in cheap editions for the next one hundred years. (My thanks to Bruce Sajdak, reference librarian extraordinaire, for helping me track this down.) The idea of understanding the animals' language would have been particularly appealing to Clare.

58. I have learned a great deal from Victor E. Neuburg's *Penny Histories*, but his claim that chapbooks like "Mother Bunch's Golden Fortune Teller" put eighteenth-

century readers in touch with British fairy tales and fairy lore is almost certainly mistaken. The fairy tales in the chapbooks he reproduces are all of French origin.

59. *Recollections of the Life of John Binns*, 18. He goes on to say: "The books now put into the hands of youth are of a more instructive character. It may, however, be doubted whether they are read with equal avidity" (18).

60. *The Autobiography of Samuel Bamford: Early Days*, 90. His description of his early reading is quite similar but more vivid: "When I first plunged, as it were, into the blessed habit of reading, faculties which had hitherto given but small intimation of existence, suddenly sprung into vigorous action. My mind was ever desiring more of the silent but exciting conversation with books" (91).

61. Quoted in Spufford, *Small Books and Pleasant Histories*, 2–3.

62. Chartier, "Figures of the 'Other,'" 151. Literacy was probably more common in the working classes and peasantry in England than it was in France.

63. Iona and Peter Opie, *The Classic Fairy Tales*, 212. Further page numbers will be given in the text. See Neuburg, *Penny Histories*, 194–95, for a reproduction of a list of Catnach's halfpenny books and the rather terrifying facing title page of a one-penny book called *The Rod*, no. 10 in the series *Houlston's Juvenile Tracts. For the Amusement and Improvement of Young Persons*. (It looks much more improving than amusing.)

64. In *On Longing* (46), Stewart quotes Charlotte Yonge's delicate description of Tom Thumb's size and acorn-cradle in her children's book *The History of Tom Thumb* (1856), stressing its "harmony of detail." Yonge's description clearly derives from chapbook passages like this one.

65. See Stewart, *On Longing*, 178 n. 23, and 119–24, for remarks on Tom Thumb and Tom Thumb weddings.

66. See Stallybrass and White, *The Politics and Poetics of Transgression*, 23: "The grotesque body, as Bakhtin makes clear, has *its* discursive norms too: impurity (both in the sense of dirt and mixed categories), heterogeneity, masking, protuberant distension, disproportion, exorbitancy, clamour, decentred or eccentric arrangements, a focus upon gaps, orifices, and symbolic filth (what Mary Douglas calls 'matter out of place'), physical needs and pleasures of the 'lower bodily stratum,' materiality and parody." All the early written versions of British tales play on the dialectic between the grotesque and the normative "normal."

67. Lurie, "Witches and Fairies," 7. Lieberman criticizes both Lang's selections and Lurie's points in "'Some Day My Prince Will Come.'"

68. Dugaw, "Chapbook Publishing and the 'Lore' of 'the Folks,'" 3. Dugaw argues that the myth of the pastoral Golden Age has determined most folklore research; "a sentimental cherishing of the folk has not disappeared from late 20th-century folklore scholarship, although the ties between this projection and the Eurocentric colonialism of the last five centuries become increasingly hard to ignore" (8).

69. See Briggs, *The Fairies in English Tradition and Literature*, 174. The phrase "the foreign invasion" is the title of chapter 20.

INTERLUDE
ONCE AGAIN

1. For an excellent anthology of little-known Victorian tales by women, see Nina Auerbach and U. C. Knoepflmacher's *Forbidden Journeys*. A surprising number of these tales are framed and narrated by older women, often as they spin or do needle-work.

2. See her *Nouveaux contes de fées pour les petits enfants*, first published in 1856 and then often reprinted by the Librairie Hachette (Paris) from 1917 on in the children's series Bibliothèque Rose Illustrée.

3. Sara Maitland, "A Feminist Writer's Progress," 17.

4. Kroeber, *Retelling/Rereading*, 9.

5. Maitland, "The Wicked Stepmother's Lament," in *Angel Maker*, 222.

6. For a fine discussion of reversals in contemporary rewritings, both comic and serious, see Zipes's introduction to his collection *Don't Bet on the Prince*, particularly 13–26.

7. Maxine Kumin, "The Archaeology of a Marriage," in *The Retrieval System*, 35–37. Kumin chose not to reprint this poem in any later collection.

8. Bacchilega, *Postmodern Fairy Tales*, 34.

9. Atwood, *Bluebeard's Egg and Other Stories*, 131–64. Atwood's story has often been reprinted, perhaps most handily in Zipes's anthology of feminist rewritings *Don't Bet on the Prince*, 160–82. For an excellent discussion of the story, see Bacchilega, *Postmodern Fairy Tales*, 113–16.

CHAPTER FOUR
NEW FRAMES FOR OLD TALES

1. For a telling discussion of the limitations of the AT classifications, see Blackwell, "Laying the Rod to Rest," 29–31. In "Gender-Related Biases in the Type and Motif Indexes of Aarne and Thompson," Torberg Lundell has also shown how this feature of the AT index reveals its gender bias.

2. Goodman, "The Telling and the Told," 801. This essay is in part a rebuttal of claims that we can ever find the one "true" or "original" version of any story.

3. See Irwin, "What's in a Frame?" 28. While Irwin sets out clear definitions of the frame-tale as a genre or "performance context" (an unusual and useful contribution), she makes two claims that I would contest. She insists that the frame-tale actually "bridges the gap" between oral and literate culture or "textualizes the oral tradition"; I would argue that it simply simulates or mimics an oral tale-telling situation, as Nicole Belmont suggests in her *Poétique du conte*, 56. (As evidence for her claim, Irwin cites Linda Dégh's discovery of frame-tales in the twentieth-century Hungarian oral tradition. These frame-tales, however, could certainly have been influenced

by written texts.) She also says that the frame-tale waned with the Middle Ages, a common belief among medievalists; all of the frame-tales I will discuss, however, date from the Renaissance or much later.

4. Lämmert, *Bauformen des Erzählens*, 48. Though many people have written about specific framed narratives, particularly the *Canterbury Tales*, it seems strange that so few narratologists have written about this structural device, given its lasting and cross-cultural popularity. As Barthes observed, "our society takes the greatest pains to conjure away the coding of the narrative situation" (*Image—Music—Text*, 116).

5. Byatt, "Fairy Stories," 6 (my emphasis).

6. The question of *how* they knew Basile remains open. According to N. M. Penzer in vol. 2 of his translation of Basile, the *Pentamerone* was not translated into standard Italian until 1747 or into French until 1777 (and even then only a few tales were translated). Both the *Enzyklopädie des Märchens* and Rouger, the editor of the Garnier edition of Perrault's *Contes*, show that almost all the tales Perrault wrote have possible sources in Basile, but do not show how he learned of them, if he did. Soriano suggests that Perrault's brother Pierre, whose Italian was excellent, may have translated the difficult Neapolitan dialect informally for his brother (*Les contes de Perrault*, 116). In *From the Beast to the Blonde*, Warner asserts that Lhéritier knew Basile's text, but gives no evidence for this (172).

7. For excellent discussions of Basile's framing technique, see Canepa, "Basile's Quest for the Literary Fairy Tale," 42–52, and *From Court to Forest*, 81–95.

8. Blackwell "Laying the Rod to Rest," 31.

9. Letter to Schiller (August 17, 1795), quoted in Jane K. Brown, *Goethe's Cyclical Narratives*, 9. I have learned a great deal from Brown's discussion of Goethe's relationship to Boccaccio and his use of the frame.

10. Goethe, *Sämtliche Werke*, 9:1114.

11. Barth, *Lost in the Funhouse*, ix.

12. Bacchilega, *Postmodern Fairy Tales*, 36. Her whole second chapter, "The Framing of 'Snow White'" (28–48), has been very useful. See also Kernan, Brooks, and Holquist, *Man and His Fictions*, 400, for a brief but telling discussion of Barth's "Frame-Tale."

13. See Victoria Sanchez, "A. S. Byatt's *Possession*," for a much fuller discussion of the role of folklore and folk motifs in the novel. She omits any discussion of Gode's Breton tale, however (and misspells Christabel throughout).

14. Byatt, *Possession*, 59. Further page numbers will be given in the text.

15. Interestingly enough, this is one of the very few of the Grimms' tales that includes an embedded story, the princess's tale of how she came to be enclosed in a glass coffin.

16. Byatt, "Ice, Snow, Glass," 73.

17. Byatt, "Fairy Stories," 4.

18. See Byatt in "Fairy Stories": "George Eliot in *Adam Bede* took an experience of her own Methodist aunt, who had accompanied an infanticide to the scaffold . . .

and wove it together with all the resonance of *Faust* and Wordsworth's ballad ["The Thorn"] to make something simple and terrible. I wanted to touch the *simple horror* Eliot had aimed for—I wanted to tell that story in a new-old form. And in doing so, I wanted to make a hidden clue in a very modern scholarly detective story that was part of my own postmodern novel" (5; my emphasis).

19. Byatt is almost certainly echoing the narrative structure of Emily Brontë's *Wuthering Heights*, which also begins with and returns obsessively to a "box bed," the "oak closet."

20. Byatt, "Fairy Stories," 8.

21. Kroeber, *Retelling/Rereading*, 9.

22. Dore Ashton, *A Joseph Cornell Album*, 23.

23. *Joseph Cornell's Theater of the Mind*, ed. Mary Ann Caws, 131, 373. Quotations from Cornell's diaries and letters will be identified by page numbers keyed to this edition.

24. Charles Simic, *Dime-Store Alchemy*, 52.

25. See Deborah Solomon's brilliant description of *Setting for a Fairy-Tale* in *Utopia Parkway*, 140–42. Some other titles in the series include *Le Chant du Rossignol*, *Untitled (Pink Castle)*, and *Untitled (Rose Palace)*.

26. See, for example, the untitled constructions, figs. 58–63, in the 1980 Museum of Modern Art catalog *Joseph Cornell*, ed. Kynaston McShine.

27. Simic quotes the entire diary entry for that day in *Dime-Store Alchemy*, 8–9. I suspect that Cornell's destination on Fifty-ninth Street was the Argosy Bookshop, the source of much of his best printed matter. His purchases may sound random, but in fact he was often following several lines of thought and acquisition at the same time.

28. A copy of the book still exists in Box 106 in the Joseph Cornell Study Center at the Smithsonian Museum of American Art. Many of the pages are missing; all are separated from the binding and out of order. About seventy pages show the rusty marks of a paper clip (including several pages from another book); the top page of this bundle is labeled "Contes des Fées" in Cornell's handwriting. It seems close to certain that the pages he used for the *Nouveaux Contes de Fées* box came from this book. (My thanks to one of my research assistants, Katie Peebles, for tracking it down.)

29. Ashbery, "Cornell: The Cube Root of Dreams," 63. Ashton, in her *Joseph Cornell Album*, claims that Cornell was influenced not by Mondrian but rather by "obsolete forms having gridlike character: old type-boxes, dovecotes, and the compartmented cabinets used by collectors of insects and fauna" (82). (Writing in 1974, she did not have access to Cornell's diaries.) I believe that Cornell was fascinated by the conjunction of Mondrian's ascetic constructions and the "obsolete forms" Ashton mentions. See also the catalog *Joseph Cornell/Marcel Duchamp—In Resonance* for correspondences between his work and another "modern" artist's.

30. Byatt, "Ice, Snow, Glass," 72–73.

31. "I wish I could approach your genius for expressing to people how you think about them and what they do. But I do want to tell you that I think of you and the *uncanny magic* of the things you make." Mark Rothko in a letter to Cornell, quoted by Solomon, *Utopia Parkway*, 198 (AAA, roll 1056, date indecipherable) (emphasis mine).

32. For more on the enclosed box and the miniature, see Stewart, *On Longing*, particularly 54–69. As she says, "The miniature world remains perfect and uncontaminated by the grotesque so long as its absolute boundaries are maintained. Consider, for example, the Victorian taste for art (usually transformed relics of nature) under glass or Joseph Cornell's glass bells" (68).

33. Kumin, "How It Was," xxviii.

34. I give the page numbers for Sexton's poems from *Transformations* (*T*) and from the *Complete Poems* (*CP*). My thanks to my colleague Susan Van Dyne for stimulating thoughts and suggestions about Sexton over the years.

35. Linda Gray Sexton, *Searching for Mercy Street*, 160. See also Diane Wood Middlebrook, *Anne Sexton*, 114, and Rose Lucas, "A Witch's Appetite," 77.

36. Letter to Paul Brooks (ca. June 1968), in Linda Gray Sexton and Ames, *Anne Sexton: A Self-Portrait*, 325.

37. I am reminded of Maurice Sendak's wild things and their threat: "We'll eat you up—we love you so" (*Where the Wild Things Are*). Sendak once said that his wild things derived from his terrifying aunts and uncles, who ate his family's food and threatened to "eat him up" too. See Tatar's wonderful essay "Table Matters: Cannibalism and Oral Greed," in *Off with Their Heads!*, particularly 190–93, 196.

38. Alicia Ostriker speaks of Sexton's "deflating techniques" in "That Story," 13. But Sexton blows the tales up as a pop artist might, before she deflates them with well-aimed barbs.

39. Bettelheim, *The Uses of Enchantment*, 149.

40. Letter to Stanley Kunitz (December 23, 1970), in Linda Gray Sexton and Ames, *Anne Sexton: A Self-Portrait*, 371.

41. Letter to Kurt Vonnegut (November 17, 1970), in Linda Gray Sexton and Ames, *Anne Sexton: A Self-Portrait*, 367.

42. Jennifer Waelti-Walters, *Fairy Tales and the Female Imagination*, 142.

43. Letter to Paul Brooks (October 14, 1970), in Linda Gray Sexton and Ames, *Anne Sexton: A Self-Portrait*, 362.

44. Donoghue, *Kissing the Witch*, 2. Subsequent citations are given in the text.

45. Compare Jane Eyre's despair on the roof of Thornfield: "Anybody may blame me who likes, when I add . . . that then I longed for a power of vision which might overpass that limit" (chapter 12).

46. As Tatar and many others have pointed out, Wilhelm Grimm gradually transformed a series of wicked mothers into stepmothers in successive editions of the tales; see *The Hard Facts*, 36–38.

47. See Bottigheimer, "Tale Spinners," and Tatar, *The Hard Facts*, 123–33, for interesting discussions of the many variants of the tale.

48. For wonderful examples of play with the frame, frame breaking, and frame dissolving, in life and in literature, see Erving Goffman, *Frame Analysis*, 345–438.

49. Barth, *Lost in the Funhouse*, ix.

CHAPTER FIVE
THE ART OF TRANSLITERATION

1. Here I always hear an echo of Saint Paul's admonition to the Corinthians: "It is better to marry than to burn" (1 Cor. 7:9). Broumas, like Saint Paul, is talking about sexual passion; she is particularly engaged in finding words to express it. As she said in an interview with Karla Hammond, the poem "came out like a manifesto—not in the sense of being rhetorical, but in articulating my position as a writer" (34).

2. Lisel Mueller, *Alive Together*, 9. My thanks to Micala Sidore for bringing Mueller's fairy-tale poems to my attention.

3. Karen Rowe, " 'Fairy-born and human-bred' ," 69.

4. "Fairy Tale Liberation," 42.

5. Gornick, "Taking a Long Hard Look at 'The Princess and the Pea,' " 166.

6. Atwood, *Surfacing*, 65.

7. Cixous and Clément, *La jeune née*, 119–20. The following translation is by Betsy Wing, *The Newly Born Woman*, 165–66.

8. Cixous and Clément, *La jeune née*, 67.

9. Lurie, "Witches and Fairies," 6.

10. In thinking about the gendered subject, I have found Elspeth Probyn's arguments and imagery very helpful: "[A] gendered self is constantly reproduced within the changing mutations of difference. . . . One way of imaging this self is to think of it as a combination of acetate transparencies: layers and layers of lines and directions that are figured together and in depth, only then to be re-arranged again" (*Sexing the Self*, 1). Another helpful metaphor, this one from Jeanette Winterson's *Sexing the Cherry*: "The self is not contained in any moment or any place, but it is only in the intersection of moment and place that the self might, for a moment, be seen vanishing through a door, which disappears at once" (87). See also Wendy Mulford's questions in "Notes on Writing" about the "construction" of the self: "Who was this 'I' speaking? What was speaking me? How far did the illusion of selfhood, that most intimate and precious possession, reach? How could the lie of culture be broken up if the lie of the self made by that culture remained intact?" (31).

11. Felicity A. Nussbaum, *Autobiographical Subject*, 15.

12. Bernheimer, *Mirror, Mirror on the Wall*, xviii.

13. Benjamin, *Selected Writings*, 1:408.

14. The inadequacies of this translation have long been apparent. The original title—*A Model Childhood*—revealed the pervasive failure of the translators to catch the nuances of ordinary spoken German; though the title has been corrected to *Patterns of Childhood*, the subtitle has still not been added—and the mistaken translation still turns up in the text (36). Though I have based my translation on theirs, I have

often been forced to modify their versions of the text and to supply translations of missing passages. My thanks to Lisa Harries-Schumann for thoughtful suggestions. (The passages the translators leave out are often passages in which Wolf insists on moving between her present, writing self and her earlier selves. The omissions transform the text into a much more conventional memoir.) Page references in the text are to the German original and to the translation by Molinaro and Rappolt.

15. See Brodzki, "Mothers, Displacement, and Language," for a fascinating discussion of Wolf's use of pronouns, particularly 257–58.

16. Mueller, "Curriculum Vitae," in *Alive Together*, 6.

17. Steedman, *Landscape for a Good Woman*, 13. Further page numbers will be given in the text.

18. Bernheimer, *Mirror, Mirror on the Wall*, 250–51. Oates's essay is a strange mixture of perceptive remarks and old myths; she still seems to believe that Perrault and the Grimms were "archivists" (247) and that "the fairy tale derives from childhood" (252).

19. Rosellen Brown, in "It Is You the Fable Is About," interprets the story in a different way: "I know that in the mermaid's voicelessness Andersen captured one of our—I mean humans'—primal terrors. . . . He gave us an implicit judgment of the limitations of mere beauty, beauty unendowed with self" (62). For Steedman, however, the absence of voice means not the absence of self but rather the inability to express the self forcefully in the world. Both Brown and Steedman, however, suppress the pious Christian "happy ending" of the tale, the possibility of the Little Mermaid's gaining an everlasting soul. Like Mary McCarthy, they resist the "morals lurking like fish eyes peering out from between [Andersen's] stories in the depths of clear water" (*How I Grew*, 5).

20. Byatt, "Ice, Snow, Glass," 83.

21. For a helpful discussion of fragmentation in women's autobiography, see Sidonie Smith, "Autobiographical Manifestoes," 434–35.

22. Bacchilega, *Postmodern Fairy Tales*, 10.

23. See also Adrienne Rich's poem "The Snow Queen," in *The Fact of a Doorframe*, 19–20: "Under my ribs a diamond splinter now / Sticks, and has taken root; I know / Only this frozen spear that drives me through."

24. Broumas, *Beginning with O*, 21. Further page numbers will be given in the text.

25. See also Broumas's lines in *Caritas*, #2: " I lie / between your sapling thighs, my tongue / flat on your double-lips, giving / voice, giving / voice." Quoted in Carruthers, "The Re-Vision of the Muse," 310.

26. This is a slight misquotation. The last lines of Sexton's poem actually read this way: "The Joy that isn't shared, I've heard, / dies young" (*CP* 455). In "Cinderella" (*Beginning with O*, 87) Broumas also echoes a line from Elizabeth Bishop's "Sestina" twice: "I know what I know."

27. Carruthers, "The Re-Vision of the Muse," 305.

28. Hammond, "Interview with Olga Broumas," 37.

29. Carter, introduction to *The Old Wives' Fairy Tale Book*, x.

30. Salman Rushdie, introduction to Angela Carter's collection *Burning Your Boats*, xiv.

31. On the relationship of Carter's tale to Beaumont's, see Anny Crunelle-Vanrigh, "The Logic of the Same and *Différance*," particularly 119–26. Crunelle-Vanrigh seems to miss, or misunderstand, the references in the tale to d'Aulnoy.

32. I will give page references first to the Penguin paperback edition of *The Bloody Chamber* (*BC*), then to Carter's posthumous collected stories, *Burning Your Boats* (*BB*).

33. In her chapter on revisions of fairy tales, also called "Twice upon a Time," in *The Disobedient Writer*, Walker points to Carter's mockery of the *conteuses'* tales (76). But I don't think she sees the way Carter also depends on and pays homage to the earlier versions.

34. The scene in which the tiger's tongue reveals the beauty of her animal self parallels the scene at the end of "Wolf Alice" where the Duke's humanity is finally revealed or "brought into being by [the wolf child's] soft, moist, gentle tongue" (*BC* 126; *BB* 228). Carter is interested in the possibility of transition from one state to another, transformation rather than transcendence.

35. For a long and brilliant discussion of Carter's two "Beauty and the Beast" tales, see Bacchilega, *Postmodern Fairy Tales*, 89–102. As she says about "The Courtship of Mr. Lyon," Carter's "text exposes the machinations of its magic without explicitly renouncing it, leaving the reader to reflect on the power of words and looks" (91).

36. See Seifert's useful comments on "Le Mouton" in *Fairy Tales, Sexuality and Gender*, 160–65.

37. See Gayle Rubin's groundbreaking 1975 essay, "The Traffic in Women."

38. Mary Kaiser, "Fairy Tale as Sexual Allegory," 33. This brief essay is one of the best things written about Carter's intertextual play and its significance.

39. As Kaiser points out, Carter here is working out some of the implications of her analysis in *The Sadeian Woman*; the heroine of "The Bloody Chamber," like Sade's Justine, is "obscene to the extent to which she is beautiful (*Sadeian Woman*, 57).

40. See, for example, Patricia Duncker, "Re-Imagining the Fairy Tales," and Robin Sheets, "Pornography, Fairy Tales, and Feminism." In contrast, Elaine Jordan, in "The Dangers of Angela Carter," argues that the tale is a rewriting of Colette, "a quarrel with another, intensely admired, woman writer" (129), not to be oversimplified by simple study of the characters and their interactions. Jordan's polemical re-readings of "The Bloody Chamber" have been very useful.

41. Carter, "Notes from the Front Line," 71.

42. Carter, "Notes from the Front Line," 70.

43. Atwood, "Running with the Tigers," 132.

44. My reading here is analogous to Mary Russo's of female spectacle in Carter's novel *Nights at the Circus* in her *The Female Grotesque*: "I would read Fevvers' act [the act of the female flyer] as a reminder that the spectacle which conceals work is itself produced, and revamping spectacle shows up and diverts this cultural production" (177).

Conclusion

Twice-Told Tales

1. Rich, from *A Wild Patience Has Taken Me This Far* (1981) in *The Fact of Doorframe*, 307.

2. Byatt, "Fairy Stories," 2. One of Byatt's acts of homage to her predecessors, the *conteuses*, has been to translate d'Aulnoy's story "Le serpentin vert" (The great green worm) in Warner's volume *Wonder Tales*.

3. Carter, "Afterword to *Fireworks*," in *Burning Your Boats*, 459.

4. Here is a very selective list for further reading: Donald Barthelme, *Snow White*; Robert Coover, "The Gingerbread House," in *Pricks and Descants*, and his recent, troubling *Briar Rose*; Jeanette Winterson's twelve reworkings of "The Twelve Dancing Princesses" in *Sexing the Cherry*; Margaret Atwood's novel *The Robber Bride*, as well as many of her short stories in addition to "Bluebeard's Egg"; Monique Wittig's sardonic references to "Snow White" in *Les Guerrillères*; Caryl Churchill's Joycean dramatic fantasia on British fairy tales *The Skriker*. This list, of course, only scratches the surface of the fairy-tale transformations of the last twenty-five years.

5. See Bacchilega, *Postmodern Fairy Tales*, particularly 19–25.

6. Here, as elsewhere in the book, I am indebted to Kroeber's *Retelling/Rereading* for its insistence on the nature and importance of retelling stories. As he says, "Storytelling is perhaps humanity's primary tool for *changing* reality" (13).

7. Rich, *The Fact of a Doorframe*, iv.

8. Rich, from *Snapshots of a Daughter-in-Law* (1963), in *The Fact of a Doorframe*, 42.

9. Rich, "Twenty-One Love Poems," XIII, from *The Dream of a Common Language* (1978), in *The Fact of a Doorframe*, 242.

10. I refer again to a phrase in Rushdie's introduction to the posthumous collection of Carter's stories, *Burning Your Boats*, xiv.

11. Carter, introduction to *The Old Wives' Fairy Tale Book*, xxi.

12. Kroeber, *Retelling/Rereading*, 48.

Aarne, Antti. *The Types of the Folktale: A Classification and Bibliography*. Translated and enlarged by Stith Thompson. 2d rev. ed. FF communications. Helsinki: Suomalainen Tiedeakatemia, 1981.

Abel, Elizabeth, Marianne Hirsch, and Elizabeth Langland, eds. *The Voyage In: Fictions of Female Development*. Hanover, NH: University Press of New England, 1983.

Ashbery, John. "Cornell: The Cube Root of Dreams." *Art News* 66 (Summer 1967): 56–64.

Ashton, Dore, ed. *A Joseph Cornell Album*. New York: Viking Press, 1974.

Ashton, John. *Chap-Books of the Eighteenth Century*. 1882. New York: Benjamin Blom, 1966.

Atwood, Margaret. *Bluebeard's Egg and Other Stories*. 1983. Boston: Houghton Mifflin, 1986.

————. "Running with the Tigers." In *Flesh and the Mirror: Essays on the Art of Angela Carter*, edited by Lorna Sage, 117–35. London: Virago, 1994.

————. *Surfacing*. New York: Simon and Schuster, 1972.

Auden, W. H. "Grimm and Andersen." In *Forewords and Afterwords*, selected by Edward Mendelson, 198–208. New York: Random House, 1973.

Auerbach, Nina, and U. C. Knoepflmacher, eds. *Forbidden Journeys: Fairy Tales and Fantasies by Victorian Woman Writers*. Chicago: University of Chicago Press, 1992.

Aulnoy, Marie-Catherine le Jumel de Barneville, Baronne de. *Contes*. Vols. 1–2. Edited by Jacques Barchilon and Philippe Hourcade. Édition du tricentenaire. Paris: Société des Textes Français Modernes, 1997–1998.

————. *Contes nouveaux ou les fées à la mode*. Paris: Veuve de Theodore Girard, 1698. A later edition (Paris, 1711) seems to be identical.

————. *Histoire d'Hipolyte, comte de Duglas*. 1690. Reprint, Geneva: Slatkine, 1979.

[————.] *The History of the Tales of the Fairies, Newly done from the French*. London, B. Harris, 1716.

————. *Nouveaux contes des fées*. 1697. Reprint, Amsterdam: Estienne Roger, 1725.

[Auneil, Louise de Bossigny, Comtesse d'.]. *La tiranie des fées détruite; nouveaux contes*. Paris: Veuve R. Chevillon, 1702.

Baader, Renate. *Dames de Lettres: Autorinnen des preziösen, hocharistokratischen und 'modernen' Salons (1649–1698)*. Stuttgart: Metzler, 1986.

Bacchilega, Cristina. *Postmodern Fairy Tales: Gender and Narrative Strategies*. Philadelphia: University of Pennsylvania Press, 1997.

Bakhtin, M. M. *The Dialogic Imagination*. Edited by Michael Holquist. Austin: University of Texas Press, 1981.

Bamford, Samuel. *The Autobiography of Samuel Bamford: Early Days*. Edited by W. H. Chaloner. London: Frank Cass, 1967.

Barchilon, Jacques. *Le conte merveilleux français: De 1690 à 1790*. Paris: Champion, 1975.

Barth, John. *Lost in the Funhouse: Fiction for Print, Tape, Live Voice*. 1968. New York: Bantam, 1978.

Barthes, Roland. *Image—Music—Text*. Translated by Stephen Heath. New York: Hill and Wang, 1977.

———. *Mythologies*. Translated by Annette Lavers. New York: Hill and Wang, 1972.

Basile, Giambattista. *The Pentamerone*. Vols. 1 and 2. Translated and edited by N. M. Penzer. London: John Lane the Bodley Head, 1932.

Bate, W. Jackson. *The Burden of the Past and the English Poet*. Cambridge: Harvard University Press, 1970.

Bauman, Richard. "Conceptions of Folklore in the Development of Literary Semiotics." *Semiotica* 39 (1982): 1–20.

Beasley, Faith E. *Revising Memory: Women's Fiction and Memoirs in Seventeenth-Century France*. New Brunswick, NJ: Rutgers University Press, 1990.

Beaumont, Jeanne-Marie Le Prince de. *Magazin des enfans*. 1756. La Haie & Leide, chez Pierre Gosse Junior et Daniel Pinet, Elie Luzac, Fils, 1774.

Belmont, Nicole. *Poétique du conte: Essai sur le conte de tradition orale*. Paris: Gallimard, 1999.

Benjamin, Walter. *Briefe* Edited by Gershom Scholem and Theodor W. Adorno. Frankfurt am Main: Suhrkamp, 1966.

———. *Gesammelte Schriften*. Edited by Rolf Tiedemann and Hermann Schweppenhäuser. Frankfurt am Main: Suhrkamp, 1977–.

———. *Selected Writings*. Vol. 1 (1913–1926). Edited by Marcus Bullock and Michael W. Jennings. Cambridge: Harvard University Press, 1996.

———. "The Storyteller: Reflections on the Work of Nikolai Leskov." In *Illuminations*, edited by Hannah Arendt, translated by Harry Zohn. New York: Schocken Books, 1968.

Bernard, Catherine. *Inés de Cordoüe: Nouvelle espagnole*. 1696. Reprint, Geneva: Slatkine, 1979.

Bernheimer, Kate, ed. *Mirror, Mirror on the Wall: Women Writers Explore Their Favorite Fairy Tales*. New York: Doubleday Anchor, 1998.

Bersani, Leo. *The Culture of Redemption*. Cambridge: Harvard University Press, 1990.

Bettelheim, Bruno. *The Uses of Enchantment: The Meaning and Importance of Fairy Tales*. 1976. New York: Vintage Books, 1989.

Binns, John. *Recollections of the Life of John Binns*. Philadelphia: Printed and for Sale by the Author, 1854.

Blackwell, Jeannine. "Fractured Fairy Tales: German Woman Authors and the Grimm Tradition." *Germanic Review* 62 (1987): 162–74.

———. "Laying the Rod to Rest: Narrative Strategies in Gisela and Bettina von Arnim's Fairy-Tale Novel *Gritta*." *Marvels and Tales* 11 (1997): 24–47.

Bloom, Harold. *The Anxiety of Influence: A Theory of Poetry*. New York: Oxford University Press, 1973.

Bottigheimer, Ruth. *Grimms' Bad Girls and Bold Boys: The Moral and Social Vision of the Tales*. New Haven: Yale University Press, 1987.

———. "Tale Spinners: Submerged Voices in Grimms' Fairy Tales." *New German Critique* 27 (1982): 141–50.

———, ed. *Fairy Tales and Society: Illusion, Allusion, and Paradigm*. Philadelphia: University of Pennsylvania Press, 1986.

Bourdieu, Pierre, Roger Chartier, and Robert Darnton. "Dialogue à propos de l'histoire culturelle." *Actes de la recherche en sciences sociales* 59 (1985): 86–83.

Bradbury, Nancy Mason. *Writing Aloud: Storytelling in Late Medieval England*. Urbana: University of Illinois Press, 1998.

Briggs, K[atharine] M. *The Fairies in English Tradition and Literature*. Chicago: University of Chicago Press, 1967.

Brodzki, Bella. "Mothers, Displacement, and Language in the Autobiographies of Nathalie Sarraute and Christa Wolf." In *Life/Lines: Theorizing Women's Autobiography*, edited by Brodzki and Celeste Schenck, 243–59. Ithaca: Cornell University Press, 1988.

Brooks, Peter. *Reading for the Plot: Design and Intention in Narrative*. New York: Knopf, 1984.

Broumas, Olga. *Beginning with O*. Yale Series of Younger Poets, 72. New Haven: Yale University Press, 1977.

Brown, Jane K. *Goethe's Cyclical Narratives:* Die Unterhaltungen deutscher Ausgewanderten *and* Wilhelm Meisters Wanderjahre. Chapel Hill: University of North Carolina Press, 1975.

Brown, Marshall. *Turning Points: Essays in the History of Cultural Expressions*. Stanford: Stanford University Press, 1997.

Brown, Rosellen. "It Is You the Fable Is About." In Bernheimer, *Mirror, Mirror on the Wall*, 50–63.

Buck-Morss, Susan. *The Dialectics of Seeing: Walter Benjamin and the Arcades Project*. Cambridge: MIT Press, 1989.

Burke, Peter. *Popular Culture in Early Modern Europe*. New York: Harper Torchbooks, 1978.

Butor, Michel. "On Fairy Tales." Translated by Remy Hall. In *European Literary Theory and Practice, from Existential Phenomenology to Structuralism*, edited by Vernon W. Grass, 349–62. New York: Dell, 1973.

Byatt, A[ntonia] S[usan]. *The Djinn in the Nightingale's Eye: Five Fairy Stories*. 1994. New York: Vintage International, 1998.

———. "Fairy Stories: The Djinn in the Nightingale's Eye." *http://www.asbyatt.com/fairy.html*

———. "Ice, Snow, Glass." In Bernheimer, *Mirror, Mirror on the Wall*, 64–84.

———. *Possession: A Romance*. New York: Random House, 1990.

Calvino, Italo. *Italian Folktales*. Translated by George Martin. New York: Harcourt, Brace, Jovanovich, 1980.

Canepa, Nancy L. *From Court to Forest: Giambattista Basile's Lo Cunto de li cunti and the Birth of the Literary Fairy Tale*. Detroit: Wayne State University Press, 1999.

———. " 'Quanto'nc'è da ccà a lo luoco dove aggio da ire': Giambattista Basile's Quest for the Literary Fairy Tale." In Canepa, *Out of the Woods*, 37–80.

———, ed. *Out of the Woods: The Origins of the Literary Fairy Tale in Italy and France*. Detroit: Wayne State University Press, 1997.

Carnell, Rachel. "It's Not Easy Being Green: Gender and Friendship in Eliza Haywood's Political Periodicals." *Eighteenth Century Studies* 32 (Winter 1998–1999): 199–214.

Carruthers, Mary J. "The Re-Vision of the Muse: Adrienne Rich, Audre Lord, Judy Grahn, Olga Broumas." *Hudson Review* 36 (1983): 293–322.

Carter, Angela. *The Bloody Chamber*. 1979. New York: Penguin, 1981.

———. *Burning Your Boats: The Collected Short Stories*. New York: Henry Holt, 1995.

———. "Notes from the Front Line." In Wandor, *On Gender and Writing*, 68–77.

———. *The Sadeian Woman, and the Ideology of Pornography*. New York: Pantheon, 1978.

———, ed. *The Old Wives' Fairy Tale Book*. New York: Pantheon, 1990.

Cashdan, Sheldon. *The Witch Must Die: How Fairy Tales Shape Our Lives*. New York: Basic Books, 1999.

Certeau, Michel de. *The Practice of Everyday Life*. Translated by Steven F. Rendall. Berkeley and Los Angeles: University of California Press, 1984.

Chartier, Roger. "Figures of the 'Other': Peasant Reading in the Age of the Enlightenment." In *Cultural History: Between Practices and Representations*, translated by Lydia G. Cochrane, 151–71. Ithaca: Cornell University Press, 1988.

———. *Forms and Meanings: Tests, Performances and Audiences from Codex to Computer*. New Cultural Studies. Philadelphia: University of Pennsylvania Press, 1995.

———. "Leisure and Sociability: Reading Aloud in Early Modern Europe." Translated by Carol Mossman. In *Urban Life in the Renaissance*, edited by Susan Zimmerman and Ronald F. E. Weissman, 103–20. Newark: University of Delaware Press, 1989.

———. "Texts, Printing, Readings." In *The New Cultural History*, edited by Lynn Hunt, 154–75. Berkeley and Los Angeles: University of California Press, 1989.

———. "Texts, Symbols, and Frenchness." *Journal of Modern History* 57 (1985): 682–95.

Chow, Rey. *Primitive Passions: Visuality, Sexuality, Ethnography, and Contemporary Chinese Cinema.* Film and Culture Series. New York: Columbia University Press, 1995.

Cixous, Hélène, and Catherine Clément. *La jeune née.* Paris: 10/18, 1975.

———. *The Newly Born Woman.* Translated by Betsy Wing. Theory and History of Literature, 24. 1975. Minneapolis: University of Minnesota Press, 1986.

Clancy, Patricia. "A French Writer and Educator in England: Mme Le Prince de Beaumont." *Studies on Voltaire and the Eighteenth Century* 201 (1982): 195–208.

Clare, John. *John Clare's Autobiographical Writings.* Edited by Eric Robinson. Oxford: Oxford University Press, 1983.

Cornell, Joseph. *Joseph Cornell's Theater of the Mind: Selected Diaries, Letters, and Files.* Edited by Mary Ann Caws. New York: Thames and Hudson, 1993.

Craveri, Benedetta. "The Lost Art." *New York Review of Books*, December 2, 1993, 40–43.

Crunelle-Vanrigh, Anny. "The Logic of the Same and *Différance*: 'The Courtship of Mr. Lyon.'" *Marvels and Tales* 12 (1998): 116–32.

Darnton, Robert. "Peasants Tell Tales: The Meaning of Mother Goose." In *The Great Cat Massacre and Other Episodes in French Cultural History*, 9–72. New York: Basic Books, 1984.

Deacon, George. *John Clare and the Folk Tradition.* London: Sinclair Browne, 1983.

Defrance, Anne. *Les contes de fées et les nouvelles de Madame d'Aulnoy (1690–98): L'imaginaire féminin à rebours de la tradition.* Geneva: Droz, 1998.

Dégh, Linda. *Folktales and Society: Story-Telling in a Hungarian Peasant Community.* Translated by Emily M. Schossberger. 1962. Bloomington: Indiana University Press, 1969.

DeJean, Joan. *Ancients against Moderns: Culture Wars and the Making of a Fin de Siècle.* Chicago: University of Chicago Press, 1997.

———. *Tender Geographies: Women and the Origins of the Novel in France.* Gender and Culture Series. New York: Columbia University Press, 1991.

De Lauretis, Teresa. *Technologies of Gender: Essays on Theory, Film, and Fiction.* Bloomington: Indiana University Press, 1987.

Donoghue, Emma. *Kissing the Witch: Old Tales in New Skins.* New York: HarperCollins, 1997.

Douglas, Mary. "The Uses of Vulgarity: A French Reading of Little Red Riding Hood." In *Thought Styles: Critical Essays on Good Taste*, 1–20. London: Sage, 1996.

Dowling, Colette. *The Cinderella Complex: Women's Hidden Fear of Independence.* New York: Simon and Schuster, 1981.

Dugaw, Diane. "Chapbook Publishing and the 'Lore' of 'the Folks.'" In Preston, *The Other Print Tradition*, 1–18.

Duncker, Patricia. "Re-Imagining the Fairy Tales: Angela Carter's Bloody Chambers." *Literature and History* 10 (1984): 3–14.

Dundes, Alan. *Interpreting Folklore*. Bloomington: Indiana University Press, 1980.

DuPlessis, Rachel Blau. *Writing beyond the Ending: Narrative Strategies of Twentieth-Century Women Writers*. Everywoman: Studies in History, Literature, and Culture. Bloomington: Indiana University Press, 1985.

Empson, William. *Some Versions of Pastoral*. 1935. Reprint, New York: New Directions, 1974.

Enzyklopädie des Märchens: Handwörterbuch zur historischen und vergleichenden Erzählforschung. Edited by Kurt Ranke et al. Berlin: de Gruyter, 1975–.

Errington, Shelly. *The Death of Authentic Primitive Art and Other Tales of Progress*. Berkeley and Los Angeles: University of California Press, 1998.

Ewers, Hans-Heino. "Erzählkunst und Kinderliteratur: Walter Benjamin's Theorie des Erzählens." In *Walter Benjamin und die Kinderliteratur*, edited by Klaus Doderer, 196–211. Weinheim and Munich: Juventa, 1988.

Farrell, Michèle L[ongino]. "Celebration and Repression of Feminine Desire in Mme d'Aulnoy's Fairy Tale: *La Chatte blanche*." *L'Esprit créateur* 29 (1989): 52–64.

Ferguson, Margaret W. "Renaissance Concepts of the 'Woman Writer.'" In *Women and Literature in Britain, 1500–1700*, edited by Helen Wilcox, 143–68. Cambridge: Cambridge University Press, 1996.

Fielding, Sarah. *The Governess, or, Little Female Academy*. 1749. Reprint, London: Pandora, 1987.

Fink, Gonthier-Louis. *Naissance et apogée du conte merveilleux en Allemagne 1740–1800*. Annales littéraires de l'Université de Besançon, 80. Paris: Les belles lettres, 1966.

Finnegan, Ruth. *Oral Poetry: Its Nature, Significance and Social Context*. Cambridge: Cambridge University Press, 1977.

Fumaroli, Marc. "Les enchantements de l'éloquence: *Les fees* de Charles Perrault ou De la littérature." In *Le statut de la littérature: Mélanges offerts à Paul Bénichou*, edited by Fumaroli, 153–86. Histoires de idées et critique littéraire, 200. Geneva: Droz, 1982.

Gaster, M[oses]. "The Modern Origin of Fairy-Tales." *Folk-lore Journal* 5 (1887): 339–51.

Genette, Gérard. "Introduction to the Paratext." *New Literary History* 22 (1991): 261–72.

———. *Seuils*. Paris: Editions du Seuil, 1987.

Gilbert, Sandra M., and Susan Gubar. *The Madwoman in the Attic: The Woman Writer and the Nineteenth-Century Literary Imagination*. New Haven: Yale University Press, 1979.

———. *Masterpiece Theater: An Academic Melodrama*. New Brunswick, NJ: Rutgers University Press, 1995.

———. *No Man's Land: The Place of the Woman Writer in the Twentieth Century*. Vol. 1, *The War of the Words*. New Haven: Yale University Press, 1988.

Ginzburg, Carlo. *The Cheese and the Worms: The Cosmos of a Sixteenth-Century Miller*. Translated by John and Anne Tedeschi. New York: Penguin Books, 1982.

———. *Ecstasies: Deciphering the Witches' Sabbath*. Translated by Raymond Rosenthal. New York: Penguin Books, 1992.

Goethe, Johann Wolfgang von. *Sämtliche Werke*. Frankfurt: Deutscher Klassiker Verlag, 1992.

Goffman, Erving. *Frame Analysis: An Essay on the Organization of Experience*. New York: Harper Colophon, 1974.

Goldthwaite, John. *The Natural History of Make-Believe: A Guide to the Principal Works of Britain, Europe, and America*. New York: Oxford University Press, 1996.

Goodman, Nelson. "The Telling and the Told." *Critical Inquiry* 7 (1981): 799–801.

Gornick, Vivian. "Taking a Long Hard Look at 'The Princess and the Pea.' " In Bernheimer, *Mirror, Mirror on the Wall*, 158–67.

Grätz, Manfred. *Das Märchen in der deutschen Aufklärung: Vom Feenmärchen zum Volksmärchen*. Stuttgart: Metzler, 1988.

Greene, Gayle, and Coppélia Kahn, eds. *Changing Subjects: The Making of Feminist Literary Criticism*. New York: Routledge, 1993.

Grimm, Jacob and Wilhelm. *Kinder- und Hausmärchen gesammelt durch die Brüder Grimm, 1812 an 1815*. Edited by Heinz Rölleke and Ulrike Marquardt. Göttingen: Vandenhoeck & Rupprecht, 1986.

Gubar, Susan. "What Ails Feminist Criticism?" *Critical Inquiry* 24 (Summer 1998): 878–902.

Guillory, John. *Cultural Capital: The Problem of Literary Canon Formation*. Chicago: University of Chicago Press, 1993.

Haase, Donald, ed. *The Reception of Grimms' Fairy Tales: Responses, Reactions, Revisions*. Detroit: Wayne State University Press, 1993.

Habermas, Jürgen. *The Structural Transformation of the Public Sphere: An Inquiry into a Category of Bourgeois Society*. Translated by Thomas Burger. Cambridge: MIT Press, 1989.

Hammond, Karla. "An Interview with Olga Broumas." *Northwest Review* 18 (1980): 33–44.

Hannon, Patricia. *Fabulous Identities: Women's Fairy Tales in Seventeenth-Century France*. Amsterdam and Atlanta: Rodopi, 1998.

———. "A Politics of Disguise: Marie-Catherine d'Aulnoy's 'Belle-Etoile' and the Narrative Structure of Ambivalence." In *Anxious Power: Reading, Writing, and Ambivalence in Narrative by Women*, edited by Carol J. Singley and Susan Elizabeth Sweeney, 73–89. SUNY Series in Feminist Criticism and Theory. Albany: State University of New York Press, 1993.

Hanson, Elizabeth. "Boredom and Whoredom: Reading Renaissance Women's Sonnet Sequences." *Yale Journal of Criticism* 10 (1997): 165–91.

Harries, Elizabeth W. "Fairy Tales about Fairy Tales: Notes on Canon Formation." In Canepa, *Out of the Woods*, 152–75.

Harries, Elizabeth W. "The Mirror Broken: Fairy Tales and Women's Autobiography." *Marvels and Tales* 14 (April 2000): 122–35.

———. "Simulating Oralities: French Fairy Tales of the 1690s." *College Literature* 23 (June 1996): 100–115.

Harth, Erica. *Cartesian Women: Versions and Subversions of Rational Discourse in the Old Regime*. Ithaca: Cornell University Press, 1992.

Hearne, Betsy. *Beauty and the Beast: Visions and Revisions of an Old Tale*. Chicago: University of Chicago Press, 1989.

Herder, Johann Gottfried. "Von Ähnlichkeit der mittlern englischen und deutschen Dichtkunst. . . ." In *Werke*, vol. 2, edited by Gunter E. Grimm, 550–62. Frankfurt: Deutscher Klassiker Verlag, 1993.

Hite, Molly. "Except thou ravish mee': Penetrations into the Life of the (Feminine) Mind." In Greene and Kahn, *Changing Subjects*, 121–28.

———. *The Other Side of the Story: Structures and Strategies of Contemporary Feminist Narrative*. Ithaca: Cornell University Press, 1989.

Hobsbawm, Eric. "Inventing Traditions." Introduction to *The Invention of Tradition*. edited by Hobsbawm and Terence Ranger, 1–14. Cambridge: Cambridge University Press, 1983.

Howe, Florence, ed. *Tradition and the Talents of Women*. Urbana: University of Illinois Press, 1991.

Hulbert, Ann. "The Great Ventriloquist: A. S. Byatt's *Possession: A Romance*." In *Contemporary British Women Writers: Narrative Strategies*, edited by Robert E. Hosmer, Jr., 55–65. New York: St. Martin's, 1993.

Hunter, J. Paul. *Before Novels: The Cultural Contexts of Eighteenth Century English Fiction*. New York: W. W. Norton, 1990.

Irwin, Bonnie D. "What's in a Frame? The Medieval Textualization of Traditional Storytelling." *Oral Tradition* 10 (1995): 27–53.

Jameson, Fredric. *The Political Unconscious: Narrative as a Socially Symbolic Act*. Ithaca: Cornell University Press, 1981.

Jarvis, Shawn C. "Trivial Pursuit? Women Deconstructing the Grimmian Model in the *Kaffeterkreis*." In Haase, *The Reception of Grimms' Fairy Tales*, 102–26.

———. "The Vanished Woman of Great Influence: Benedikte Naubert's Legacy and German Women's Fairy Tales." In *In the Shadow of Olympus: German Women Writers around 1800*, edited by Katherine R. Goodman and Edith Waldstein, 189–209. Albany: State University of New York Press, 1992.

Johnson, Barbara. *A World of Difference*. Baltimore: Johns Hopkins University Press, 1987.

Jones, Ann Rosalind. *The Currency of Eros: Women's Love Lyric in Europe, 1540–1620*. Bloomington: Indiana University Press, 1990.

Jones, Steven Swann. "On Analyzing Fairy Tales: 'Little Red Riding Hood' Revisited" and "Response to Oring." *Western Folklore* 46 (April 1987): 97–106 and 112–14.

Jordan, Elaine. "The Dangers of Angela Carter." In *New Feminist Discourses: Critical Essays on Theories and Texts*, edited by Isobel Armstrong, 119–31. New York: Routledge, 1992.

Joseph Cornell / Marcel Duchamp—in Resonance. Houston: The Menil Foundation, 1998.

Kaiser, Mary. "Fairy Tale as Sexual Allegory: Intertextuality in Angela Carter's *The Bloody Chamber*." *Review of Contemporary Fiction* 14 (1994): 30–36.

Kemp, Wolfgang. "A Shelter for Paintings: Forms and Functions of Nineteenth-Century Frames." In *In Perfect Harmony: Picture + Frame 1850–1920*, edited by Eva Mendgen, 13–25. Amsterdam: Van Gogh Museum/Kunstforum Wien, 1995.

Kernan, Alvin B., Peter Brooks, and J. Michael Holquist, eds. *Man and His Fictions: An Introduction to Fiction-Making, Its Forms and Uses*. New York: Harcourt, Brace, Jovanovich, 1973.

Klotz, Volker. *Das europäische Kunstmärchen*. Stuttgart: Metzler, 1985.

Knoepflmacher, U. C. *Ventures into Childland: Victorians, Fairy Tales, and Femininity*. Chicago: University of Chicago Press, 1998.

Kodish, Debora. "Absent Gender, Silent Encounter." *Journal of American Folklore* 100 (1987): 573–78.

Kolbenschlag, Madonna. *Kiss Sleeping Beauty Good-Bye: Breaking the Spell of Feminine Myths and Models*. New York: Doubleday, 1979.

Kroeber, Karl. *Retelling/Rereading: The Fate of Storytelling in Modern Times*. New Brunswick, NJ: Rutgers University Press, 1992.

Kumin, Maxine. "How It Was." Foreword to *The Complete Poems*, by Anne Sexton, xix–xxxiv. Boston: Houghton Mifflin, 1981.

———. *The Retrieval System*. New York: The Viking Press, 1978.

La Force, Charlotte-Rose Caumont de. *Les jeux d'esprit ou la promenade de la princesse de Conti*. Edited by de la Grange. Paris: Auguste Aubry, 1862.

[La Force.] *Les fées, contes des contes*. 1698. Paris: Medard Brunet, 1707.

Lämmert, Eberhard. *Bauformen des Erzählens*. 4th ed. Stuttgart: Metzler, 1970.

Lang, Andrew, ed. *The Blue Fairy Book*. 1889. New York: Dover, 1965.

Lappas, Catherine. " 'Seeing is believing, but touching is the truth': Female Spectatorship and Sexuality in *The Company of Wolves*." *Women's Studies* 25 (1996): 115–35.

Lewis, Philip. *Seeing Through the Mother Goose Tales: Visual Turns in the Writings of Charles Perrault*. Stanford: Stanford University Press, 1996.

Lhéritier de Villandon, Marie-Jeanne. *Oeuvres meslées*. Paris: Guignard, 1696.

[Lhéritier.] *La tour tenebreuse et les jours lumineux, contes anglois*. Paris: Veuve Claude Barbin, 1705. Reprint, Geneva: Slatkine, 1978.

Lieberman, Marcia K. " 'Some Day My Prince Will Come': Female Acculturation through the Fairy Tale." 1972. In Zipes, *Don't Bet on the Prince*, 185–200.

Lokke, Kari E. "*Bluebeard* and *The Bloody Chamber*: The Grotesque of Self-Parody and Self-Assertion." *Frontiers* 10 (1988): 7–12.

Lucas, Rose. "A Witch's Appetite: Anne Sexton's *Transformations*." *Southern Review* 26 (1993): 73–85.

Lundell, Torborg. "Gender-Related Biases in the Type and Motif Indexes of Aarne and Thompson." In Bottigheimer, *Fairy Tales and Society*, 149–63.

Lurie, Alison. "Fairy Tale Liberation." *New York Review of Books*, December 17, 1970, 42–44.

———. "Witches and Fairies: Fitzgerald to Updike." *New York Review of Books*, December 2, 1971, 6–11.

Lüthi, Max. *Once upon a Time: On the Nature of Fairy Tales*. Translated by Lee Chadeayvre and Paul Gottwald. 1970. Bloomington: Indiana University Press, 1976.

McCarthy, Mary. *How I Grew*. New York: Harcourt Brace Jovanovich, 1987.

McGavran, James Holt, Jr., ed. *Romanticism and Children's Literature in Nineteenth-Century England*. Athens: University of Georgia Press, 1991.

McGlathery, James M., ed. *The Brothers Grimm and Folktale*. Urbana: University of Illinois Press, 1991.

McShine, Kynaston, ed. *Joseph Cornell*. New York: Museum of Modern Art, 1980.

[Mailly, Chevalier . . . de]. *Les illustres fées, contes galans, dédiés aux dames*. Paris: Medard-Michel Brunet, 1698.

Maitland, Sara. *Angel Maker: The Short Stories of Sara Maitland*. New York: Henry Holt, 1996.

———. "A Feminist Writer's Progress." In Wandor, *On Gender and Writing*, 17–23.

Mandrou, Robert. *De la culture populaire aux 17e et 18e siècles: La bibliothèque bleue de Troyes*. 1964. 3d ed. Paris: Imago, 1985.

Marin, Louis. "Les enjeux d'un frontispice." *L'Esprit Créateur* 27 (1987): 49–57.

Mehlman, Jeffrey. *Walter Benjamin for Children: An Essay on His Radio Years*. Chicago: University of Chicago Press, 1993.

Middlebrook, Diane Wood. *Anne Sexton: A Biography*. Boston: Houghton Mifflin, 1991.

Miller, Nancy K. "Men's Reading, Women's Writing: Gender and the Rise of the Novel." In *Displacements: Women, Tradition, Literatures in French*, edited by Joan DeJean and Miller, 37–54. Baltimore: Johns Hopkins University Press, 1991.

———. *Subject to Change*. Gender and Culture Series. New York: Columbia University Press, 1988.

Moore, Edward [and Henry Brooke]. *Fables for the Female Sex*. London: Printed for R. Franklin, 1744.

Morris, Meaghan. *The Pirate's Fiancée: Feminism, Reading, Postmodernism*. Questions for Feminism. London: Verso, 1988.

Mortimer, Armine Kotin. "La clôture féminine des *Jeux d'Esprit*." *L'Esprit Créateur* 23 (1983): 107–16.

Mueller, Lisel. *Alive Together: New and Selected Poems*. Baton Rouge: Louisiana State University Press, 1996.

Muir, Edwin. *Collected Poems 1921–1958*. London: Faber & Faber, 1960.

Mulford, Wendy. "Notes on Writing: A Marxist/Feminist Viewpoint." In Wandor, *On Gender and Writing*, 31–41.

[Murat, . . .]. *Les contes des fées*. Vols. 1 and 2. Paris: Claude Barbin, 1698.

[Murat, Comtesse . . .]. *Histoires sublimes et allegoriques, dediées aux fées modernes*. Paris: Florentin & Claude Delaune, 1699.

Myers, Mitzi. "Impeccable Governesses, Rational Dames, and Moral Mothers: Mary Wollstonecraft and the Female Tradition in Georgian Children's Books." *Children's Literature* 14 (1986): 31–59.

———. "Romancing the Moral Tale: Maria Edgeworth and the Problematics of Pedagogy." In McGavran, *Romanticism and Children's Literature in Nineteenth-Century England*, 96–128.

Neuburg, Victor E. *The Penny Histories: A Study of Chapbooks for Young Readers over Two Centuries*. London: Oxford University Press, 1968.

Noakes, Susan. "On the Superficiality of Women." In *The Comparative Perspective on Literature: Approaches to Theory and Practice*, edited by Clayton Koelb and Noakes, 339–55. Ithaca: Cornell University Press, 1988.

Nouveau conte des fées. [Le portrait qui parle.] Metz: Brice Antoine, 1699.

Nussbaum, Felicity A. *The Autobiographical Subject: Gender and Ideology in Eighteenth-Century England*. Baltimore: Johns Hopkins University Press, 1989.

O'Brien, Geoffrey. "Recapturing the American Sound." *New York Review of Books* 45, no. 6 (April 9, 1998): 45–51.

Ong, Walter J., S.J. "Latin Language Study as a Renaissance Puberty Rite." In *Rhetoric, Romance, and Technology: Studies in the Interaction of Expression and Culture*, 113–41. Ithaca: Cornell University Press, 1971.

———. *Orality and Literacy: The Technologizing of the Word*. London: Methuen, 1982.

Opie, Iona and Peter. *The Classic Fairy Tales*. 1974. New York: Oxford University Press, 1980.

Oring, Elliott. "On the Meanings of Mother Goose." *Western Folklore* 46 (1987): 106–11.

Ostriker, Alicia. "That Story: Anne Sexton and Her Transformations." *American Poetry Review* 11 (1982): 11–16.

Palmer, Nancy and Melvin. "English Editions of French *Contes de Fées* Attributed to Mme d'Aulnoy." *Studies in Bibliography* 27 (1974): 227–32.

Perrault, Charles. *Contes*. Edited by Gilbert Rouger. Paris: Garnier, 1967.

Pickering, Samuel F. *John Locke and Children's Books in Eighteenth-Century England*. Knoxville: University of Tennessee Press, 1981.

Preston, Cathy Lynn and Michael J., eds. *The Other Print Tradition: Essays on Chapbooks, Broadsides, and Related Ephemera*. New York: Garland, 1995.

Probyn, Elspeth. *Sexing the Self: Gendered Positions in Cultural Studies*. London and New York: Routledge, 1993.

Propp, Vladimir. *Morphology of the Folktale*. 2d ed. Austin: University of Texas Press, 1968.

———. *Theory and History of Folklore*. Translated by Ariadna Y. Martin and Richard P. Martin et al. Theory and History of Literature, 5. Minneapolis: University of Minnesota Press, 1984.

Régnier-Bohler, Danielle. "Imagining the Self: Exploring Literature." In *A History of Private Life*, vol. 2, edited by Philippe Ariès and Georges Duby, translated by Arthur Goldhammer, 311–93. Cambridge: Harvard University Press, 1985.

Reiss, Timothy J. *The Meaning of Literature*. Ithaca: Cornell University Press, 1992.

Rich, Adrienne. *The Fact of a Doorframe: Poems Selected and New 1950–1984*. New York: W. W. Norton, 1984.

———. *On Lies, Secrets, and Silence: Selected Prose 1966–1978*. New York: W. W. Norton, 1979.

Richardson, Alan. *Literature, Education, and Romanticism: Reading as Social Practice, 1780–1832*. Cambridge Series in Romanticism. Cambridge: Cambridge University Press, 1994.

———. "Wordsworth, Fairy Tales, and the Politics of Children's Reading." In McGavran, *Romanticism and Children's Literature in Nineteenth-Century England*, 34–53.

Robert, Raymonde. *Le conte de fées littéraire en France de la fin du XVIIe à la fin du XVIIIe siècle*. Nancy: Presses Universitaires de Nancy, 1982.

Robinson, Lillian S. *In the Canon's Mouth: Dispatches from the Culture Wars*. Bloomington: Indiana University Press, 1997.

Roche-Mazon, Jeanne. "De qui est Riquet à la houppe?" *Revue des Deux Mondes*, July 15, 1928, 404–36.

Rose, Ellen Cronan. "Through the Looking Glass: When Women Tell Fairy Tales." In Abel, *The Voyage In*, 209–27.

Rose, Jacqueline. *The Case of Peter Pan, or The Impossibility of Children's Fiction*. New Cultural Studies. 1984. Reprint, Philadelphia: University of Pennsylvania Press, 1992.

Rowe, Karen E. " 'Fairy-born and human-bred': Jane Eyre's Education in Romance." In Abel, *The Voyage In*, 69–89.

———. "Feminism and Fairy Tales." 1979. In Zipes, *Don't Bet on the Prince*, 209–26.

———. "To Spin a Yarn: The Female Voice in Folklore and Fairy Tale." In Bottigheimer, *Fairy Tales and Society*, 53–74.

Rubin, Gayle. "The Traffic in Women: Notes on the 'Political Economy' of Sex." In *Toward an Anthropology of Women*, edited by Rayna R. Reiter, 157–210. New York: Monthly Review Press, 1975.

Rushdie, Salman. Introduction to *Burning Your Boats: The Collected Short Stories*, by Angela Carter, ix–xiv. New York: Henry Holt, 1995.

———. *Shame: A Novel*. 1983. Reprint, New York: Henry Holt, 1997.

Russo, Mary. *The Female Grotesque: Risk, Excess, and Modernity*. New York: Routledge, 1994.

Sanchez, Victoria. "A. S. Byatt's *Possession*: A Fairytale Romance." *Southern Folklore* 52 (1995): 33–51.

Schenda, Rudolf. "Telling Tales—Spreading Tales: Change in the Communicative Forms of a Popular Genre." In Bottigheimer, *Fairy Tales and Society*, 75–94.

———. *Von Mund zu Ohr: Bausteine zu einer Kulturgeschichte volkstümlichen Erzählens in Europa*. Göttingen: Vandenhoeck & Rupprecht, 1993.

Schor, Naomi. "Blindness as Metaphor." *Differences* 11 (Summer 1999): 76–105.

Schulte-Sasse, Jochen. "Art and the Sacrificial Structure of Modernity: A Sociohistorical Supplement." Afterword to *Framed Narratives: Diderot's Genealogy of the Beholder*, by Jay Caplan, 97–115. Theory and History of Literature, 19. Minneapolis: University of Minnesota Press, 1985.

Seago, Karen. "Some Aspects of the English Reception of the Grimms' *Kinder- und Hausmärchen* in the Nineteenth Century." *Zeitschrift für Kultur- und Bildungswissenschaften* 7 (1999): 41–58.

Ségur, Sophie Rostopchine, Comtesse de. *Nouveaux contes de fées pour les petits enfants*. 1856. Reprint, Paris: Librairie Hachette, 1920.

Seifert, Lewis C. *Fairy Tales, Sexuality, and Gender in France, 1690–1715*. Cambridge Studies in French. Cambridge: Cambridge University Press, 1996.

———. "*Les Fées Modernes*: Women, Fairy Tales, and the Literary Field in Late Seventeenth Century France." In *Going Public: Women and Publishing in Early Modern France*, edited by Elizabeth C. Goldsmith and Dena Goodman, 129–45. Ithaca: Cornell University Press, 1995.

———. "Female Empowerment and Its Limits: The *Conteuses'* Active Heroines." *Cahiers du dix-septième* 4 (1990): 17–34.

———. " 'Marvelous Realities': Reading the *Merveilleux* in the Seventeenth-Century French Fairy Tale." In Canepa, *Out of the Woods*, 131–51.

Sendak, Maurice. *Where the Wild Things Are*. New York: Harper and Row, 1963.

Sévigné, Marie Rabutin-Chantal, Marquise de. *Correspondance*. Edited by Roger Duchêne. Paris: Gallimard (Pléiade), 1972–1978.

Sexton, Anne. *The Complete Poems*. Boston: Houghton Mifflin, 1981.

———. *Transformations*. Boston: Houghton Mifflin, 1971.

Sexton, Linda Gray. "Bones and Black Puddings: Revisiting 'The Juniper Tree.' " In Bernheimer, *Mirror, Mirror on the Wall*, 295–317.

———. *Searching for Mercy Street: My Journey Back to My Mother, Anne Sexton*. Boston: Little, Brown, 1994.

Sexton, Linda Gray, and Lois Ames, eds. *Anne Sexton: A Self-Portrait in Letters*. Boston: Houghton Mifflin, 1977.

Sheets, Robin Ann. "Pornography, Fairy Tales, and Feminism: Angela Carter's 'The Bloody Chamber.'" *Journal of the History of Sexuality* 1 (1991): 633–57.

Sherwood, Mrs. [Martha Mary Butts]. *The Works of Mrs. Sherwood, Being the Only Uniform Edition Ever Published in the United States*. Vol. 6. New York: Harper, 1836.

Shiach, Morag. *Discourse on Popular Culture: Class, Gender, and History in Cultural Analysis, 1730 to the Present*. Stanford: Stanford University Press, 1989.

Showalter, Elaine. *A Literature of Their Own: British Women Novelists from Brontë to Lessing*. Princeton: Princeton University Press, 1977.

———, ed. *The New Feminist Criticism: Essays on Women, Literature, and Theory*. New York: Pantheon Books, 1985.

Shuman, Amy, and Charles L. Briggs. "Introduction." *Western Folklore* 52 (April 1993): 109–34.

Simic, Charles. *Dime-Store Alchemy: The Art of Joseph Cornell*. Hopewell, NJ: Ecco, 1992.

Smith, Barbara Herrnstein. "Narrative Versions, Narrative Theories." *Critical Inquiry* 7 (1980): 213–36.

Smith, Sidonie. "Autobiographical Manifestoes." In *Women, Autobiography, Theory: A Reader*, edited by Smith and Julia Watson, 433–40. Madison: University of Wisconsin Press, 1998.

Solomon, Deborah. *Utopia Parkway: The Life and Work of Joseph Cornell*. New York: Farrar, Straus and Giroux, 1997.

Soriano, Marc. *Les contes de Perrault: Culture savante et traditions populaires*. Paris: Gallimard, 1968.

Spufford, Margaret. *Small Books and Pleasant Histories: Popular Fiction and Its Readership in Seventeenth-Century England*. London: Methuen, 1981.

Stallybrass, Peter, and Allon White. *The Politics and Poetics of Transgression*. Ithaca: Cornell University Press, 1986.

Steedman, Carolyn Kay. *Landscape for a Good Woman: A Story of Two Lives*. 1986. New Brunswick, NJ: Rutgers University Press, 1987.

Stephens, John, and Robyn McCallum. *Retelling Stories, Reframing Culture: Traditional Story and Metanarratives in Children's Literature*. Children's Literature and Culture. New York: Garland, 1998.

Stewart, Joan Hinde. "Allegories of Difference: An Eighteenth-Century Polemic." *Romanic Review* 75 (1984): 283–93.

Stewart, Susan. *Crimes of Writing: Problems in the Containment of Representation*. New York: Oxford University Press, 1991.

——— *On Longing: Narratives of the Miniature, the Gigantic, the Souvenir, the Collection*. 1984. Durham: Duke University Press, 1993.

[Straparola.] *Les facecieuses nuictz du Seigneur Jean François Straparole, Avec les Fables & Enigmes, racontées par deux ieunes gentilz-hommes, & dix Damoiselles, nouvellement traduictes d'Italien en François par Jean Lonneau*. Paris: Mathurin Martin, 1573.

Summerfield, Geoffrey. *Fantasy and Reason: Children's Literature in the Eighteenth Century*. Athens: University of Georgia Press, 1984.

Tatar, Maria. *The Hard Facts of the Grimms' Fairy Tales*. Princeton: Princeton University Press, 1987.

———. *Off with Their Heads! Fairy Tales and the Culture of Childhood*. Princeton: Princeton University Press, 1992.

———, ed. *The Classic Fairy Tales*. New York: Norton Critical Edition, 1999.

Thelander, Dorothy R. "Mother Goose and Her Goslings: The France of Louis XIV as Seen through the Fairy Tale." *Journal of Modern History* 54 (September 1982): 467–96.

Thompson, Stith. *Motif-Index of Folk-Literature: A Classification of Narrative Elements in Folktales, Ballads, Myths, Fables, Mediaeval Romances, Exempla, Fabliaux, Jest-Books and Local Legends*. 6 vols. Bloomington: Indiana University Press, 1955.

Todorov, Tzvetan. *The Fantastic: A Structural Approach to a Literary Genre*. 1970. Translated by Richard Howard. Ithaca: Cornell University Press, 1975.

Tolkien, J.R.R. "On Fairy-Stories." In *Essays Presented to Charles Williams*, 38–89. Oxford: Oxford University Press, 1947.

Tompkins, Jane. *Sensational Designs: The Cultural Work of American Fiction, 1790–1860*. New York: Oxford University Press, 1985.

Trinh T. Minh-ha. *Woman, Native, Other: Writing Postcoloniality and Feminism*. Bloomington: Indiana University Press, 1989.

Trumpener, Katie. *Bardic Nationalism: The Romantic Novel and the British Empire*. Literature in History. Princeton: Princeton University Press, 1997.

Velay-Vallantin, Catherine. *La fille en garçon*. Classiques de la littérature orale. Carcassonne: Garae/Hesiode, 1992.

———. *L'histoire des contes*. Paris: Fayard, 1992.

———. "Tales as a Mirror: Perrault in the *Bibliothèque bleue*." In *The Culture of Print: Power and the Uses of Print in Early Modern Europe*, edited by Roger Chartier, 92–135. Princeton: Princeton University Press, 1989.

Verdier, Gabrielle. "Féerie et utopie dans les contes de fées féminins." *Parabasis* 7 (1995): 139–48.

———. "Figures de la conteuse dans les contes de fées feminins." *XVIIe siècle* 180 (1993): 481–99.

Viala, Alain. *Naissance de l'écrivain: Sociologie de la littérature à l'âge classique*. Paris: Editions de Minuit, 1985.

Vidal, Mary. *Watteau's Painted Conversations: Art, Literature, and Talk in Seventeenth- and Eighteenth-Century France*. New Haven: Yale University Press, 1992.

[Villiers, Abbé Pierre de.] *Entretiens sur les contes de fées et sur quelques autres ouvrages du temps, pour servir comme préservatif contre le mauvais goût*. Paris: Jacques Collombat, 1699.

Waelti-Walters, Jennifer. *Fairy Tales and the Female Imagination*. Montreal: Eden, 1982.

Walckenaer, C. A. *Lettres sur les contes des fées*. 1826. Paris: Didot Frères, 1862.

Walker, Nancy A. *The Disobedient Writer: Women and Narrative Tradition*. Austin: University of Texas Press, 1995.

Wall, Wendy. *The Imprint of Gender: Authorship and Publication in the English Renaissance*. Ithaca and London: Cornell University Press, 1993.

Wandor, Micheline, ed. *On Gender and Writing*. London: Pandora Press, 1983.

Warner, Marina. *From the Beast to the Blonde: On Fairy Tales and Their Tellers*. New York: Farrar, Straus and Giroux, 1995.

———, ed. *Wonder Tales*. New York: Farrar, Straus and Giroux, 1996.

Watson, Victor. "Jane Johnson: A Very Pretty Story to Tell Children." In *Opening the Nursery Door: Reading, Writing and Childhood 1600–1900*, edited by Mary Hilton, Morag Styles, and Watson, 31–46. London: Routledge, 1997.

Weber, Eugen. "Fairies and Hard Facts: The Reality of Folktales." *Journal of the History of Ideas* 43 (1981): 93–113.

Wesselski, Albert. *Versuch einer Theorie des Märchens*. Prager Deutsche Studien, 45. 1931. Hildesheim: Gerstenberg, 1974.

Wilner, Arlene Fish. "Education and Ideology in Sarah Fielding's *The Governess*." *Studies in Eighteenth-Century Culture* 24 (1995): 307–27.

Winnett, Susan. "Coming Unstrung: Women, Men, Narrative, and Principles of Pleasure." *PMLA* 105 (1990): 505–18.

Winterson, Jeanette. *Sexing the Cherry*. New York: Vintage International, 1991.

Wolf, Christa. *Kindheitsmuster*. 1976. Munich: Deutscher Taschenbuch Verlag, 1994.

———. *Patterns of Childhood* [originally *A Model Childhood*]. Translated by Ursule Molinaro and Hedwig Rappolt. 1980. New York: Noonday, 1990.

Ziolkowski, Jan M. "A Fairy Tale from before Fairy Tales: Egbert of Liege's 'De puella a lupelli seruata' and the Medieval Background of 'Little Red Riding Hood.'" *Speculum* 67 (1992): 549–75.

Zipes, Jack. *The Brothers Grimm: From Enchanted Forests to the Modern World*. New York: Routledge, 1988.

———. "Cross-Cultural Connections and the Contamination of the Classical Fairy Tale." In Zipes, *The Great Fairy Tale Tradition*, 845–69.

———. *Fairy Tales and the Art of Subversion: The Classical Genre for Children and the Process of Civilization*. 1983. Reprint, New York: Routledge, 1991.

———. *Fairy Tale as Myth / Myth as Fairy Tale*. The Thomas D. Clark Lectures, 1993. Lexington: University Press of Kentucky, 1994.

———. *Happily Ever After: Fairy Tales, Children, and the Culture Industry*. New York: Routledge, 1997.

———, ed. *Beauties, Beasts and Enchantment: Classic French Fairy Tales*. New York: Meridian, 1989.

————, ed. *Beauty and the Beast and Other Classic French Fairy Tales*. New York: Signet, 1997.

————, ed. *Don't Bet on the Prince: Contemporary Feminist Fairy Tales in North America and England*. 1987. New York: Routledge, 1989.

————, ed. *The Great Fairy Tale Tradition: From Straparola and Basile to the Brothers Grimm*. New York: Norton Critical Edition, 2001.

INDEX

REFERENCES to illustrations are printed in italic type. The various versions of well-known tales are indexed under the most common English name.